PDM II

Piano for the Developing Musician

Second Edition

p 79
p 80 top
p 183

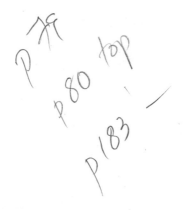

PDM II

Piano for the Developing Musician

Second Edition

Martha Hilley
The University of Texas at Austin

Lynn Freeman Olson
Composer and Consultant, New York City

West Publishing Company

St. Paul New York Los Angeles San Francisco

Credits

Cover Art: The Metropolitan Museum of Art,
Frank Lloyd Wright, window triptych
from the Avery Coonley Playhouse.
Purchase, Edward C. Moore, Jr. Gift and
Edgar J. Kaufmann Charitable Foundation Gift,
1967. (67.231.1-.3)

Cover Design: The Quarasan Group, Inc.
Copyediting: David Severtson
Composition: A-R Editions, Inc.
Music Engraving: A-R Editions, Inc.

We wish to thank the many publishers who were so kind to grant permission to reprint their works. Specific credit lines appear in the body of the text.

610 Opperman Drive
P.O. Box 64526
St. Paul, MN 55164–0526

Printed in the United States of America

99 98 97 96 95 94 93 8 7 6 5 4 3 2 1

Library of Congress Cataloging-in-Publication Data
(Revised for vol. 2)

Hilley, Martha.
PDM I (-II).

Includes index.
1. Piano—Instruction and study. 2. Music—Theory.
I. Olson, Lynn Freeman. II. Piano for the developing musician. III. Title.
MT220.H58 1989 89-753165
ISBN 0-314-48123-0 (v. 1)
ISBN 0-314-93368-9 (v. 2)

Publisher's Note

As everyone associated with the world of piano pedagogy well knows, Lynn Freeman Olson, the co-author of this book, succumbed to cancer on November 18, 1987.

Lynn was a most remarkable author. In him dwelt a rare combination of authority and kindness, of professional accomplishment and personal warmth, of undaunting self-discipline and disarming good spirits. Working with him was a stimulating challenge and a happy adventure.

Lynn was a perfectionist who, on behalf of the thousands of students to whom he devoted his life, drove himself to the highest personal and professional standards. He was proud of the books he published with West, and we were—and are—proud to be his publisher.

Contents

RELATED SKILLS AND ACTIVITIES

SUBSEQUENT REPERTOIRE

3. Supplementary Material

4. Diatonic Seventh Chords in Major and Minor/Secondary Seventh Chords

5. Altered/Borrowed Triads

6. Altered Seventh Chords/Extended Harmonies (Ninth, Thirteenth)

7. Supplementary Materials

Preface

Piano for the Developing Musician, 2nd edition, in contrast to many other keyboard texts, was researched and created for a highly specific population: the college music major who must demonstrate a variety of musical skills at the piano. I owe a debt of gratitude to group piano teachers across the country for their support of the original PDM II and their suggestions for this revision.

As with the original edition, PDM does not pamper the student. The text moves quickly but thoroughly in areas where general musical knowledge exists. It has been demonstrated time and again that when expectations are low, student achievement will be low; when expectations are higher, and the means for acquiring the requisite skills are delineated, student achievement will be far higher. Practicality is not ignored, for such aspects as reading, accompanying, harmonization, score reading, chord facility, improvisation and transposition are developed throughout the text.

You will notice some major changes in this 2nd edition. Among these is a Review Chapter which recaps the skills and activities covered in PDM I. You will also notice that an appreciable amount of piano repertoire has been eliminated from the Reading, Transposition and Subsequent Repertoire sections. These have been replaced with vocal and instrumental works, many of which will be familiar to students enrolled in the aforementioned classes. These selections will give the students experience in practical sight reading, accompanying (keyboard parts), transposition (instrumental parts and vocal accompaniments) and, most important of all, music making with their peers.

As a direct response to your comments, the Rhythm Cassette has been eliminated from this edition. Suggestions for both tonal and rhythmic accompaniments designed through use of MIDI keyboards and sequencers are included in the expanded Teacher's Manual. You will also note the inclusion of scale and chord appendices as well as a glossary.

The basic PDM chapter outline has been retained with the exception of Supplementary Chapters.

EXEMPLARY REPERTOIRE

Discoveries are based on this literature, and steps for learning are provided. A full historical range is covered.

RELATED SKILLS AND ACTIVITIES

Technique—A series of drills and etudes stresses finger and hand development, independence, and coordination.
Reading—Practicality is stressed! Many style and keys are involved, as are a variety of score configurations and clefs.
Keyboard Theory—Drills and exercises stress full understanding of the subject matter.
Harmonization—Melodies from folk and other composed sources have been extended in number and are presented for accompaniment in a wide variety of styles
Transposition—This skill of musicianship is practiced through regular execution, always based on theoretical understanding.
Improvisation—The ability to express oneself freely at the keyboard grows through frameworks based on acquired technical and theoretical skills.
Ensemble—Duet repertoire, multi-keyboard scores and instrumental scores including transposing instruments have been included.

SUBSEQUENT REPERTOIRE

Addition selections of keyboard literature appear. These are fewer in number and are offered for further study *if needed*.

We are practitioners of what might be termed a "humanistic" approach to music teaching. In this new edition you will still find stress on those aspects of music that do not change—its expressive nature, its freedom within organization, its social nature, and its eclectic qualities—all applied to the individual as a unique music maker. These things we teach, and we happen to be teaching them through the piano keyboard.

Acknowledgments

Whoever says "if you can do one revision, you've got the rest of them made" is definitely a person who has never done multiple second editions. You tend to establish strong attachments to your favorite skills, drills and repertoire in a first edition and, at times, those are hard to let go. However, I listened to those of you out there that are using PDM II, plus those of you that *are not* using PDM II, and this second edition is a direct result of your advice.

I wish to thank those who took the time to respond to my letter requesting suggestions for this edition: Nancy Rice Baker, University of Wisconsin-Eau Claire; Russell Bliss, Nassau Community College; Stephen Busch, Colorado State University; Angeline Case-Newport, Memphis State University; Sandy Coryell, Millikin University; Betty Anne Diaz, Columbus College; Anna Farina, University of Central Florida; Joann Feldman, Sonoma State University; Helen Galloway (retired), Winona State University; Tanya Gille, University of Colorado at Boulder; Patricia Graham, Peabody Conservatory of Music; Joyce Grill, University of Wisconsin-La Crosse; Patricia Halbeck, Austin Peay State University; Gordon P. Howell, Bethel College; Michael Keller, University of Wisconsin-Stevens Point; Frances Larimer, Northwestern University; Jerry E. Lowder, Ohio State University; Madeline Hsu, Boise State University; Claudia McCain, Western Illinois State University; John T. O'Brien, Columbus College; Naomi Oliphant, University of Louisville; Larry Rast, Northern Illinois University; Joan Reist, University of Nebraska-Lincoln; Larry Scully, Valdosta State College; Joanne Smith, University of Michigan; Rebecca Shockley, University of Minnesota; Paul Stroud, California State University-Long Beach; Tom Wade, Glassboro State College; Dallas Weekley and Nancy Arganbright, University of Wisconsin-La Crosse; Gary Wolf, University of Central Florida; Jeanette Constance Wong, California Baptist College; and very special thanks to Steve Perry, Mark Sullivan and Marienne Uszler, University of Southern California. For any omissions, I do apologize.

Thanks also to West Publishing personnel Clark G. Baxter (acquisition editor), Jayne Lindesmith (production editor) and David Severtson (copy editor), whose dedication to music and editorial expertise produced this second edition; Kathy Morton deserves praise for her assistance with permissions. Special thanks to James Schnars for his timely and attentive work in procuring permissions. And as always, to Lynn and all of the memories I have of our work together, I am forever grateful.

Martha Hilley

Review of Skills Learned in PDM I, Second Edition

As with any new beginning, it is perhaps best to take a moment to reflect and review what has come before. The next few pages will deal with selected portions from PDM I 2/e. This review will quickly show those entrance skills assumed at the start of PDM II. These skills (and others) listed will conform to actual headings for activities in PDM I, as this method best describes what has been covered.

This chapter need not take a large amount of your class time. Instead, you might use it as a type of diagnostic.

REVIEW OF SKILLS

TECHNIQUE

In PDM I, technique, other than traditional scale fingerings, related primarily to the repertoire. There may be value, however, in reviewing scale fingerings to assess your "digital dexterity."

All scales are to be played hands together, over two octaves. Play the scales according to the finger combinations shown here. Note that scales do not always *begin* with the same fingering for the tonic note.

Keys of D♭/C♯, C♭/B, and G♭/F♯ major; B♭/A♯, A♭/G♯, E♭/D♯ and B minor.

RH	2	3	[1]	2	3	4	[1]	2	3	[1]	2	3	4	[1]	2
LH	3	2	[1]	4	3	2	[1]	3	2	[1]	4	3	2	[1]	3

Keys of C, D, E, G, A and A♭ major; C, D, E, G, A, C♯ and F♯ minor.

RH	1	2	(3)	1	2	(3)	4	[1]	2	(3)	1	2	(3)	4	5
LH	5	4	(3)	2	1	(3)	2	[1]	4	(3)	2	1	(3)	2	1

Keys of F major and F minor.

RH	1	2	3	4	1	2	3	1	2	3	4	1	2	3	4
LH	5	4	3	2	1	3	2	1	4	3	2	1	3	2	1

Keys of E♭ major and B♭ major.

RH	3	1	2	3	4	1	2	3	1	2	3	4	1	2	3
LH	3	2	1	4	3	2	1	3	2	1	4	3	2	1	3

RH	4	1	2	3	1	2	3	4	1	2	3	1	2	3	4
LH	3	2	1	4	3	2	1	3	2	1	4	3	2	1	3

Chromatic Scales.

- White key to black key—1 to 3 (RH) or 3 to 1 (LH)
- White key to white key—1 to 2 (RH) or 2 to 1 (RH)

READING

The range of reading in PDM I was from basic "intervallic" to an SATB choral score. The following excerpts, with suggestions, will give an overview of the skills covered previously.

In *any* reading activity, the primary goal is to develop the ability to continue—no matter what. On the subject of sight reading there are many approaches that would take volumes to cover. Instead, you might wish to follow the five Ts:

- Think key
- Think intervals
- Think shapes
- Think meter
- Think logic in your fingering

Intervallic playing should start with the instant recognition of abstract intervals

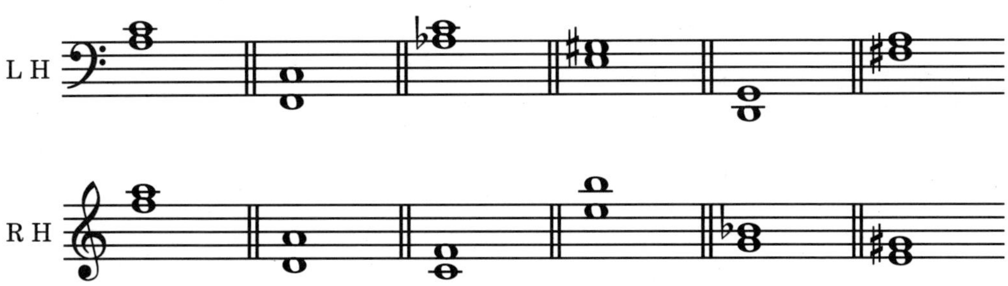
L H
R H

and lead to the recognition of these intervals within a piece of music.

dim. e rit.

Choral playing requires recognition of intervallic relationships and melodic motion between staves.

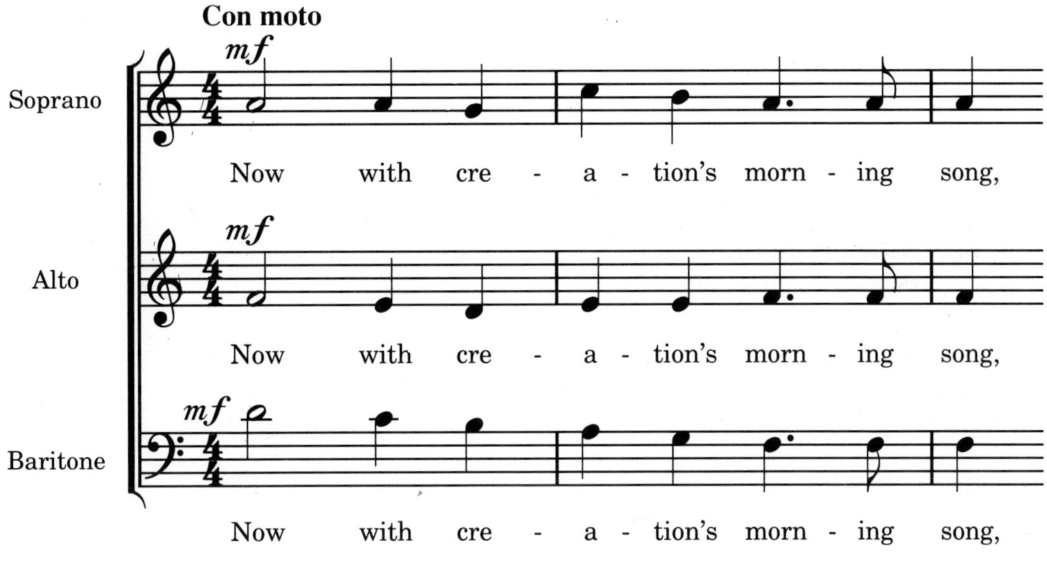
Con moto
Soprano
Alto
Baritone
mf
Now with cre - a - tion's morn - ing song,
Now with cre - a - tion's morn - ing song,
Now with cre - a - tion's morn - ing song,

To accompany an instrumental or vocal solo, reduce the printed score by leaving some notes out of the right-hand accompaniment.

Violin

Piano

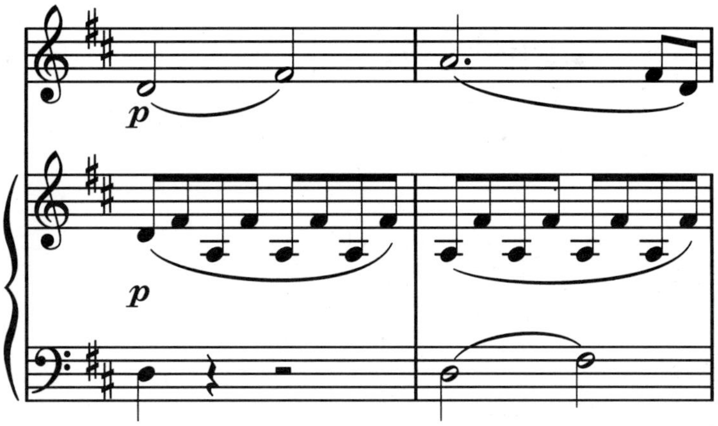

Voice

Piano

Schlafe, mein Prinzchen, schlaf ein, es ruhn nun Schäfchen und Vö-ge - lein,

KEYBOARD THEORY

Starting with basic diatonic triads and progressing through secondary dominants, the keyboard theory presented in PDM I was also closely tied to the repertoire.

Following are five areas that represent the theoretical knowledge you are assumed to have. Realize, however, that it is one thing to know something and quite another to be able to apply that knowledge. It is this practical application that any piano class must emphasize.

Diatonic Triads

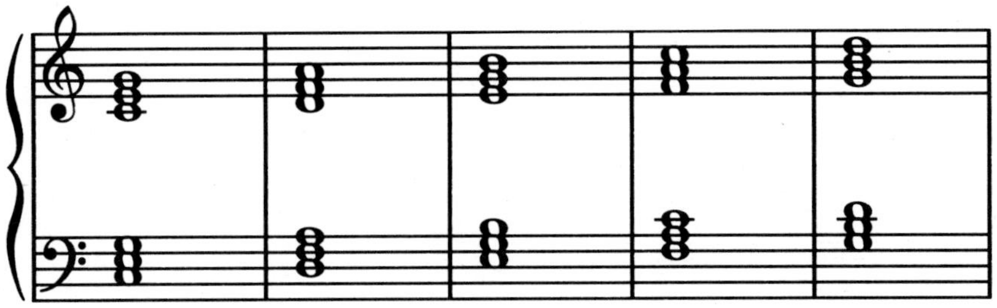

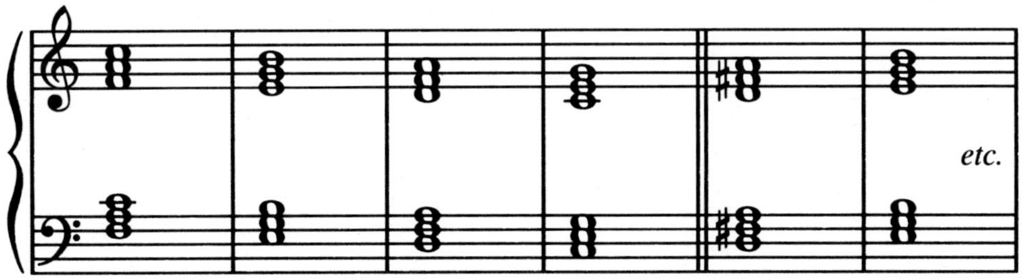

Closest Position Chords

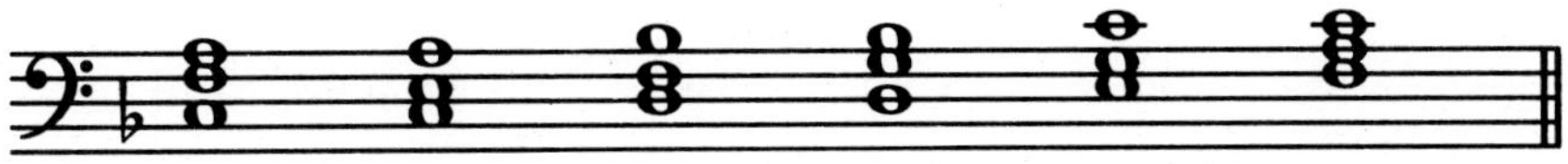

Modes

- Ionian—1st degree (major scale)
- Dorian—2nd degree
- Phrygian—3rd degree
- Lydian—4th degree
- Mixolydian—5th degree
- Aeolian—6th degree (natural minor)
- Locrian—7th degree

Think the key of D♭ major and play a scale beginning on the second degree and ending on the second degree an octave higher. This is the E♭ *Dorian* mode.

Think the B major key signature and play a scale beginning on the second scale degree and ending on C♯ an octave above. This is the C♯ Dorian mode.

Minor

All minor scales are derived from their relative majors and use the same key signatures. The natural minor scale can be observed within the major scale pattern, beginning on the sixth scale degree.

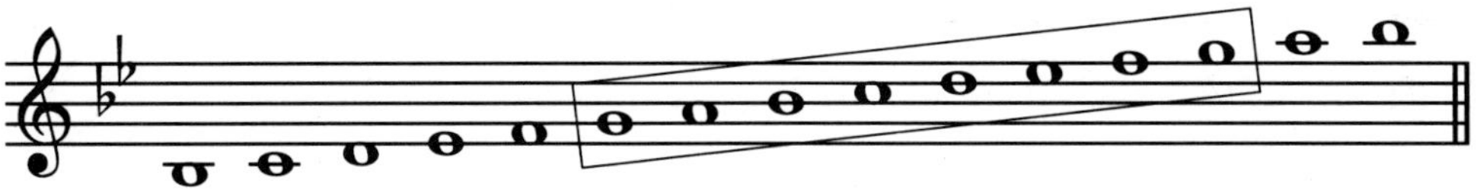

There are two commonly used altered forms of the natural minor scale. The *harmonic* form is the result of the major quality of the dominant seventh chord and therefore uses an accidental to produce a leading tone that is a half step below tonic.

The *melodic* form uses an additional accidental in the ascending pattern to avoid the awkward augmented second.

When descending, the melodic scale returns to the natural form of the minor.

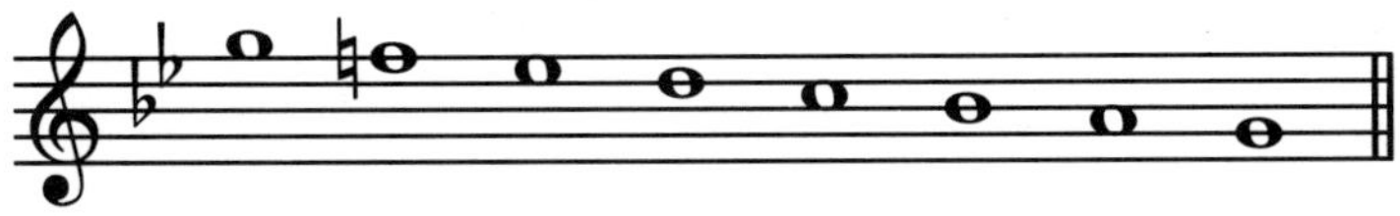

Following are the closest position triads in minor.

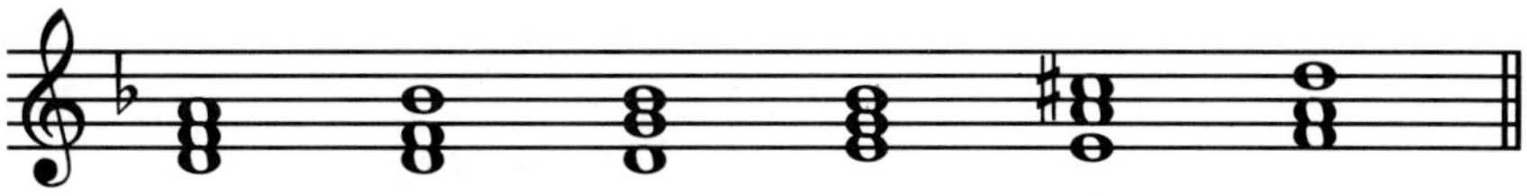

i VI iv ii V i

Secondary Dominants

V/vi	vi	(C major)
V/ii	ii	(G major)
V/iii	iii	(F major)

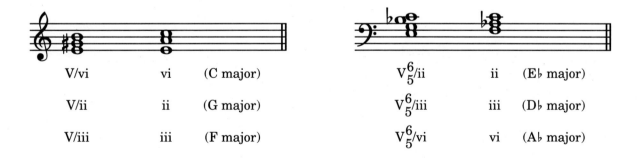

V^6_5/ii	ii	(E♭ major)
V^6_5/iii	iii	(D♭ major)
V^6_5/vi	vi	(A♭ major)

A secondary dominant is nothing more than a V7 that has been "borrowed" and will be given right back.

HARMONIZATION

All harmonization exercises (in this volume and the previous one) are directly related to the theoretical concepts presented. All of the aforementioned keyboard theory areas, with the exception of modes, were covered extensively in PDM I. The harmonic implication of modes will be covered in PDM II.

The following examples will give an opportunity for you to review harmonies and styles of accompaniments.

Diatonic Triads

Diatonic triads can add interest to a melody by adding harmony, from its simplest possible harmonization

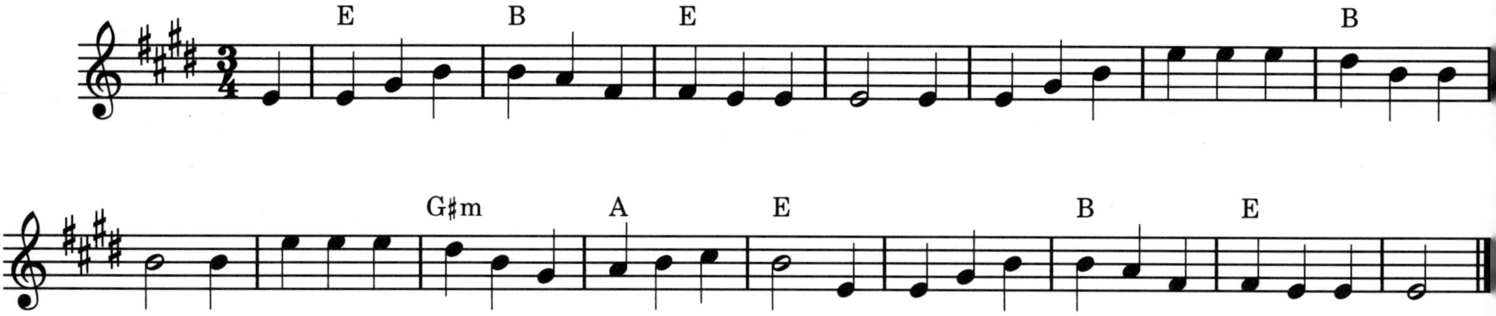

to one of more interest through chord substitution using diatonic triads and the dominant seventh.

Roman Numeral/Guitar Symbols

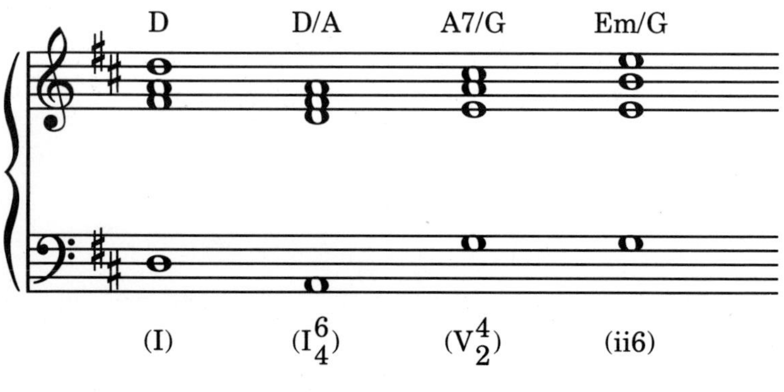

Minor

Two-Handed Accompaniment

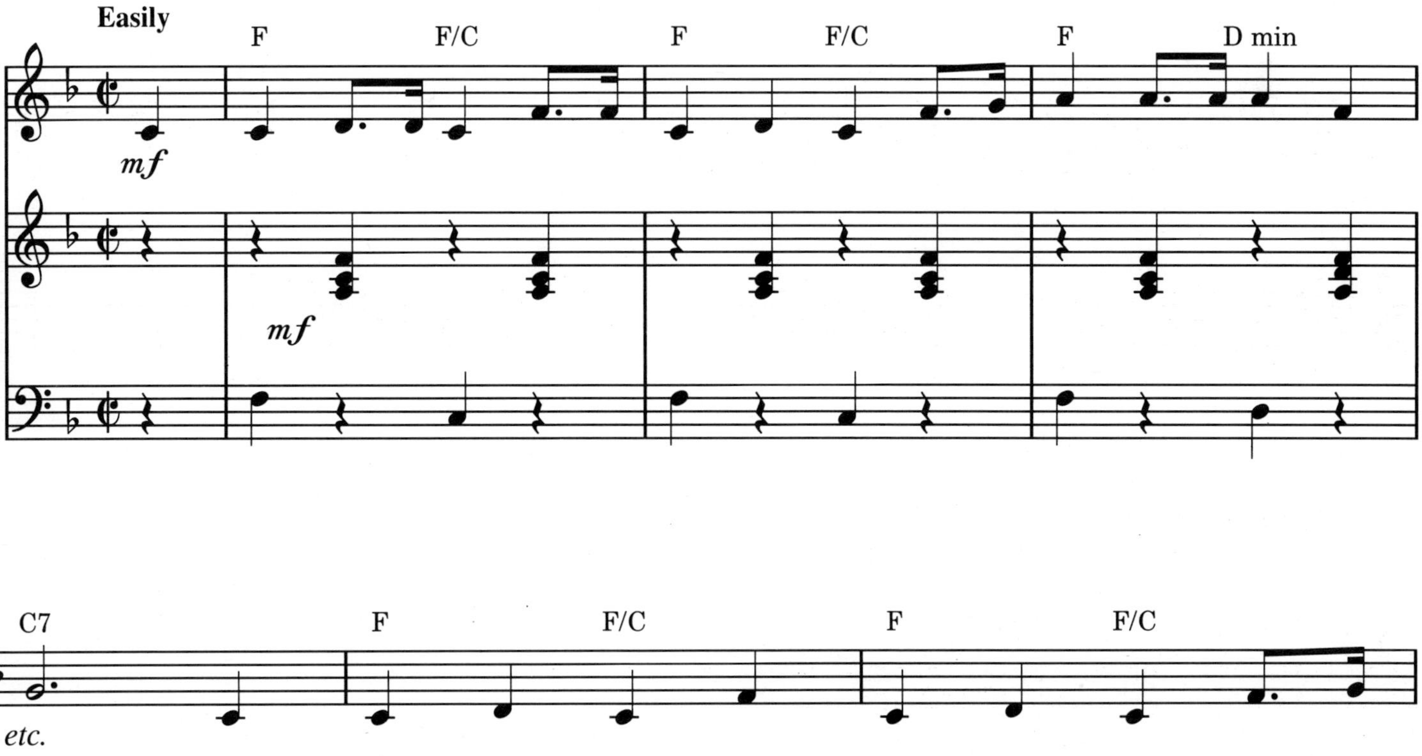

Broken Chord

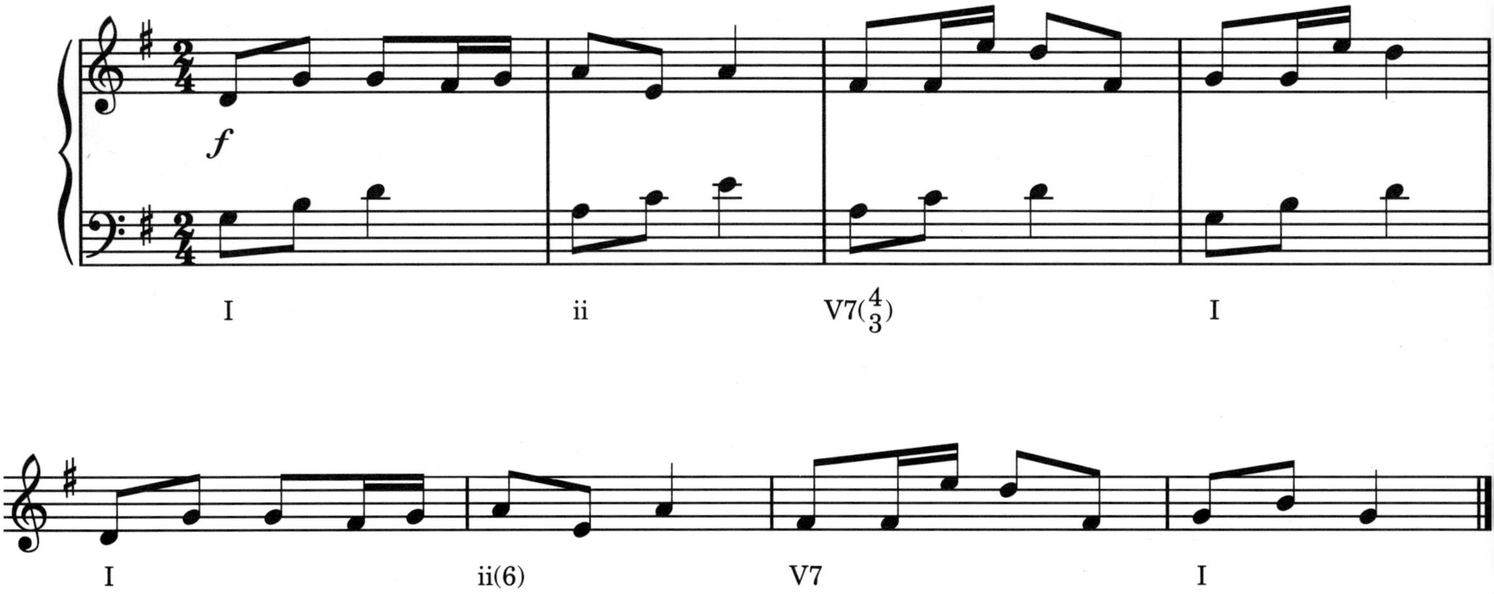

Keyboard Style

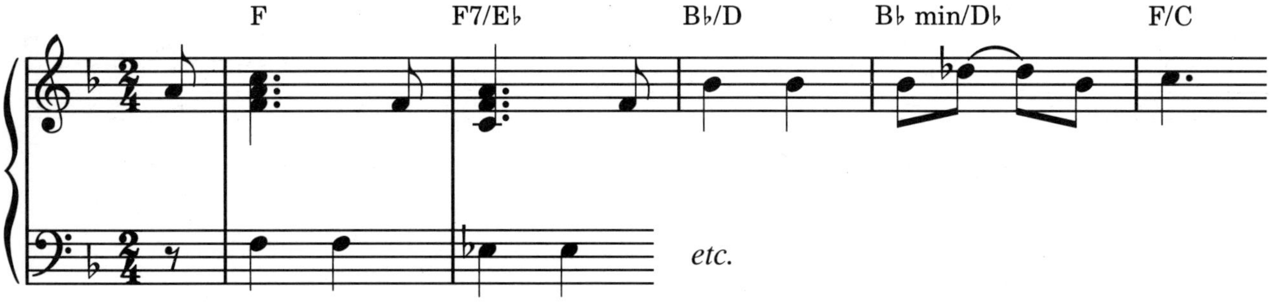

Two-Handed Broken Chord

TRANSPOSITION

Transposition is a chance to apply your skills and knowledge in basic theory directly to the keyboard. The tenor vocal line and the B♭ clarinet were the only two "transposing" parts included in PDM I. Other transposing instruments are used extensively in PDM II.

There are two basic rules for success in transposition:

- Think key
- Think function

If done correctly, transposition can be one of the easiest keyboard skills to acquire.

Of Melody with Chords

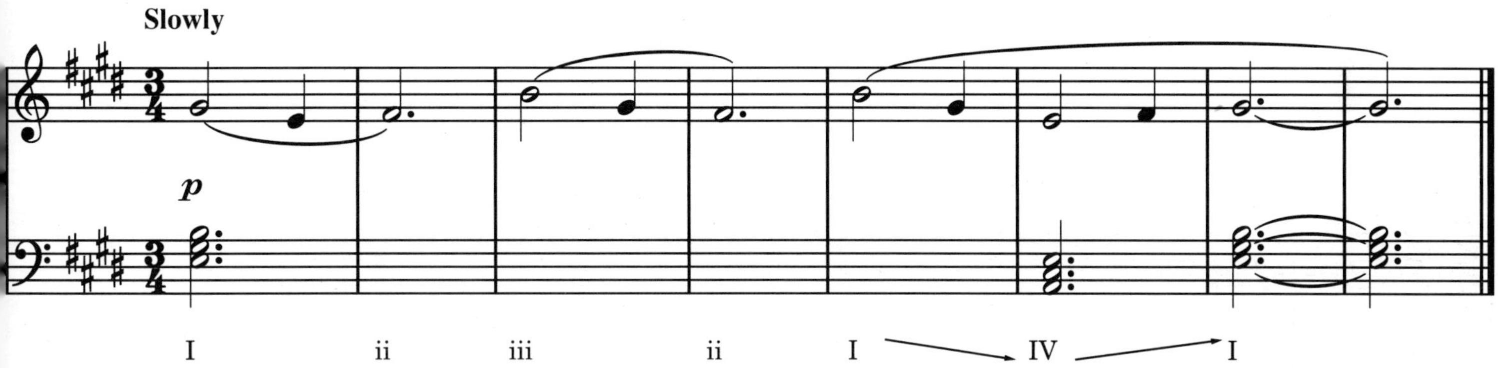

using a broken-chord accompaniment.

Of Pieces

Play in G major and A major.

Of Tenor Vocal Line

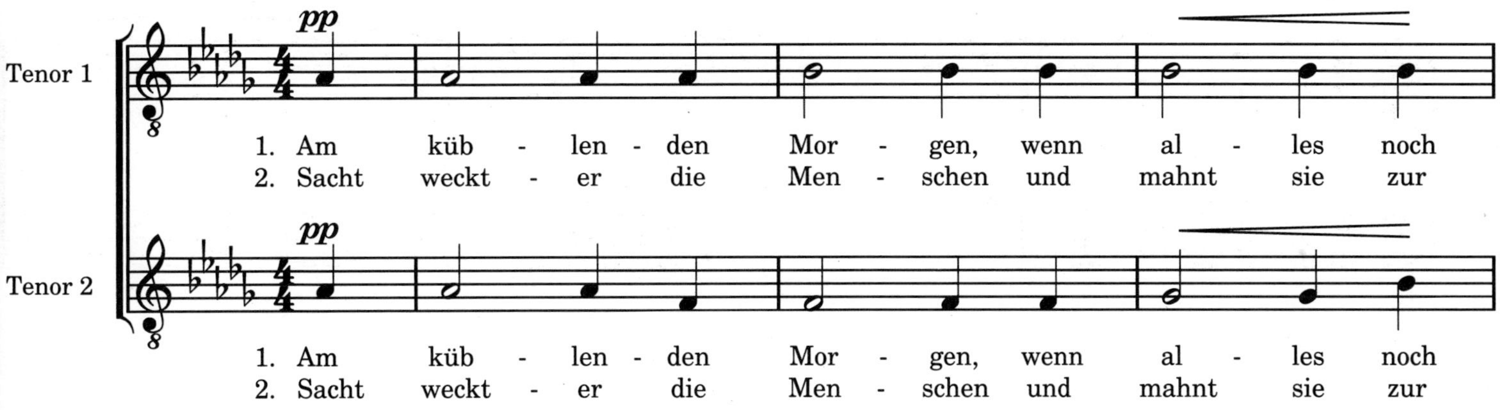
Tenor 1
pp
1. Am küb - len - den Mor - gen, wenn al - les noch
2. Sacht weckt - er die Men - schen und mahnt sie zur
Tenor 2
pp
1. Am küb - len - den Mor - gen, wenn al - les noch
2. Sacht weckt - er die Men - schen und mahnt sie zur

Of Harmonic Progressions

D major

$\frac{6}{8}$ I I | V7/vi vi | iii IV | V7/ii ii |

V7/V V | V7/iii iii | V7/IV ii^{6}_{5} | V7 I :||

Also in:

B♭ major
E♭ major

IMPROVISATION

This is one of the most enjoyable—and intimidating—keyboard skills one can learn. As musicians, we are taught to be "correct," if not "perfect," in our art. Besides wanting to perfect our skills on the piano, most of us have this secret desire to be able to sit down at the instrument and play spontaneously and wonderfully.

Unfortunately, it rarely works that way. Most of us have to work at it. The old saying that you have to be born with the ability to improvise is not true, however. This does not mean that we can all become the Mozarts or Taylors or Marsalises of the 1990s; but the ability to improvise is a possibility for any and all musicians. And inspirational playing is based on knowledge. It is the rare individual who simply walks to the keyboard and "lets it happen" without needing any instructions.

There were a variety of improvisational activities in PDM I, all of which stem from theoretical concepts. This review will deal with five basic areas of improvisation.

On a Given Progression

Play the progression in each of the indicated keys. Use left-hand chord roots while improvising a right-hand melody based on chord tones.

E major $\frac{4}{4}$ I | vi | IV | ii | V | I ii6 | I^6_4 V7 | I ||

D major $\frac{3}{4}$

F major $\frac{6}{8}$

Black-Key

The following melodies may be played using black keys only.

- *Amazing Grace*
- *Auld Lang Syne*

Play through each and improvise an ostinato bass.

The blues pentascale is scale degrees 1, 4, and 5 of a major pentascale, with a flat 3 and a flat 5.

a. Expansion

b. Full Blues Scale

c. Walking Bass

Typical Progression for Twelve-Bar Blues

I	IV	I	I
IV	IV	I	I
V	IV	I	V (I to end)

Example of Blues "Scat" Rhythms

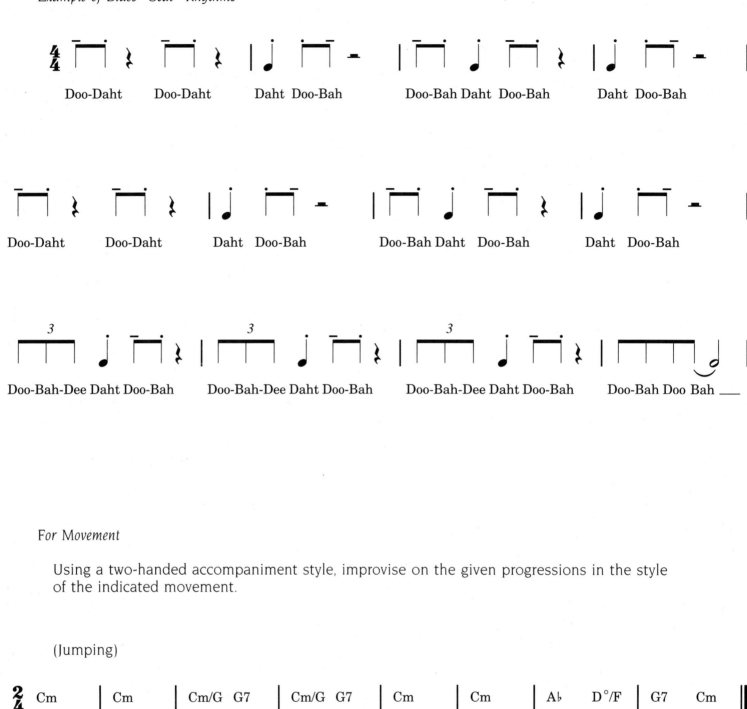

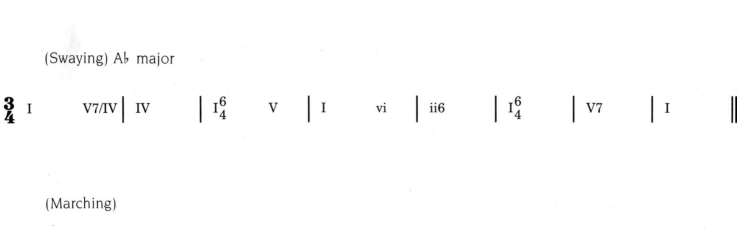

Doo-Daht Doo-Daht Daht Doo-Bah Doo-Bah Daht Doo-Bah Daht Doo-Bah
Doo-Daht Doo-Daht Daht Doo-Bah Doo-Bah Daht Doo-Bah Daht Doo-Bah
3 3 3
Doo-Bah-Dee Daht Doo-Bah Doo-Bah-Dee Daht Doo-Bah Doo-Bah-Dee Daht Doo-Bah Doo-Bah Doo Bah ___

For Movement

Using a two-handed accompaniment style, improvise on the given progressions in the style of the indicated movement.

(Jumping)

2/4 Cm | Cm | Cm/G G7 | Cm/G G7 | Cm | Cm | A♭ D°/F | G7 Cm ||

(Swaying) A♭ major

3/4 I V7/IV | IV | I_4^6 V | I vi | ii6 | I_4^6 | V7 | I ||

(Marching)

4/4 E | B7 | C♯m E/G♯ | C♯7/G♯ | F♯m/A | E/B B7 | E ||

becomes:

1.

EXEMPLARY REPERTOIRE

RELATED SKILLS AND ACTIVITIES

SUBSEQUENT REPERTOIRE

The ii–V7–I Progression

EXEMPLARY REPERTOIRE **Lemonade** Lynn Freeman Olson

INQUIRY

1. Scan the piece. Observe:
   - Chord shapes
   - Form
   - Harmonic progression
2. Determine fingering.

PERFORMANCE

1. Block right-hand chord shapes.
2. Play as written. Count aloud.

Lemonade

LYNN FREEMAN OLSON

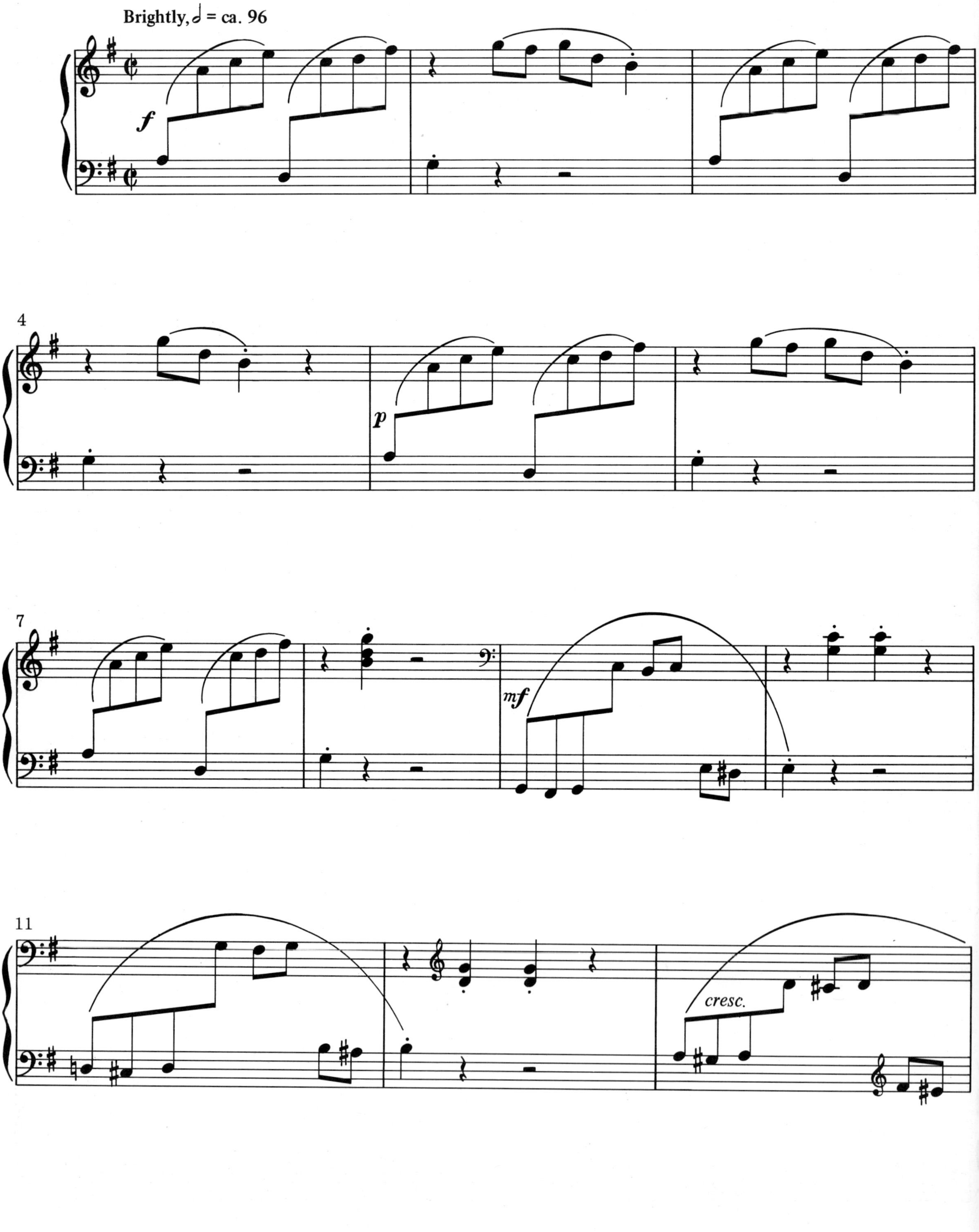

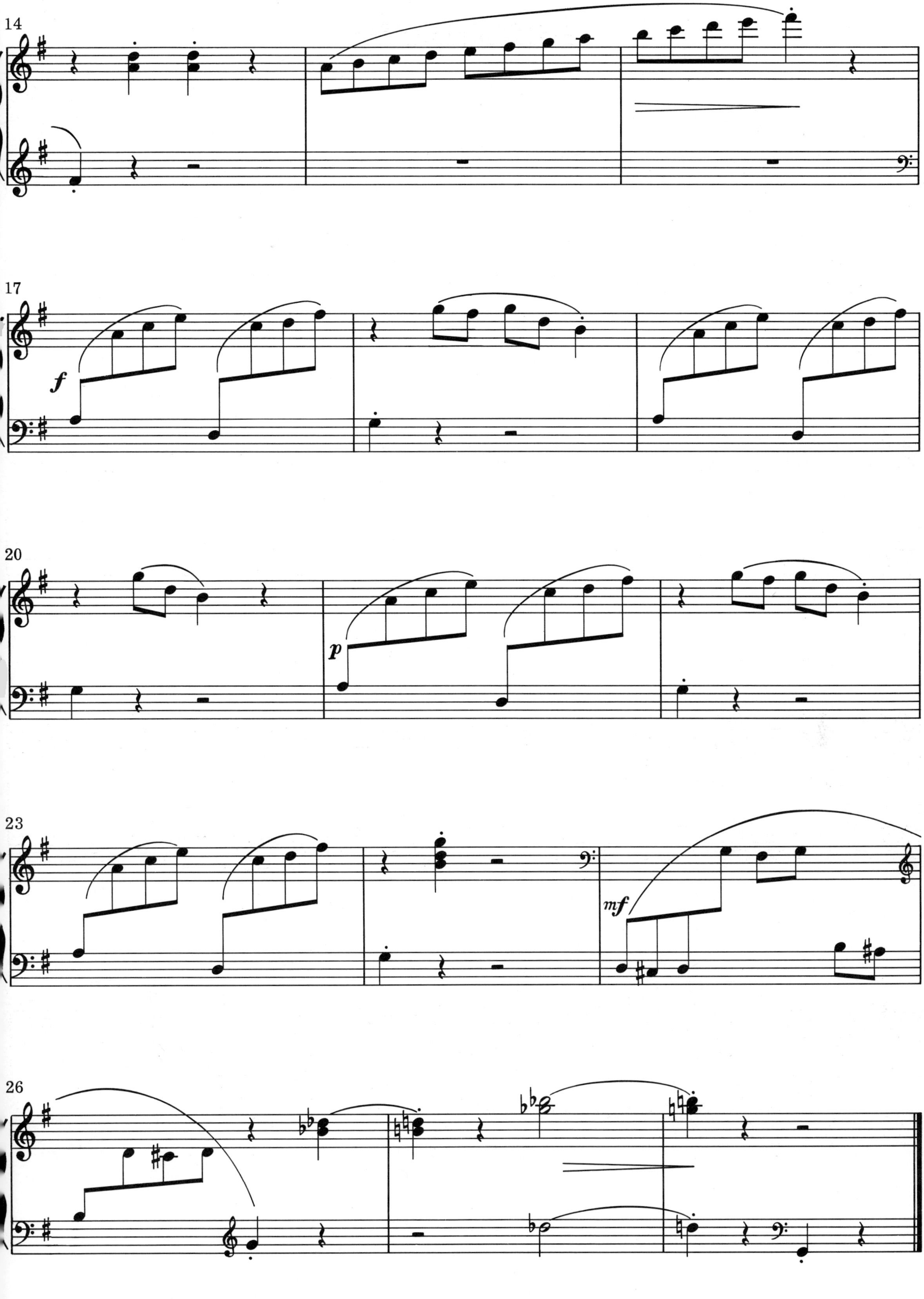
14
17
f
20
p
23
mf
26

RELATED SKILLS AND ACTIVITIES

TECHNIQUE

1. C♯ minor and F♯ minor scales use the same fingering combinations as their relative major scales.

						START ↓									
RH:	1	2	3	1	2	3	4	1	2	3	1	2	3	4	1
LH:	5	4	3	2	1	3	2	1	4	3	2	1	3	2	1
						↑ START									

2. Play *Pleasant Morning.*

Pleasant Morning

STREABBOG (JEAN-LOUIS GOBBAERTS)
(1835–1886)

Allegro moderato

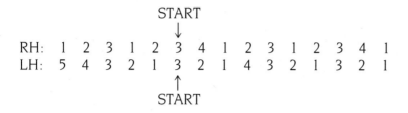

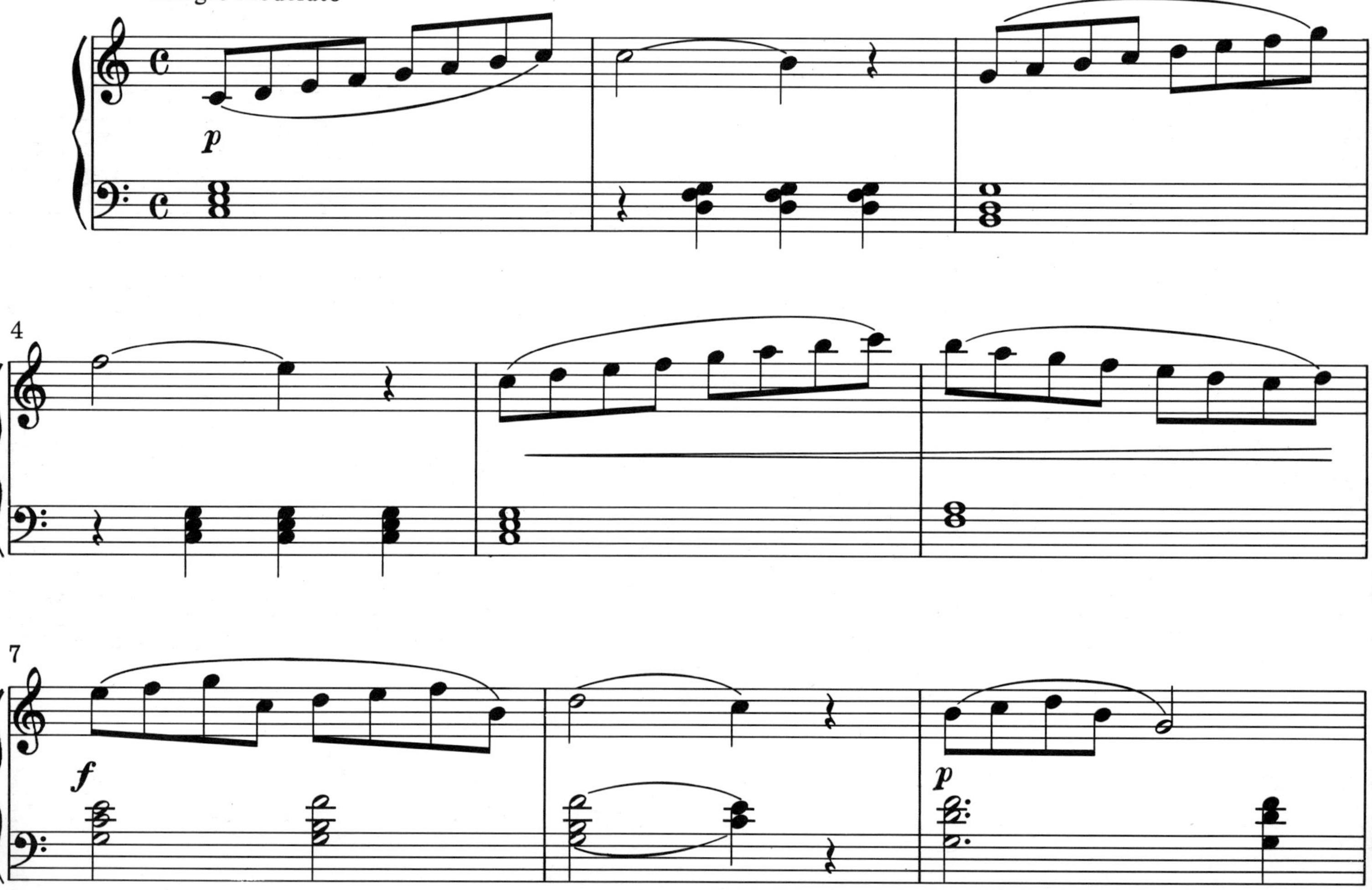

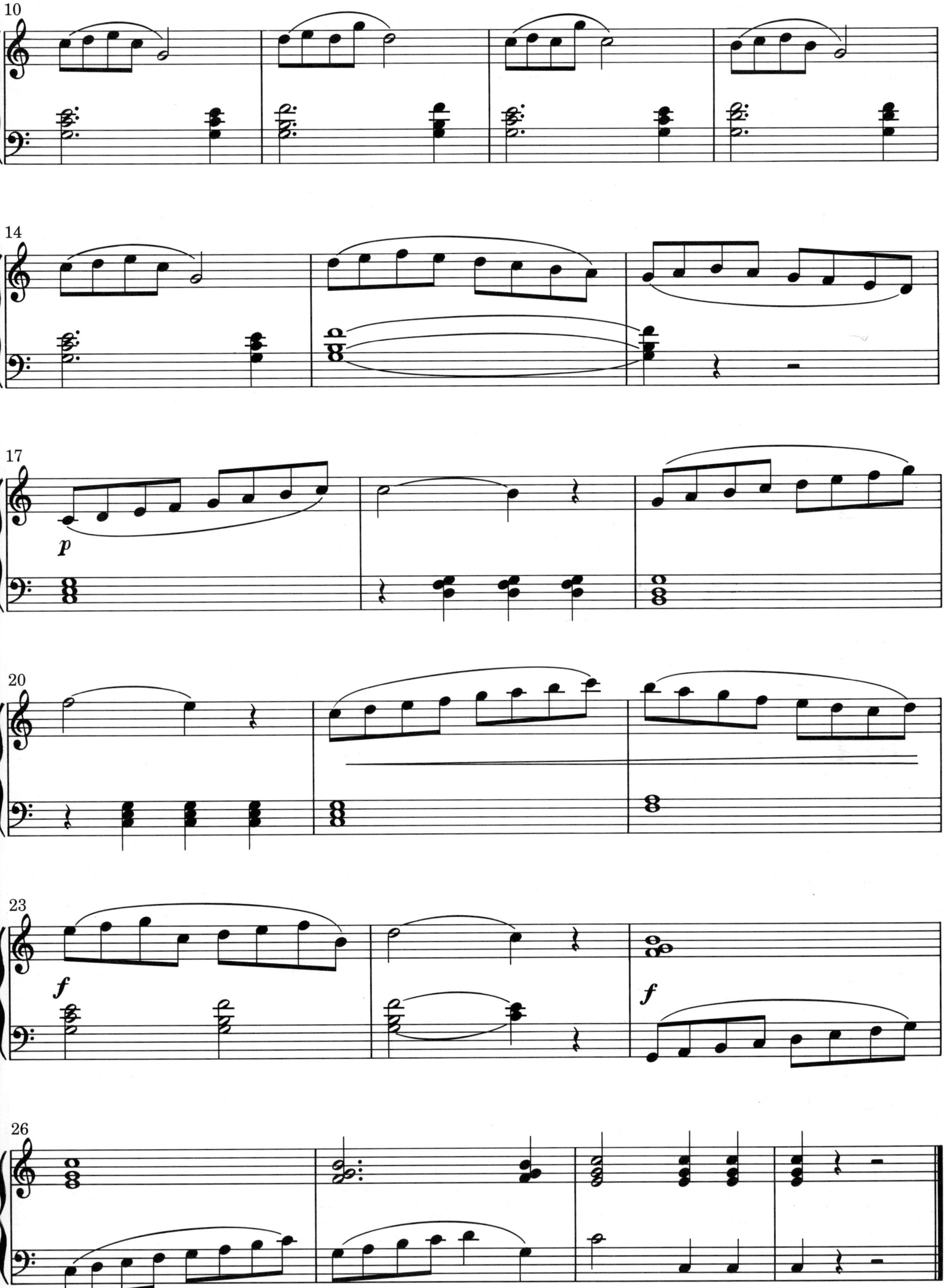
10
14
17
p
20
23
f
f
26

READING

1. The alto clef positions middle C on the third line of the staff.

Play the following viola excerpt using alto clef.

String Quartet in E-Flat Major

(Viola excerpt)

WOLFGANG AMADEUS MOZART
(1756–1791)

2. Play the following viola line from *Bassa imperiale*. Then choose a partner and play as an ensemble.

Bassa imperiale

ANONYMOUS
18th Century

3. When learning to read chorale-style pieces such as hymns, a good plan is to play through while focusing only on the soprano and bass lines.

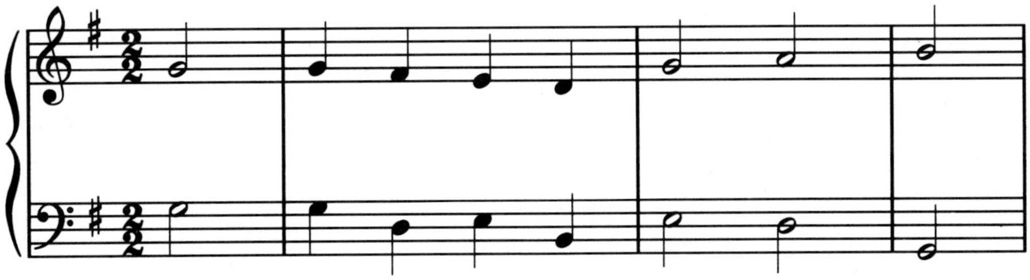

Next, repeat and add another voice that you will play no matter how difficult it may be. (Alto will often be easier, and we suggest this. The tenor line may be more satisfying at times to the ear, but it sometimes must be played by RH.)

Finally, play all four voices, keeping in mind that the soprano-bass combination is to be maintained with surety.

Old Hundredth

Genevan Psalter
(1551)

4. Play all four parts at once.

Erlaube mir, feins Mädchen

(Original key—A♭ major)

JOHANNES BRAHMS
(1833–1897)

Lieblich
p
Soprano 1 2
1. Er - lau - be mir, feins Mäd - chen, in den Gar - ten zu
Alto 1 2
p
4
gehn, dass ich dort mag schau - en, wie die
7
Ro - sen so schön. Er - lau - be sie zu

10
bre - chen, es ist die höch - ste Zeit; ih - re
13
Schön - heit, ih - re Ju - gend hat mir mein Herz er - freut.

5. Apply the principles of chorale-style reading outlined on pages 25–26.

Were You There?

(Voice excerpt)

American Folk Hymn

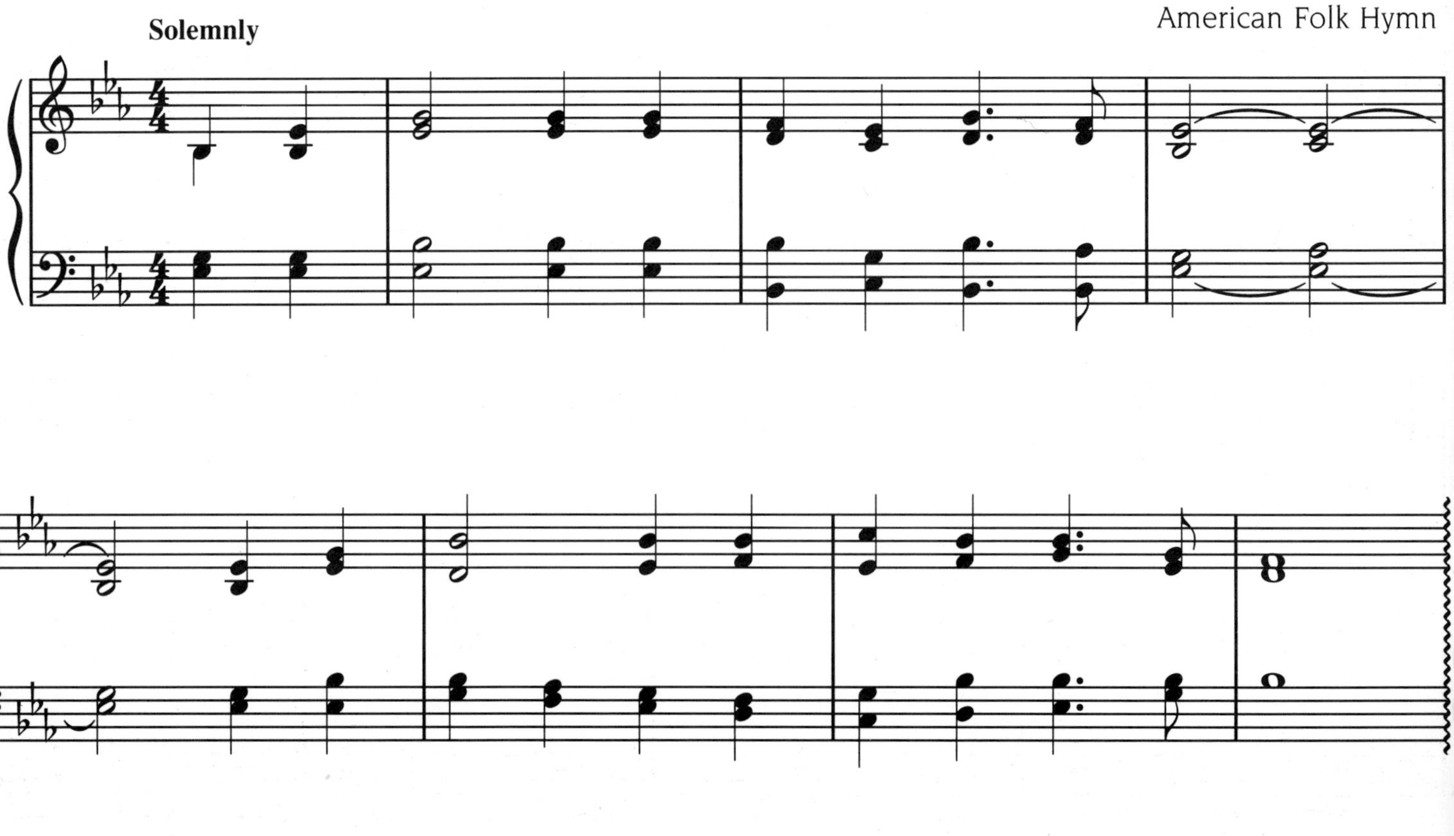
Solemnly

6. Before reading the accompaniment for *Come raggio di sol,* play the following "preparation." This is what the eye should see—*only what is different.*

Come raggio di sol

(Voice excerpt)

ANTONIO CALDARA
(1670–1736)

KEYBOARD THEORY

1. Play a V^4_3–I^6_3 chain chromatically from C up to C. Begin with the right hand, then play it again with the left hand.

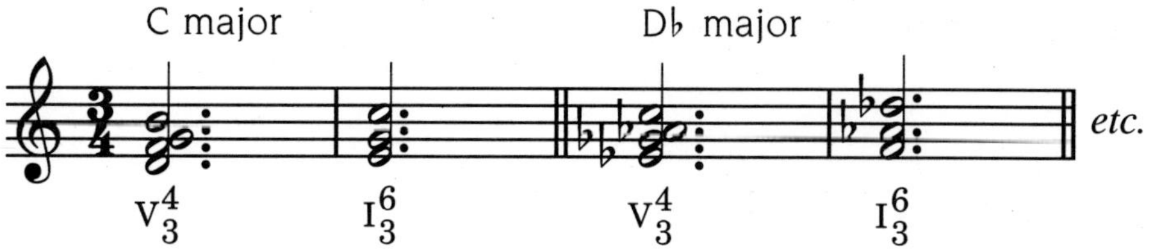

Add left-hand roots as the right hand plays the chord chain.

2. The most basic type of authentic cadence is twofold: dominant to tonic. The dominant area is strengthened by preceding it with the subdominant or substituting another chord for the subdominant (such as the supertonic—ii).

   The ii–V7–I cadence appears frequently. For smooth voice leading (and because melodic content often dictates), the form is commonly ii6–V7–I.

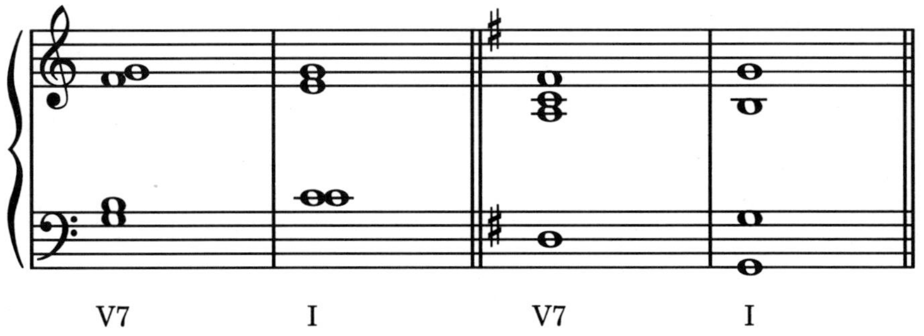

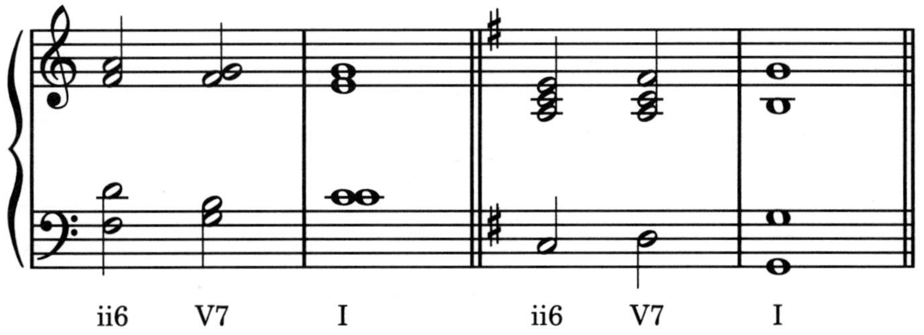

3. Play ii6–V7–I progressions in the following keys. Your teacher will set the tempo and give a measure of rest between each new key:

A E♭ D A♭ G D♭

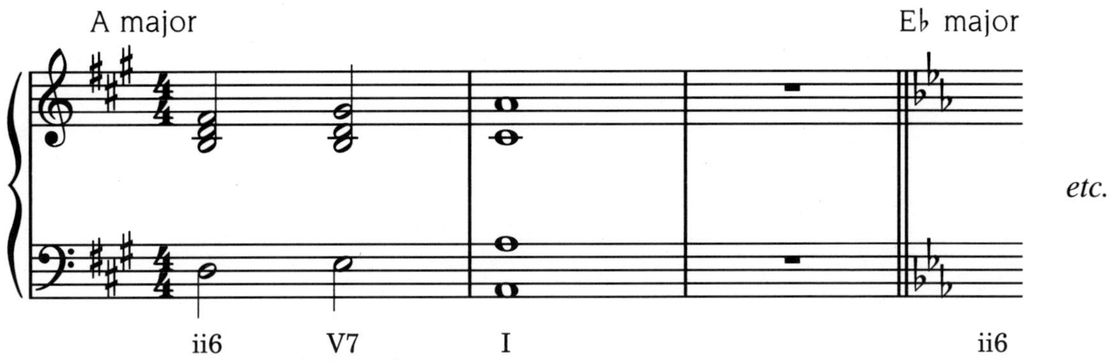

HARMONIZATION

1. Choose from I, ii, V6, V7.

M'appari tutti' amor

from the opera *Martha*

FRIEDRICH von FLOTOW
(1812–1883)

2. Review the V^4_3–I^6_3 theory exercise. Furnish missing Roman numerals before playing.

The Flowers That Bloom in the Spring

from *The Mikado*

SIR ARTHUR SULLIVAN
(1842–1900)

4
etc.
V4/3 of vi
8
f
V7 of V
11
(unis.)
14
p
17
I
mf
20
f
vi
23
ii6/5

3. Choose from I, V^4_3, V^6_5, ii6, I6, V7, V7/IV, and IV.

With a lilt Irish

4. Determine the harmony for the following and play in keyboard style.

Dennis Hymn Tune

LOWELL MASON
(1792–1872)

1. Transpose this Thomas Arne hymn to the key of G♭ major. Think *totally* in the new key—use the score as a directional guide. Refer to the suggestions for chorale style under Reading (pages 25–26).

Arlington

THOMAS A. ARNE
(1710–1778)

With joy

2. Play the following as a round in the key written. As the fourth group plays the last measure of the melody, the teacher will call for a new key. From that point on, at the downbeat of the last measure in each phrase, a new key will be called. Continue until the fourth group has played the melody two more times.

To Portsmouth!

Lively

MELVILL

3. With all transposing instruments, *think in concert key* rather than transposing each note. For clarinets in B♭, think down a whole step.

- In what key will you play the clarinet part?
- Play both parts.

Three Duos

(Excerpt)

LUDWIG van BEETHOVEN
(1770–1827)

4. Choose a partner and perform this excerpt from Donahue's *Divertimento for B♭ Clarinet*.

Lullaby

(B♭ clarinet excerpt)

ROBERT L. DONAHUE

8
rit.
a tempo
p
rit.
p a tempo
12
16
p
p
legato
20

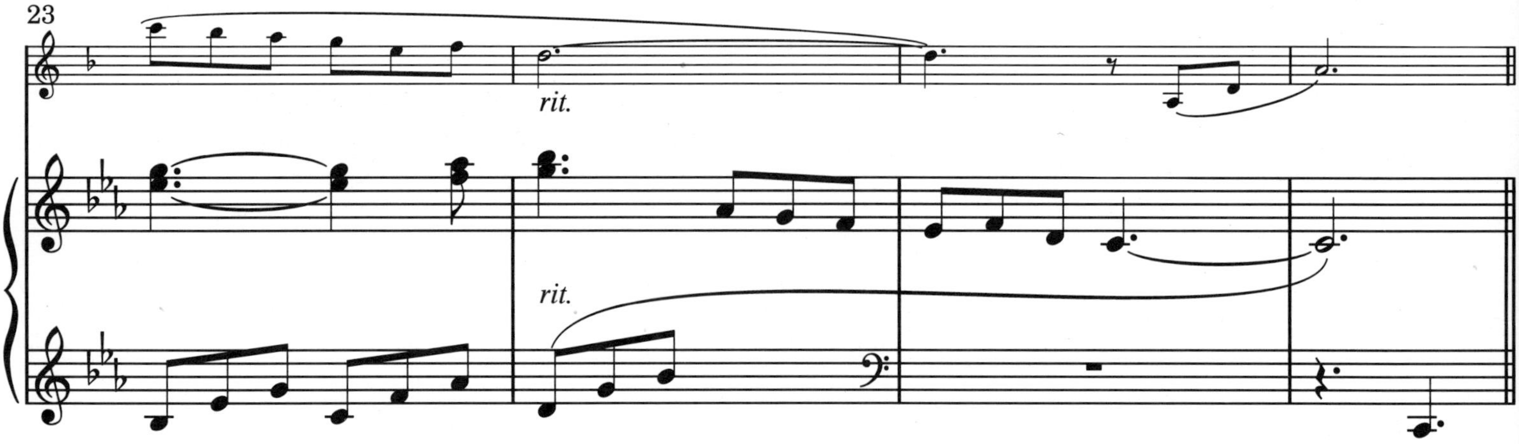

IMPROVISATION

1. Play the Mozart "A" section as written (with repeat), then substitute an improvised "B" section with a return to the written "A."

Burleske

LEOPOLD MOZART
(1719–1787)

2. Based on the harmonies of *Burleske*, improvise a piece "in the style" of Leopold Mozart. Consider the following characteristics:

- Use of sequence in melody
- Use of repetition
- Bass uses only one interval throughout

ENSEMBLE

1. Perform the following once as written. Perform again with these options:

- Parts 2 and 3 become one part.
- On the repeat, part 1 should play a solo improvisation based on the harmonic structure; the second ending as written may be used for the close of the solo improvisation.

The ii–V Doodle

MARTHA HILLEY

2. Choose a partner and perform *Allegro in E Minor.*

Allegro in E Minor

ANTON DIABELLI
(1781–1858)

7
ff
p
ff
p
10
cresc.
cresc.
13
f
ff
f
ff

SUBSEQUENT REPERTOIRE

1. Before reading, pay special attention to the rhythm of the ornament figures.

One Voice Singing

from A *Set of Six*

JOSEPH SCRIVENER

2. Practice the "layering" effect of the left hand.

B♭ F g d c B♭ Cm7 F7 B♭

Sarabande

JOHANN PACHELBEL
(1653–1706)

2.

EXEMPLARY REPERTOIRE

RELATED SKILLS AND ACTIVITIES

SUBSEQUENT REPERTOIRE

Harmonic Implications of Common Modes

EXEMPLARY REPERTOIRE **Lydian Nocturne** Robert D. Vandall

INQUIRY

1. Scan the piece. Observe:

   - Broken chord accompaniment
   - Clef changes
   - Lydian scalar passages

PERFORMANCE

1. Determine a fingering for left-hand accompaniment figure.

2. Start practice with bars 11–18. Why?

Lydian Nocturne

Lydian Mode

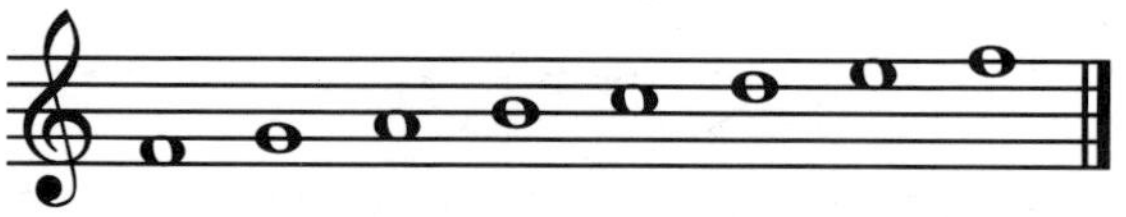

ROBERT D. VANDALL

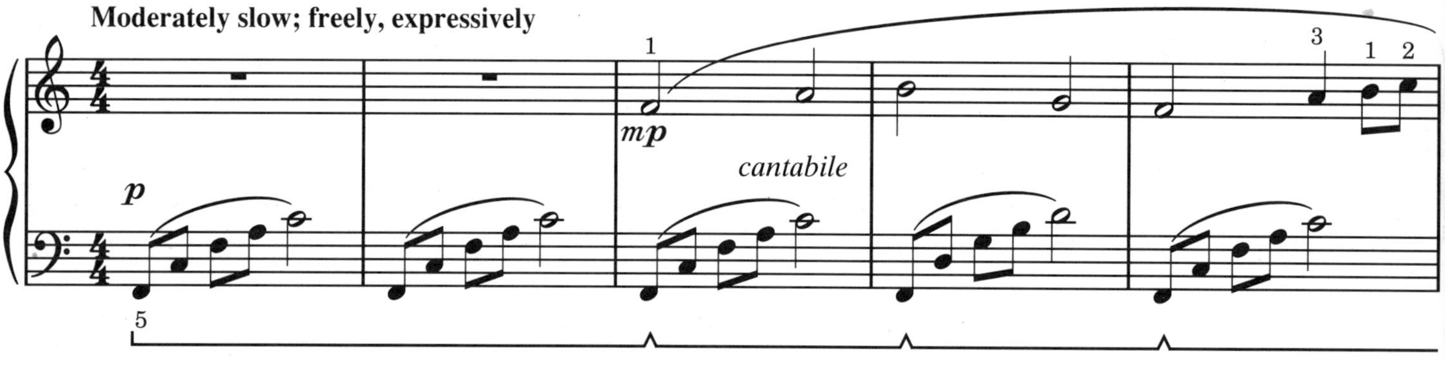

15
19
8va
p
cresc.
f
23
mf
dim.
p
(8va)
27
a tempo
rit.
mp
31
loco
rit.

RELATED SKILLS AND ACTIVITIES

TECHNIQUE

1. A♭/G♯ minor, B♭/A♯ minor, and E♭/D♯ minor scales use the same fingering combinations as their relative majors:

G♭ major

RH: 2 3 4 1 2 3 1 2 3 4 1 2 3 1 2
LH: 4 3 2 1 3 2 1 4 3 2 1 3 2 1 4

E♭ minor ↓

RH: 3 1 2 3 4 1 2 3 1 2 3 4 1 2 3
LH: 2 1 4 3 2 1 3 2 1 4 3 2 1 3 2

2. Observe clef changes and sequence before playing.

Prelude in C Minor

GIUSEPPE CONCONE, Op. 37
(1801–1861)

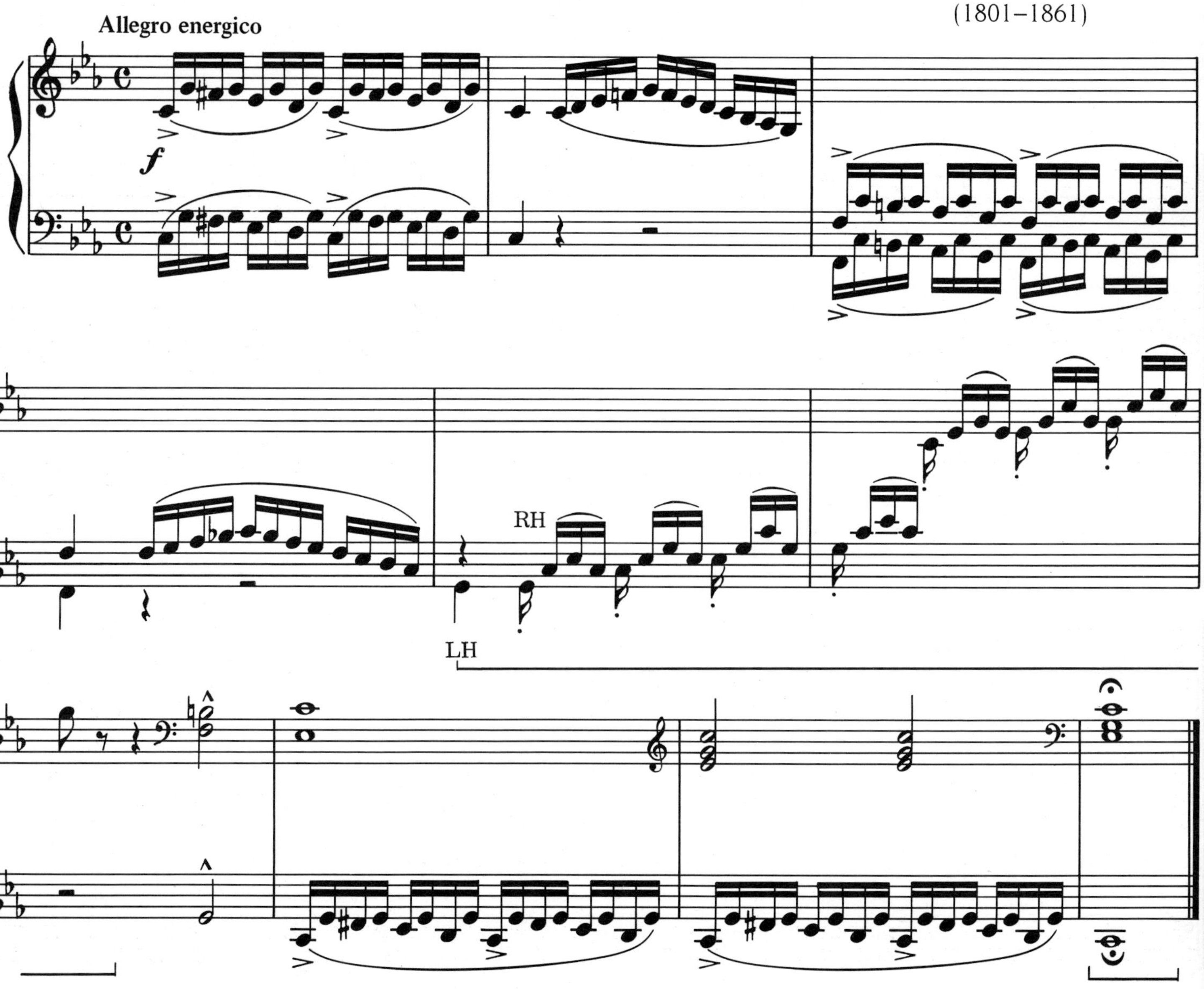

READING

1. In the following Haydn excerpt, play the soprano and alto parts in one hand as you conduct with the other.

Psalm 50

(Excerpt)

FRANZ JOSEPH HAYDN
(1732–1809)

Un poco allegro
Soprano
Alto
Bass
mf
Sein Au - ge sieht, was wir nie sehn:
Sein Au - ge sieht, was wir nie sehn:
Sein Au - ge sieht, was wir nie sehn:
5
Wie Zei - ten auf und nie - der - gehn,
10
wie Zei - ten auf und nie - der - gehn.

2. Play the following combinations in the excerpt from the Beethoven *Menuetto and Trio*:

- Violin I and cello
- Violin II and cello
- Violin I and violin II

Then play as a three-part ensemble.

Menuetto and Trio

(Excerpt)

LUDWIG van BEETHOVEN
(1770–1827)

3. As a class, discuss possible simplifications of this accompaniment. Choose a partner and perform.

Vom Tode

LUDWIG van BEETHOVEN
(1770–1827)

Mäßig und cher langsam als geschwind
Voice
Piano
p
pp
Mei - ne Le - bens - zeit ver - streicht, stünd - lich
7
eil ich zu dem Gra - be, und was ist's, das ich viel -
f
13
leicht, das ich noch zu le - ben ha - be?
sf
p
cresc.
f
p

20
Denk, o Mensch, an dei - nen Tod! Säu - me
27
nicht, denn eins ist not, säu - me nicht, denn eins
cresc.
f
sf
p
34
ist not, säu - me nicht, denn eins ist not!
cresc.
p
42

3. Play violin II and viola together. Notice parallel and oblique motion.

String Quartet in E-Flat Major

(Violin II and viola excerpt)

WOLFGANG AMADEUS MOZART
(1756–1791)

4. Play both parts.

Duo in C Major

(Excerpt)

JOHANN GEORG ALBRECHTSBERGER
(1736–1809)

5. In *Chautauqua Hymn Tune* on page 54 play soprano, alto, and bass, then add tenor voice. Keep a steady tempo regardless of any mistakes that may occur.

Chautauqua Hymn Tune

WILLIAM SHERWIN
(1826–1888)

6. The clarinet part must be transposed down a whole step in order to be played on a keyboard. Simply think in the key of B-flat and read intervals.

- Play the clarinet line
- Play the accompaniment
- Choose a partner and play as an ensemble

Sonata for B-Flat Clarinet

(Excerpt)

JOHANN BAPTIST WANHAL
(1739–1813)

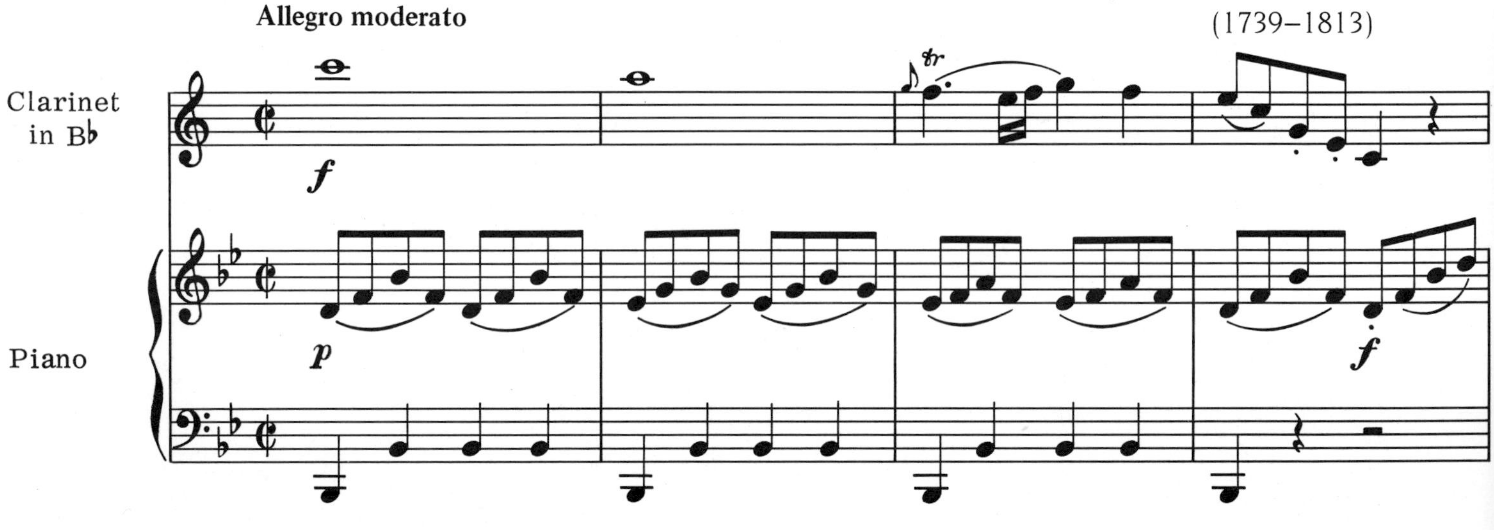

KEYBOARD THEORY

1. The harmony in modal music is diatonic to the particular scale. Modes can be divided into major and minor categories.

Major	**Minor**
Ionian	Dorian
Lydian	Phrygian
Mixolydian	Aeolian

The harmonies resulting from building triads on modal scale tones tend to diffuse the strong traditional sense of tonic. For example, in Dorian, Mixolydian, and Aeolian modes, the dominant is a minor triad; in Phrygian, the dominant is diminished.

Play diatonic triads for the following modal scales.

Example:

D Phrygian:

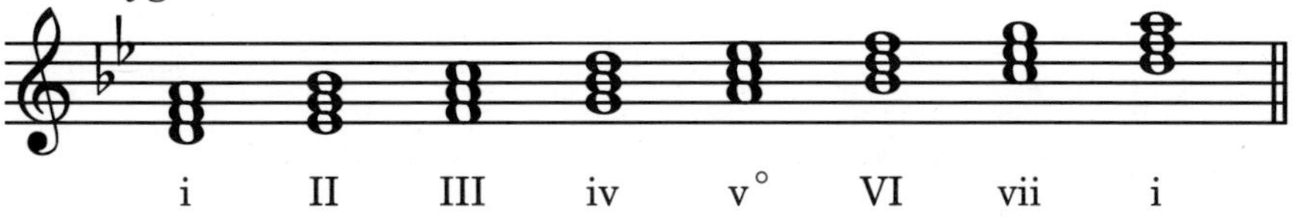

A Dorian
B♭ Mixolydian
E Lydian
C Phrygian

2. In the following examples, indicated harmonies represent progressions characteristic of the mode. Complete each harmonization using chords that will highlight the mode.

It is occasionally appropriate to harmonize modal melodies in ways not associated with eighteenth-century common practice because of the special characteristics of certain modes. Although modal harmonies should use only pitches from the mode in question, occasional accidentals (such as a raised 7th or a lowered 6th) may occur as the tasteful choice.

HARMONIZATION

1. Use left-hand broken chord accompaniment.

Iris

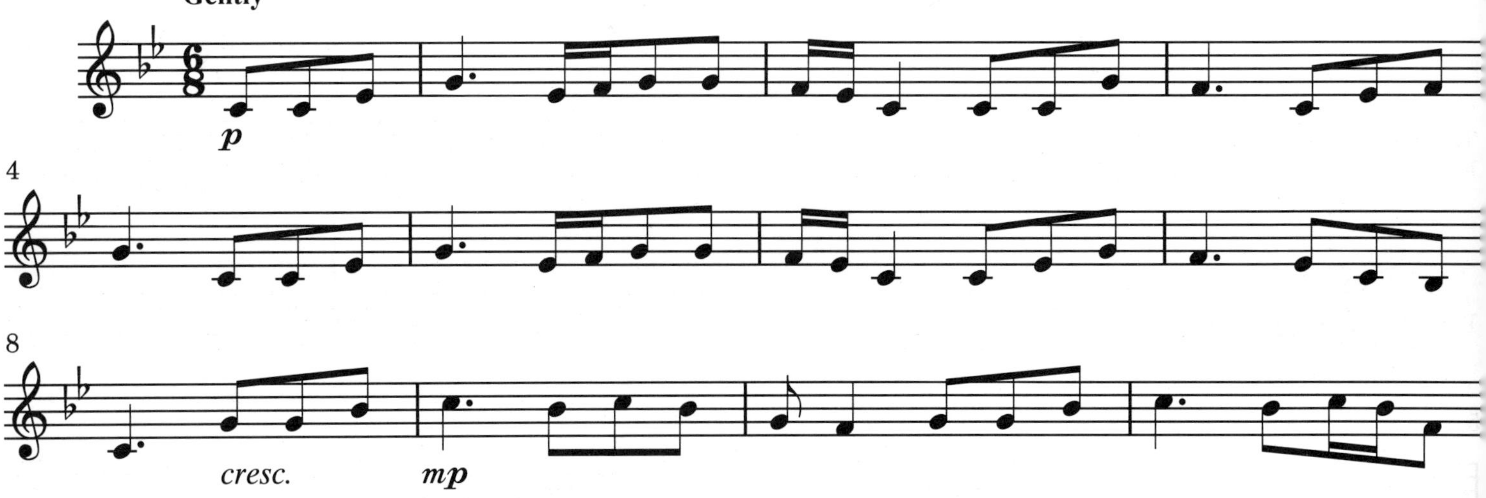

2. On what mode is the following American melody based?

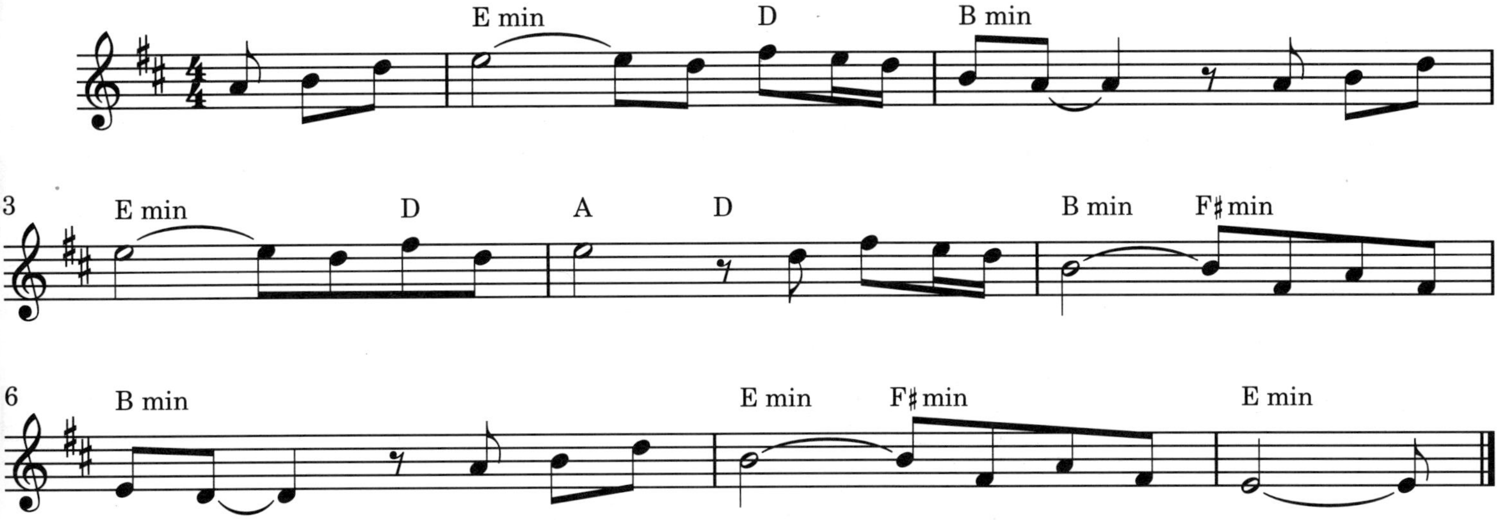

Harmonize using a "strumming" style accompaniment:

TRANSPOSITION

1. Play the following adaptation of Telemann's *Menuett*. In what key must the trumpet part be played when performed on the keyboard?

Menuett

(Adapted excerpt)

GEORG PHILIPP TELEMANN
(1681–1764)

2. Transpose this theme for horn in F. Think in the key of E♭ major.

Theme

from *Theme and Variations*

FRANZ STRAUSS, Op. 13
(1822–1905)

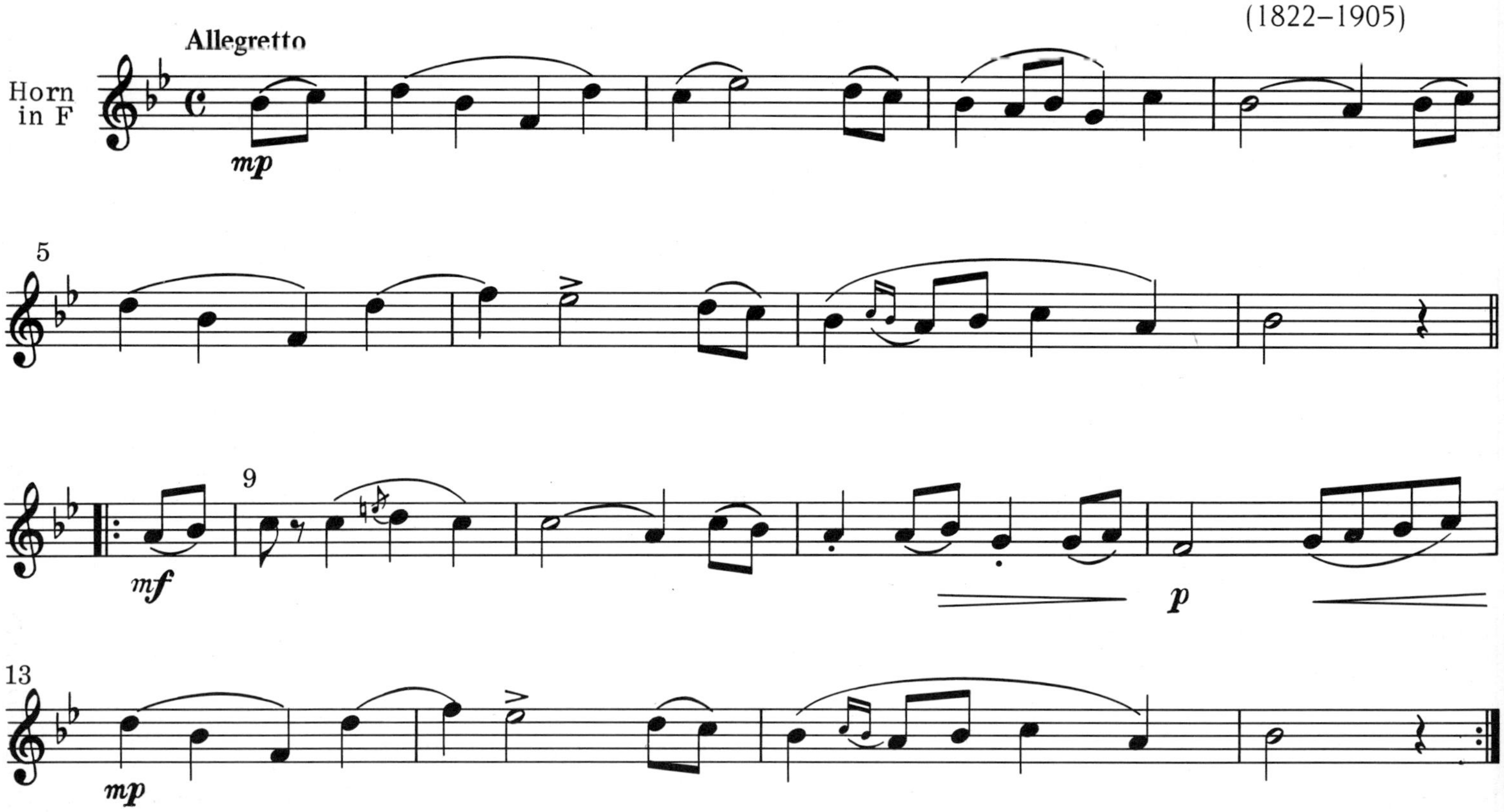

3. Analyze the Gurlitt, then transpose to E♭ major and A♭ major.

Das artige Kind

from *First Lessons*

CORNELIUS GURLITT, Op. 117, No. 19
(1820–1901)

IMPROVISATION

1. Determine the tonal center for each of the following and improvise melodically above the given bass.

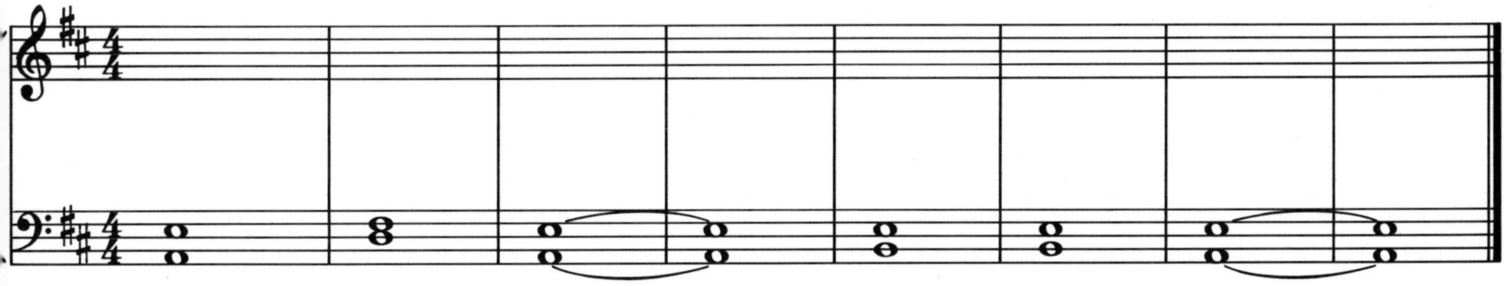

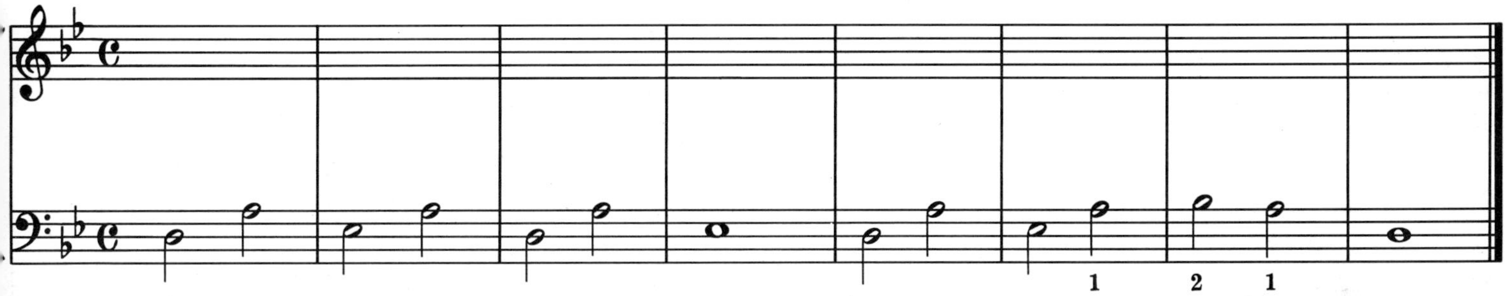

2. Dorian mode is useful in minor blues improvisation due to its compatibility with minor-minor seventh chords. If playing blues in "F minor," the I chord would use F Dorian, the IV chord B-flat Dorian, and the V chord C Dorian. The example below uses Dorian mode for melodic improvisation. Complete the 12-bar pattern using Dorian fragments.

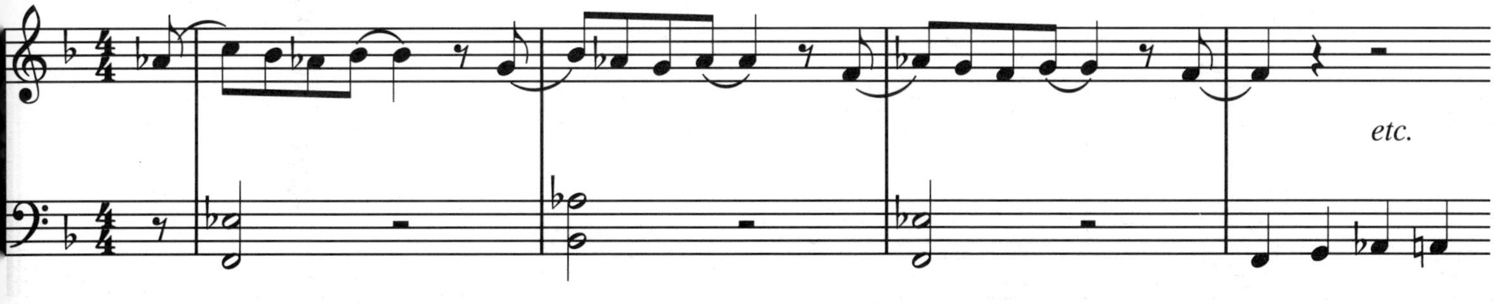

ENSEMBLE

1. Choose a partner and practice playing in the following order: RH of each part, LH of each part. Listen carefully for balance.

Now Sleep Gently

Norwegian
Arranged by Lynn Freeman Olson

SUBSEQUENT REPERTOIRE

1. Identify the traditional passamezzo progression.

Thursday 10/9

Passamezzo

Italian, 16th century
Realization, Lynn Freeman Olson

Quickly, 𝅗𝅥 = ca. 138

2. The A section of *Bright Orange* is divided into the following groups of measures: 3 + 3 + 3 + 6.

- Divide the class into four groups and *patsch* the rhythm of this section in a round-robin fashion.
- Determine the sections and groups of measures for the balance of the piece. *Patsch*.
- Play left-hand triads while tapping the right-hand rhythm patterns on a flat surface.
- Play as written.

Bright Orange

from *Sketches in Color*

ROBERT STARER
(1924–)

21
27
f
32
ff
mf
38
f
43
ff
8va
sfz

3.

Supplementary Material

READING

1. Scan quickly for common tones and repeated pitches.

Maryton Hymn Tune

H. PERCY SMITH
(1825–1898)

2. Look for chord shapes in accompaniment.

Reverie

(Excerpt)

CLAUDE DEBUSSY
(1862–1918)
Arranged by Herman A. Hummel

3. Look for harmonic structure.

Sonatina

WOLFGANG AMADEUS MOZART
(1756–1791)
Arranged by Jay Ernst

4. Note clef changes.

Menuett

(Excerpt)

FRIEDRICH KUHLAU
(1786–1832)
Edited by H. Voxman

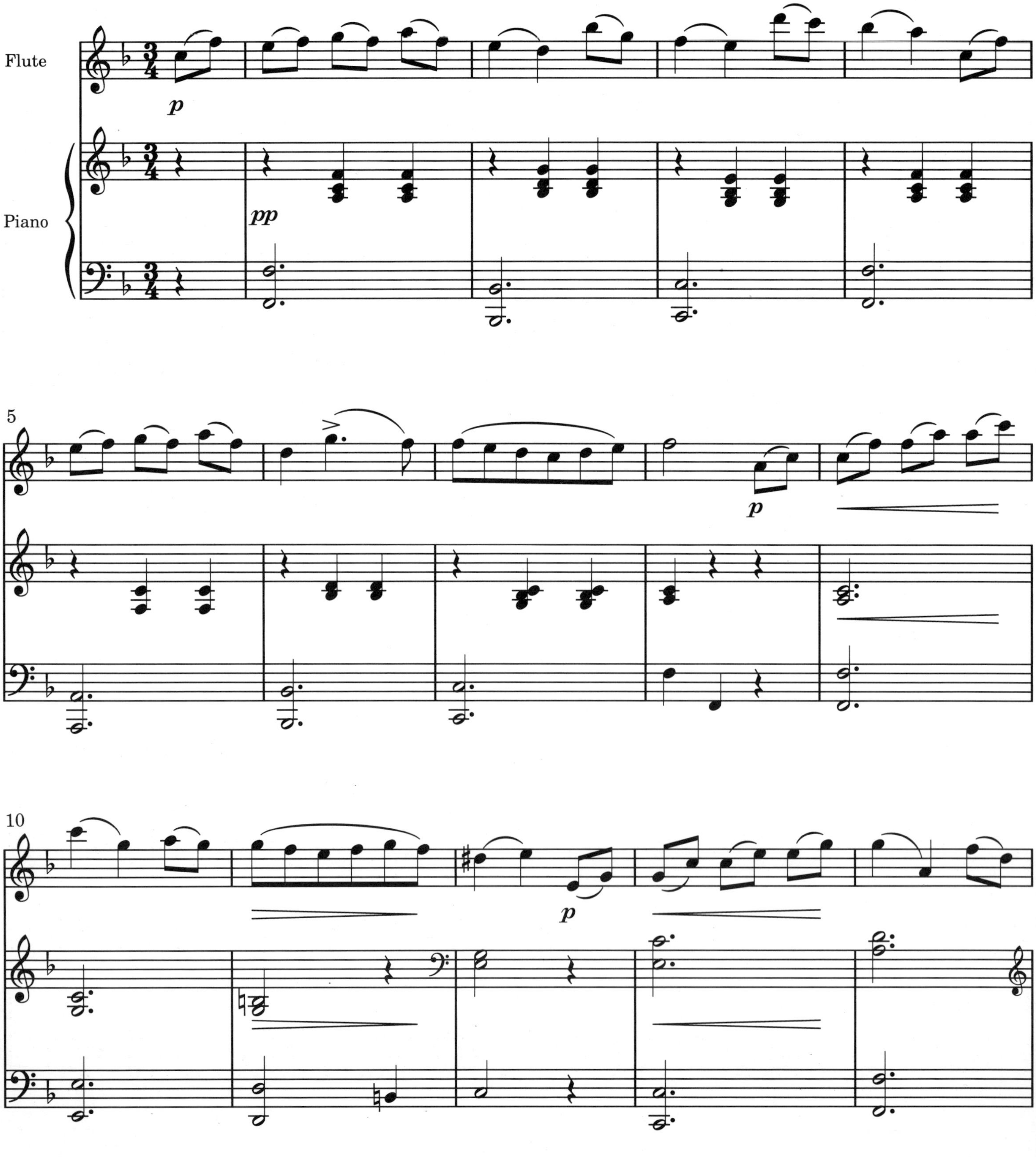

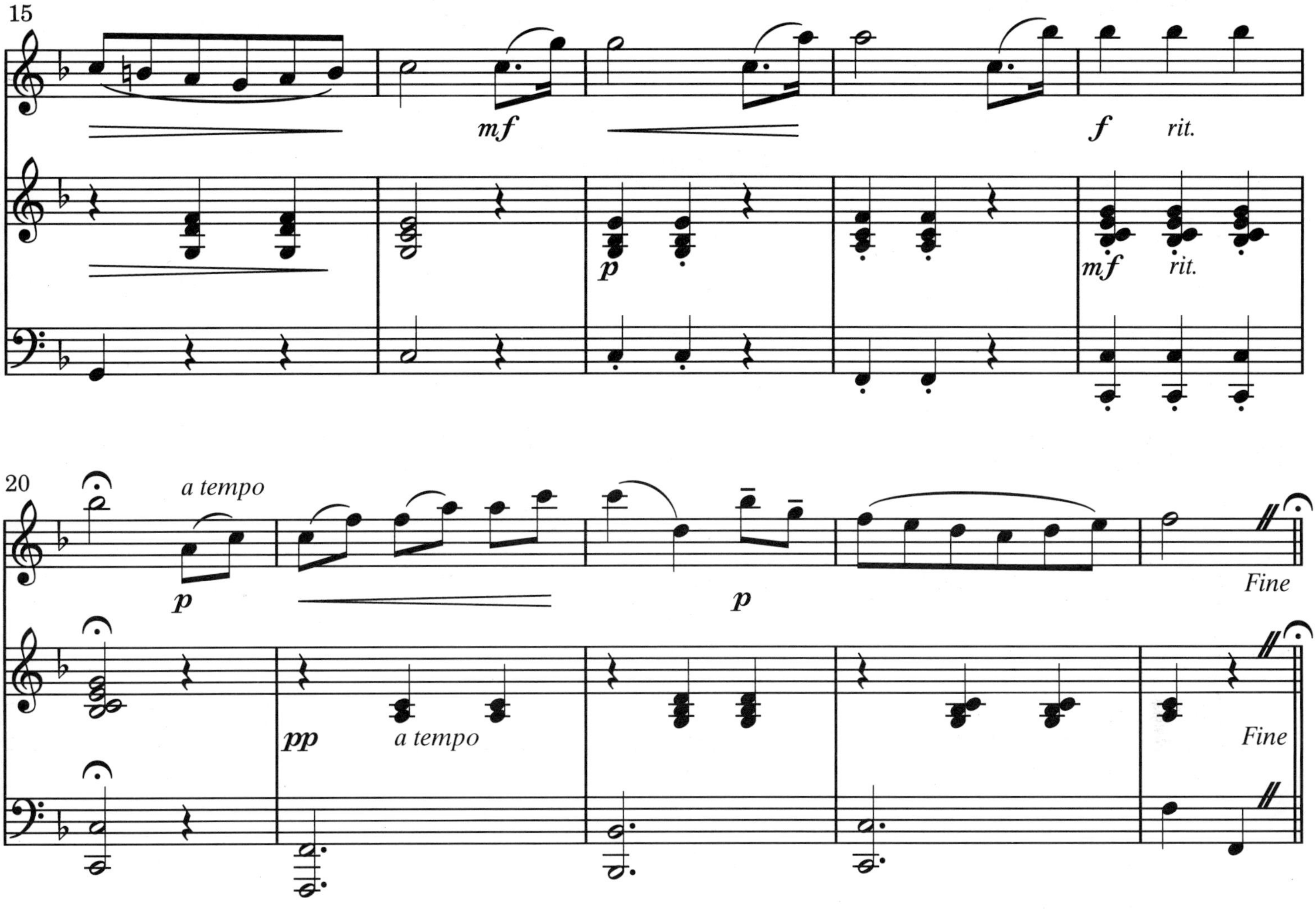

5. Play the right hand accompaniment as blocked chords first. Then choose a partner and play as written.

Sonate

(Excerpt)

LUDWIG van BEETHOVEN, Op. 24, No. 5
(1770–1827)

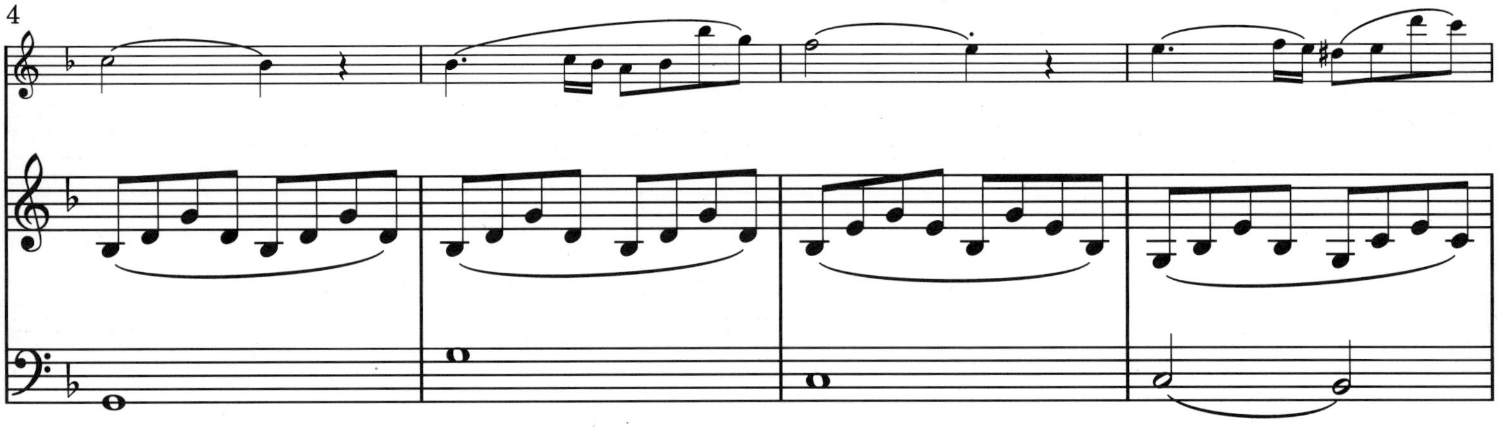

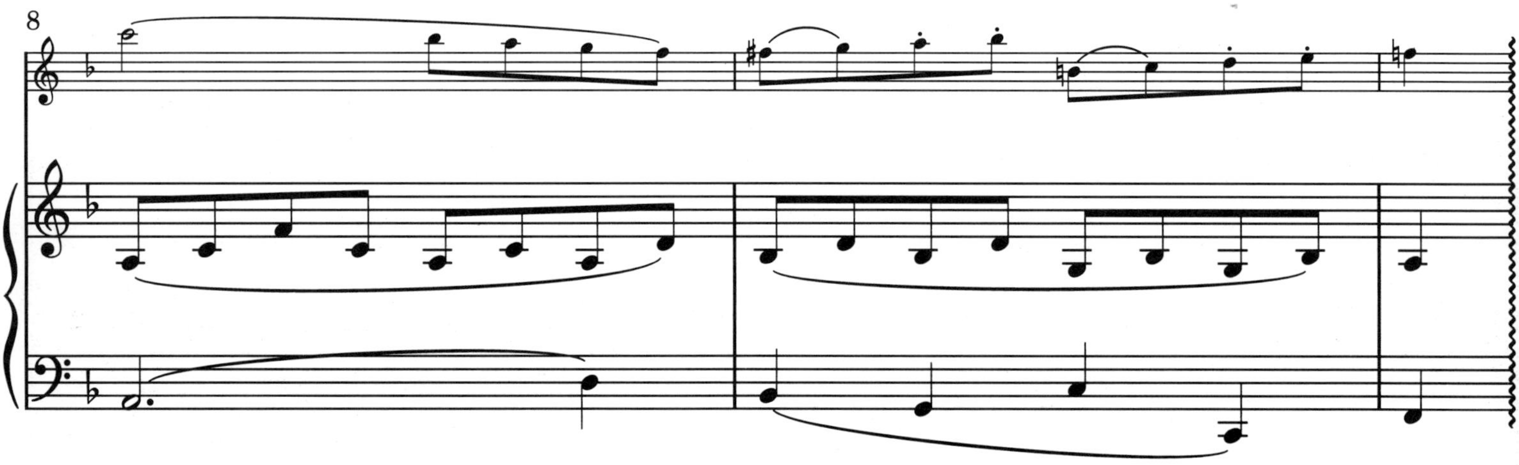

6. Simplify the accompaniment and perform.

Sebben, crudele

(Excerpt)

ANTONIO CALDARA
(1670–1736)

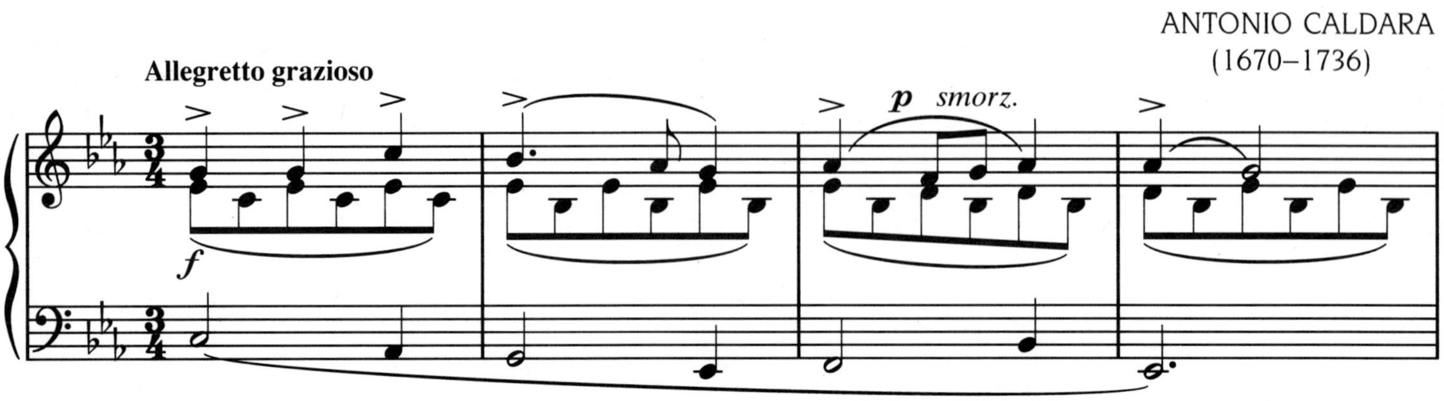

5
p
cresc.
Seb - ben, cru - de - le, mi fai lan - guir, sem - pre fe -
p
cresc.
10
piú cresc.
rit.
a tempo
de - le, sem - pre fe - de - le ti vo - glio a - mar.
a tempo
piú cresc.
rit.
15
deciso
p

7. Play the following combinations:

- SB
- AT
- SAT
- ATB
- SATB

The Carol of the Angels

(Excerpt)

JOHN JACOB NILES
(1892–1980)

Larghetto ♩. = 44
Soprano
Alto
Tenor
Bass
pp
Lu - le, lu - lay, lu - le, lu - lay, lu - le, lu - lay,
Lu - le, lu - lay, lu - le, lu - le, lu - lay,
Lu - lay, lu - le, lu - lay, lu - le,
Lu - lay, lu - le, lu - lay, and
4
p
lu - le, lu - lay, Lu - le, lu - lay, and lull - a - by,
lu - le, lu - lay, Lu - le, lu - lay,
lull - a - by, Lu - le, lu - lay,
lull - a - by, Lu - le, lu - lay,

7
by - by lu - le, lu - lay, As Ma - ry holds Him to her heart,
lu - le, lu - lay, As Ma - ry holds Him, He
lu - le, lu - lay, As Ma - ry holds
lu - le, lu - lay, lull - a - by, As Ma - ry holds Him, He
11
He sleeps the night a - way, He sleeps the night a - way.
sleeps the night a - way.
Him, He sleeps the night a - way.
sleeps, He sleeps the night a - way.

8. Play all parts.

Quartet in G Major

(Rondo—excerpt)

WOLFGANG AMADEUS MOZART, K. 80
(1756–1791)

9. Play the *Corrente* as an ensemble (primo—violin I and II; secondo—continuo).

Corrente

ARCANGELO CORELLI
(1653–1713)

19
26
33
40

Tuesday : Oct. 14

1. Choose a partner and perform using the suggested accompaniment pattern.

Teach to the class
1) Play melody/chord first
2) Play again w/ acc. pattern only - no melody
Make up lyrics

My Home's in Montana

American

Mon tan a is pur ty the cows they ain't dir ty The

green grass grows just like it does here at home I

think I would like to live just like a cow - I roam

aim less ly chew - ing my cud eve ry day

Suggested Accompaniment Pattern

etc.

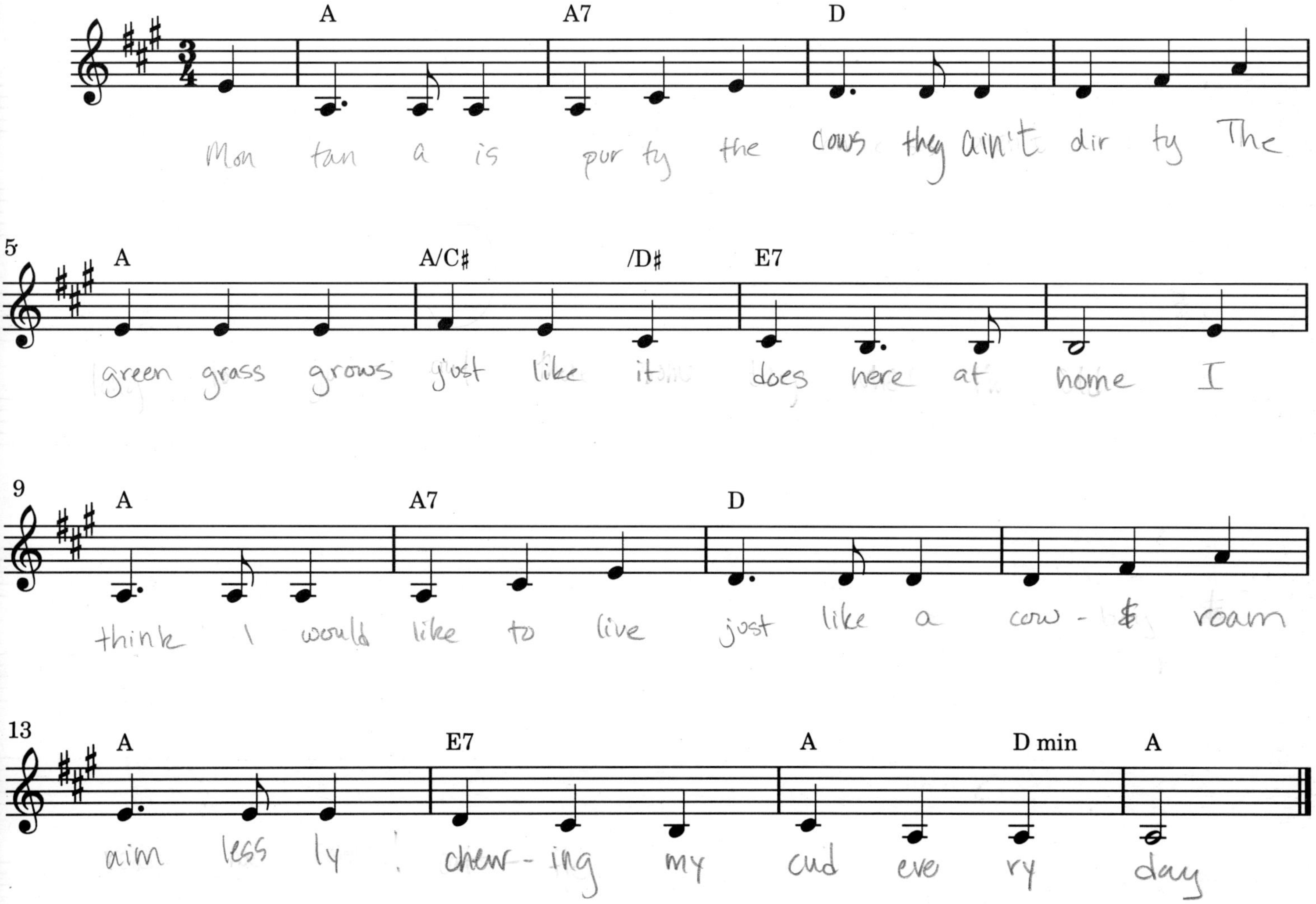

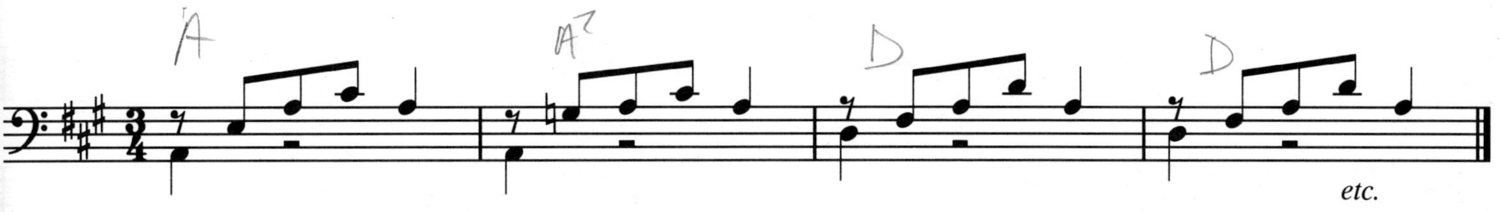

2. Determine harmonies and perform in an appropriate style.

All Night, All Day

Spiritual

All night, all day, An - gels watch-ing o - ver me, my Lord.
5
Fine
All night, all day, An - gels watch-ing o - ver me.
9
If I lay me down to sleep, An - gels watch-ing o - ver me, my Lord.
If I die be - fore I wake,
13
D.C. al Fine
Pray the Lord my soul to keep, An - gels watch-ing o - ver me.
Pray the Lord my soul to take,

3. Play verse by ear.

Joshua Fit da Battle of Jericho

Spiritual

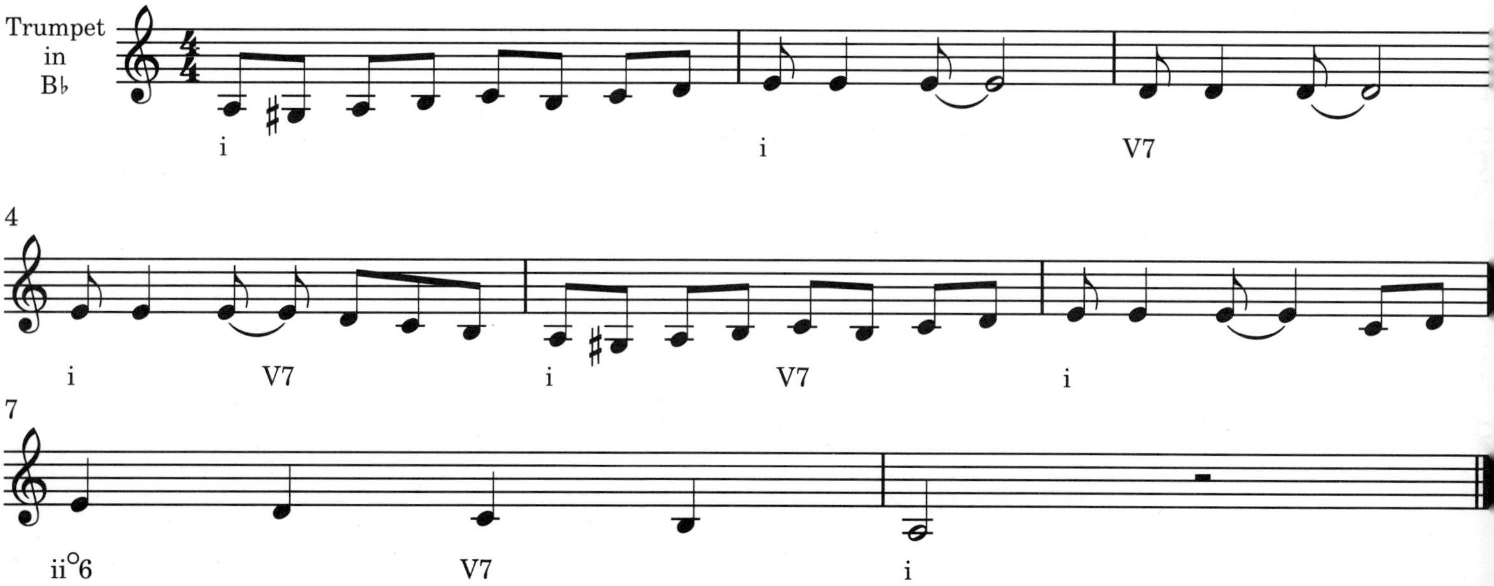
Trumpet in B♭
i
i
V7
4
i
V7
i
V7
i
7
ii°6
V7
i

4. Accompany *Myrtilla* in a similar manner, varying the pattern as necessary for faster harmonic changes. Furnish missing harmonies before playing.

Myrtilla

THOMAS ARNE
(1710–1778)

5. Furnish harmonies and play.

We Gather Together

Netherlands Folk Hymn

6. Harmonize using a style of your choice.

On the Banks of the Wabash

PAUL DRESSER

7. Harmonize in keyboard style.

WOLFGANG AMADEUS MOZART
(1756–1791)
Adapted by Lynn Freeman Olson

Moderato

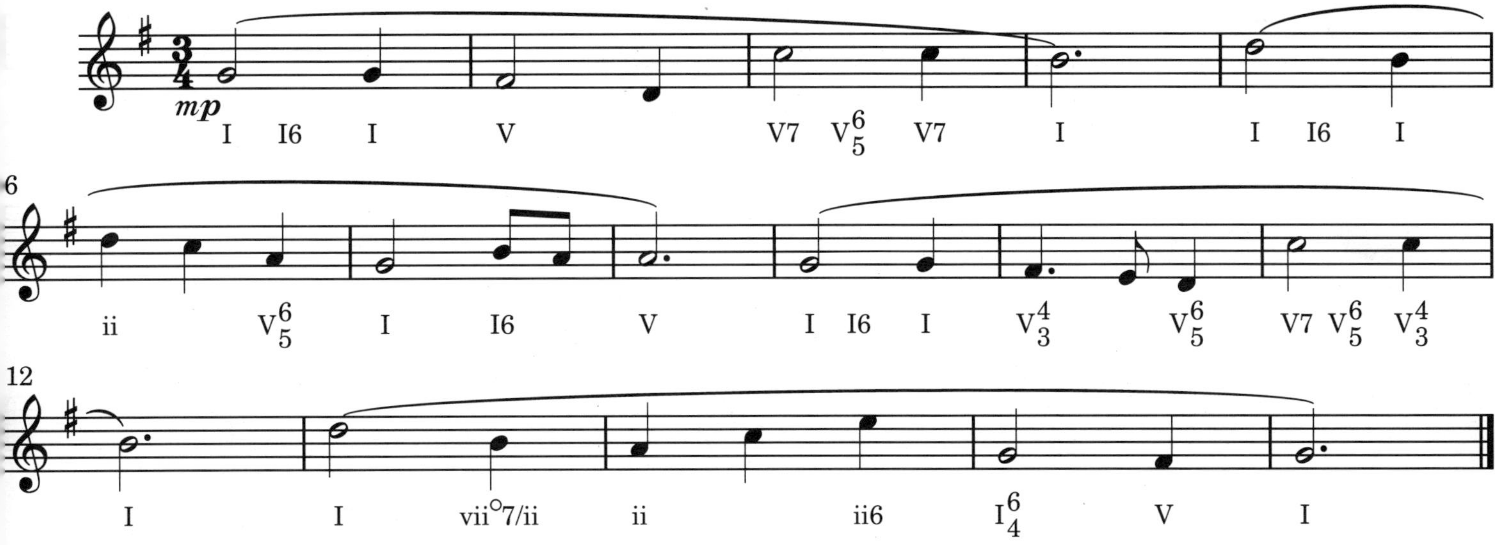

TRANSPOSITION

1. Transpose *Study in* G to the keys of D♭ major, F major, and G♭ major.

Study in G

LUDVIG SCHYTTE, Op. 108, No. 12
(1848–1909)

Moderato

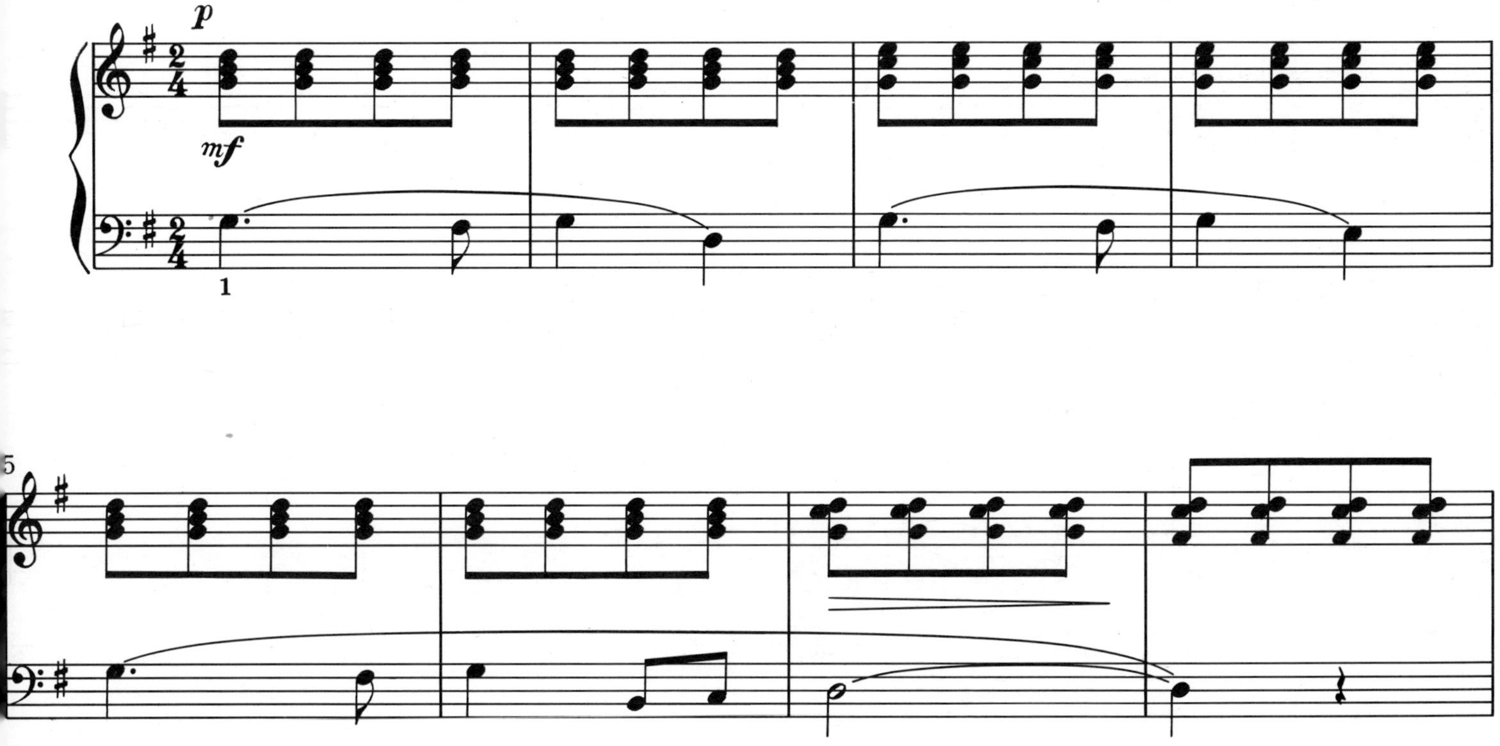

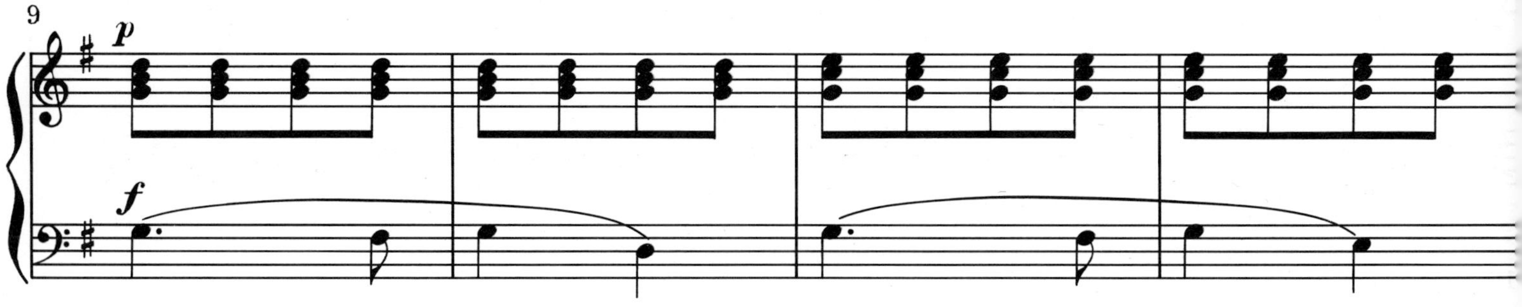

2. Transpose to G Dorian. Do not play in written key.

Wayfarin' Stranger

Irish

3. Transpose the Czerny excerpt through F major using half-step modulation between each key.

Study in C Major

(Excerpt)

CARL CZERNY, Op. 139, No. 2
(1791–1857)

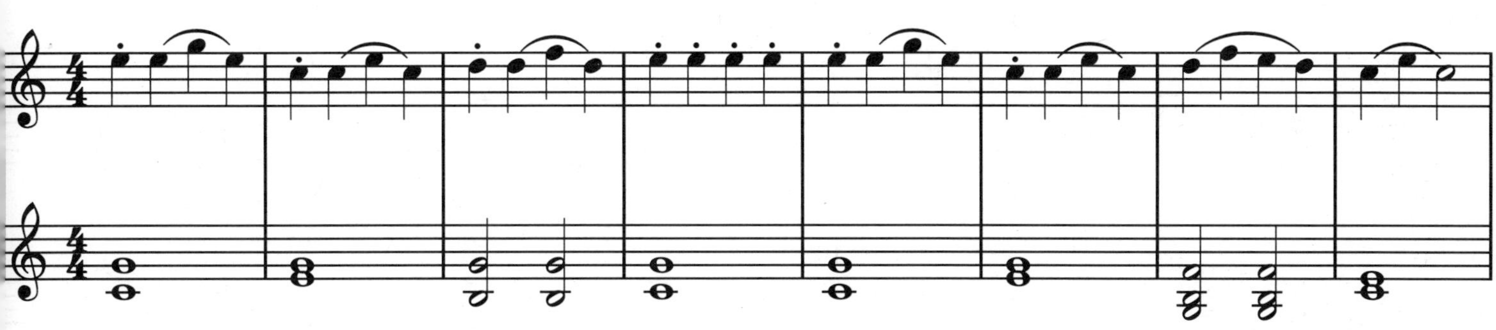

4. On what mode is the Járdányi based? Play as written. Change the tonal center to E♭ and play again.

Ugra-Bugra

PÁL JÁRDÁNYI
(1920–1966)

Allegretto, ♩ = ca. 126

5. Play in the keys of A♭ major and A major.

St. Agnes

JOHN B. DYKES
(1823–1876)

4.

EXEMPLARY REPERTOIRE

RELATED SKILLS AND ACTIVITIES

SUBSEQUENT REPERTOIRE

Diatonic Seventh Chords in Major and Minor/ Secondary Seventh Chords

EXEMPLARY REPERTOIRE **Prelude in C Major** Muzio Clementi

INQUIRY

1. Scan the piece. Observe:
    - Chordal outlines
    - Bass motion
    - Roulade effects

PERFORMANCE

1. Block the chordal outlines in the first eight measures, maintaining the pulse—

2. Practice the written roulade (measures 9–12).

3. Play as written at a slow tempo.

4. In *An Introduction to the Art of Playing on the Pianoforte*, Clementi states, "The pause 𝄐 renders the note longer at pleasure; and in certain cases, the composer expects some embellishments from the performer; but the pause on a rest only lengthens, at pleasure, the silence." In bar 14, improvise a right-hand roulade while sustaining the left-hand harmony.

5. Play as written, including your improvisation.

Prelude in C Major

MUZIO CLEMENTI
(1752–1832)

RELATED SKILLS AND ACTIVITIES

TECHNIQUE

1. Play the following arpeggio drills.

a.

b.

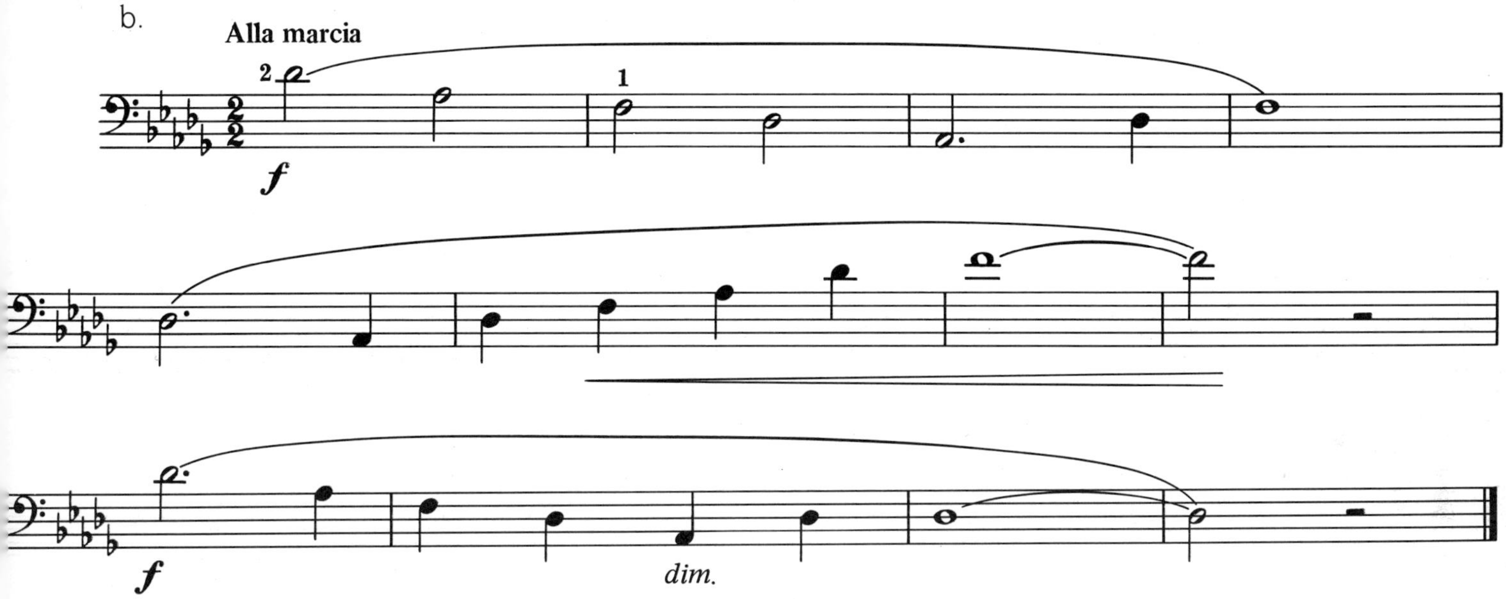

2. Play these seventh shapes.

a.

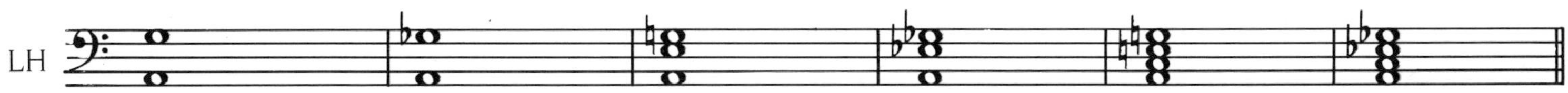

b.

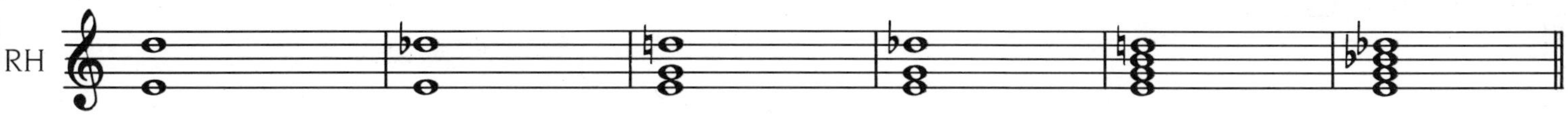

c.

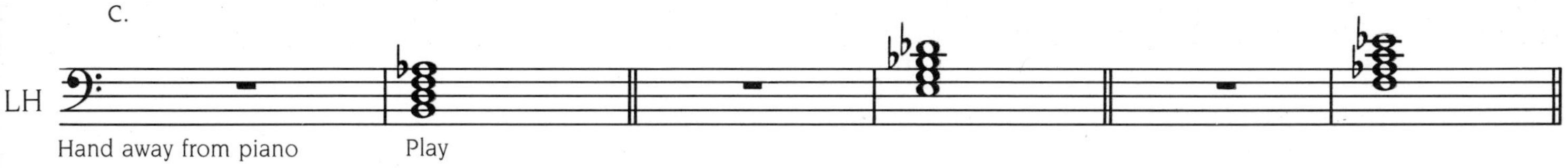

d.

READING

1. Play the viola and bass lines together. Then, choose a partner and perform as an ensemble.

Bourrée

JOHANN PACHELBEL
(1653–1706)

2. Think key signature!

Adeste Fideles

Traditional
Arranged by M. Hilley

3. Play the flute and bass lines of the Kuhlau excerpt. Then play the accompaniment as another person plays the flute solo.

Theme

from *Variations on a Scottish Song*

FRIEDRICH KUHLAU, Op. 104
(1786–1832)

4. Play the vocal lines of the Mozart excerpt as your teacher plays the accompaniment.

Die Zauberflöte

(Excerpt)

WOLFGANG AMADEUS MOZART, K. 620
(1756–1791)

Allegro
1st Lady
2nd Lady
3rd Lady
Piano
p
Du Jüng - ling, schön und lie - be-voll, du trau - ter Jüng - ling,
dolce
le - be wohl! bis ich dich wie - der - seh, bis ich
le - be wohl! bis ich dich wie - der - seh, bis
f
p
dich wie - - der - seh,
ich dich wie - der -
bis ich dich wie - der -

11
1
bis ich dich wie - der - seh,
2
seh, bis ich dich wie - der - seh,
3
seh, bis ich dich wie - der - seh,

5. Play these combinations: Violin I and violin II or violin I and viola

String Quartet in E-Flat

(Violin I, violin II, viola excerpt)

WOLFGANG AMADEUS MOZART
(1756–1791)

Violin I
Violin II
Viola

6. Accompany a classmate.

O del mio dolce ardor

(Excerpt)

CHRISTOPH WILLIBALD von GLUCK
(1714–1787)

Moderato
Voice
Piano
p dolcissimo
p
O del mio dol - ce ar -
3
dor bra - ma - to og - get -
5
to, bra - ma - to og - get - to,

7. Observe use of consecutive thirds, fourths, and sixths before playing.

Toplady Hymn Tune

THOMAS HASTINGS
(1784–1872)

KEYBOARD THEORY

1. In a major key, diatonic seventh chords fall into one of four categories.

Major Seventh	Minor Seventh	Major-Minor Seventh	Half-Diminished Seventh
I7	ii7	V7	$\text{vii}^{\varnothing}7$
IV7	iii7		
	vi7		

Play the diatonic seventh chords in each white-key major scale as shown. Use the keys of C, D, E, F, G, and A.

C major

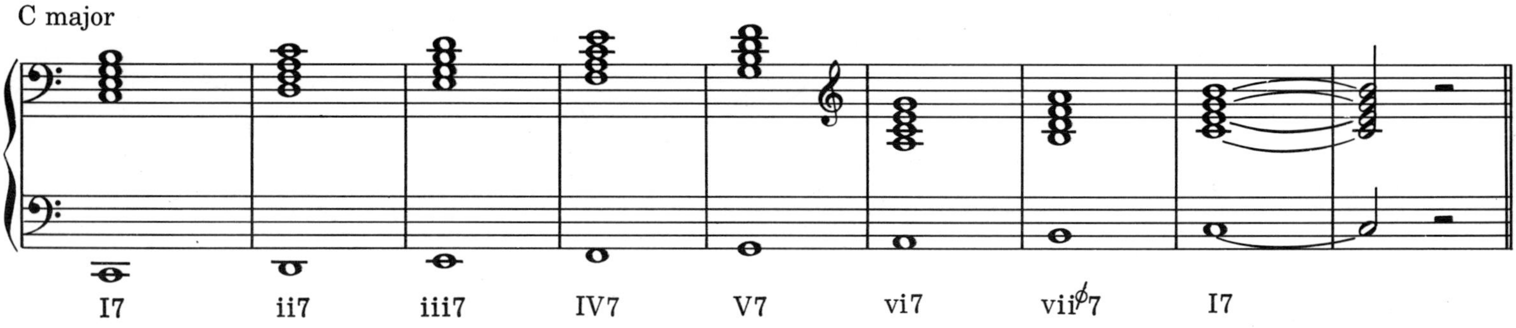

D major

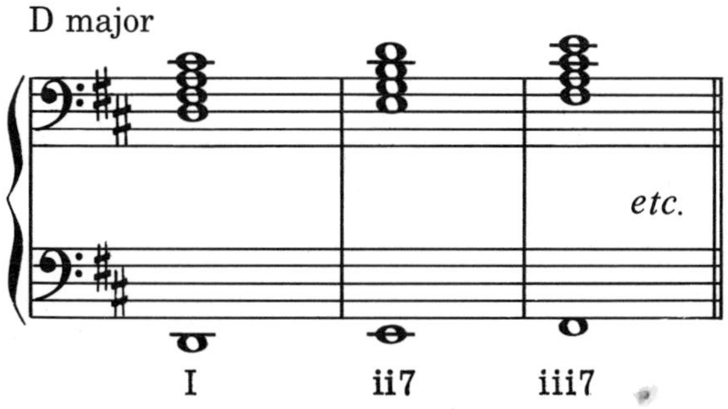

E major

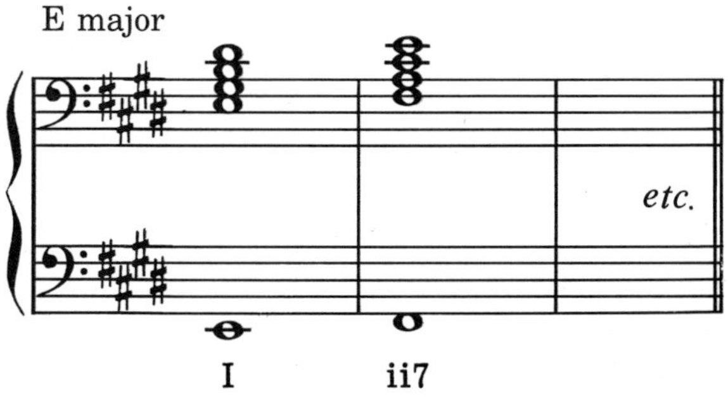

2. Play the following seventh chords in C minor. Notice the raised seventh degree in the i7 (creating a minor-major seventh chord).

C minor

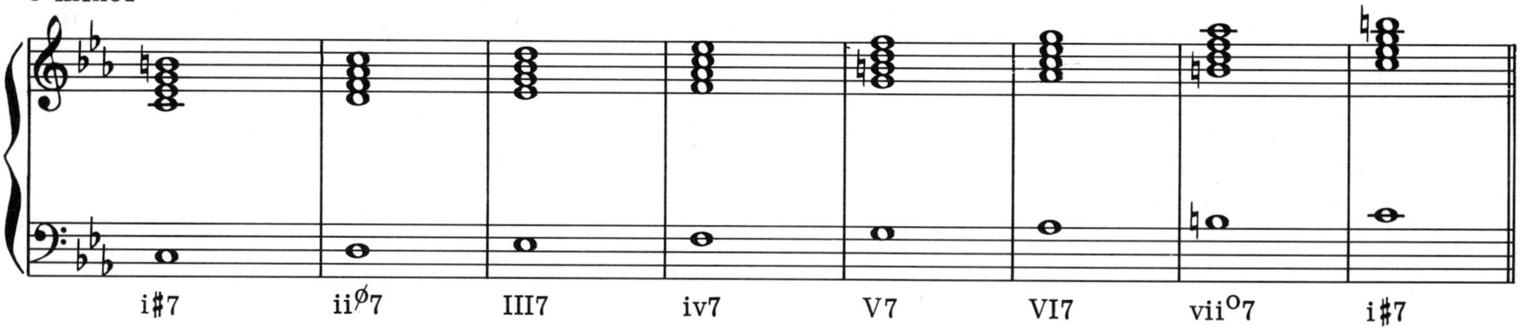

3. Play the preceding example of minor-key seventh chords in the keys of D, G, A, and B minor.

4. There are many ways to write lead sheet notation of seventh chords.

Key of C:	I7	CΔ7 or C maj 7
	ii7	D-7 / D min 7
	iii7	E-7 / E min 7
	IV7	FΔ7 / F maj 7
	V7	G7
	vi7	A-7 / A min 7
	vii^{ø}7	B-7♭5/ B min 7♭5

A designation of G^{sus} or G^{sus}C is a suspended fourth above the root.
A triad with an added sixth is shown as C6 (CEGA).

5. Play the following progression in a relaxed tempo, keyboard style. Use common tones between chords.

Ballad

4/4 E♭Δ7 | C-7 | B♭-7 E♭7 | A♭Δ7 F-7 | F-7 | B♭7 |

C-7 C-7/B♭ | A♭Δ7 A♭Δ7/G | F-7 | B♭7 | E♭Δ7 | E♭6 ||

6. Just as triads and seventh chords are at times chromatically altered to function as V or V7, so may triads and seventh chords be chromatically altered to function as vii or vii°7. There are two widely accepted designations for these chords (note the difference in resolution):

G major:

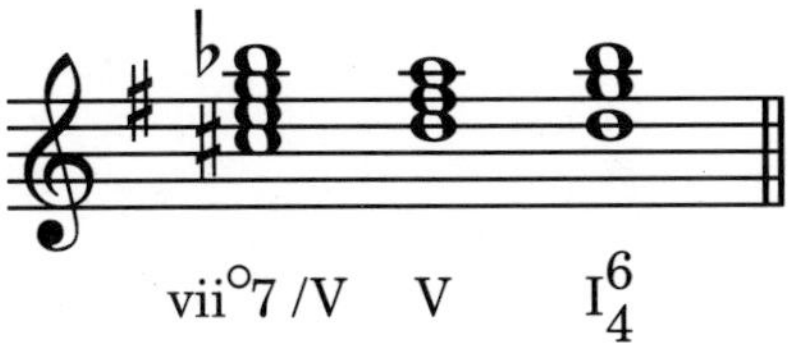

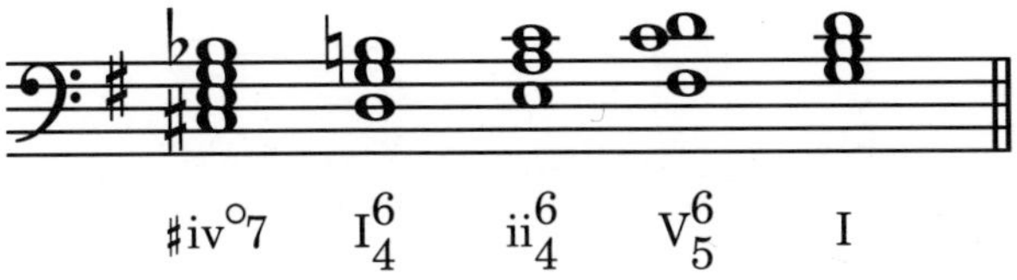

7. Analyze the following examples with special attention to the use of diatonic and/or secondary seventh chords.

Prelude in B-Flat Major

MUZIO CLEMENTI, Op. 43
(1752–1832)

Andante

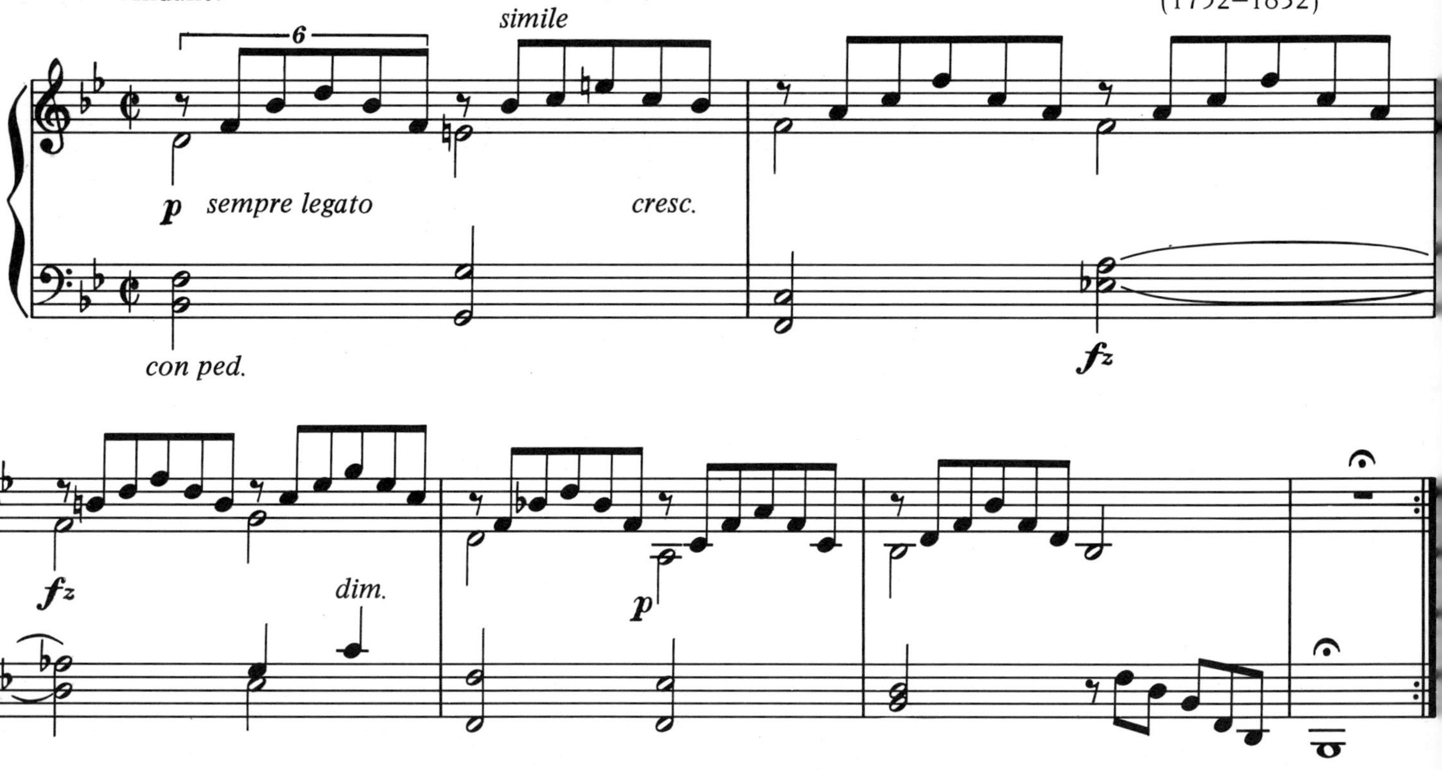

Sonata in F Major

(Excerpt)

WOLFGANG AMADEUS MOZART, K. 332
(1756–1791)

Allegro

HARMONIZATION

1. *Amazing Grace* uses dominant seventh, secondary seventh, and diatonic seventh chords. Harmonize with a half-step modulation at the end of each verse.

Amazing Grace

American

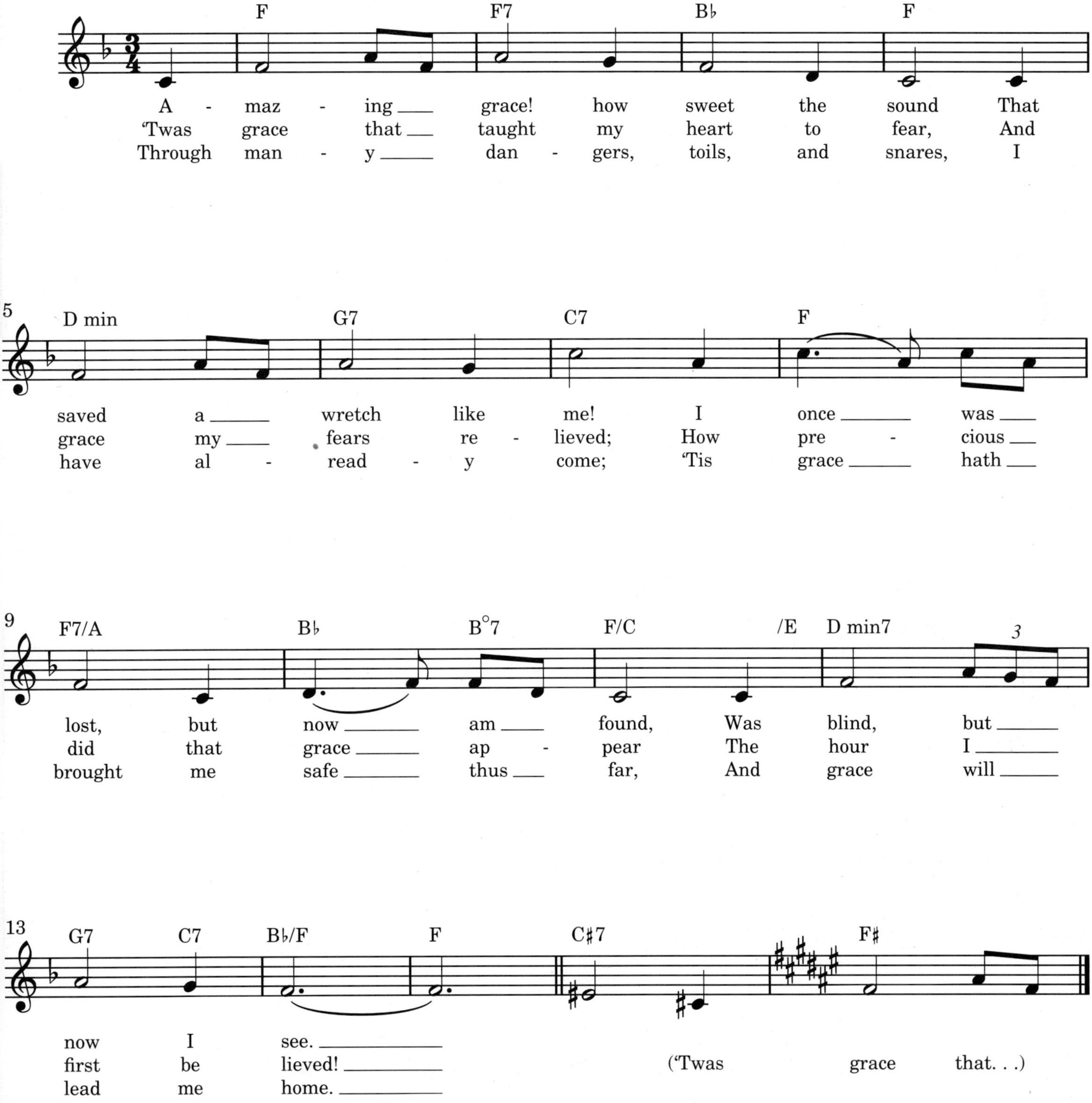
F F7 B♭ F
A - maz - ing grace! how sweet the sound That
'Twas grace that taught my heart to fear, And
Through man - y dan - gers, toils, and snares, I
5
D min G7 C7 F
saved a wretch like me! I once was
grace my fears re - lieved; How pre - cious
have al - read - y come; 'Tis grace hath
9
F7/A B♭ B°7 F/C /E D min7
3
lost, but now am found, Was blind, but
did that grace ap - pear The hour I
brought me safe thus far, And grace will
13
G7 C7 B♭/F F C♯7 F♯
now I see.
first be lieved!
lead me home.
('Twas grace that. . .)

2. Complete in the style indicated.

Take Me Out to the Ball Game

ALBERT VON TILZER
Words by Jack Norworth

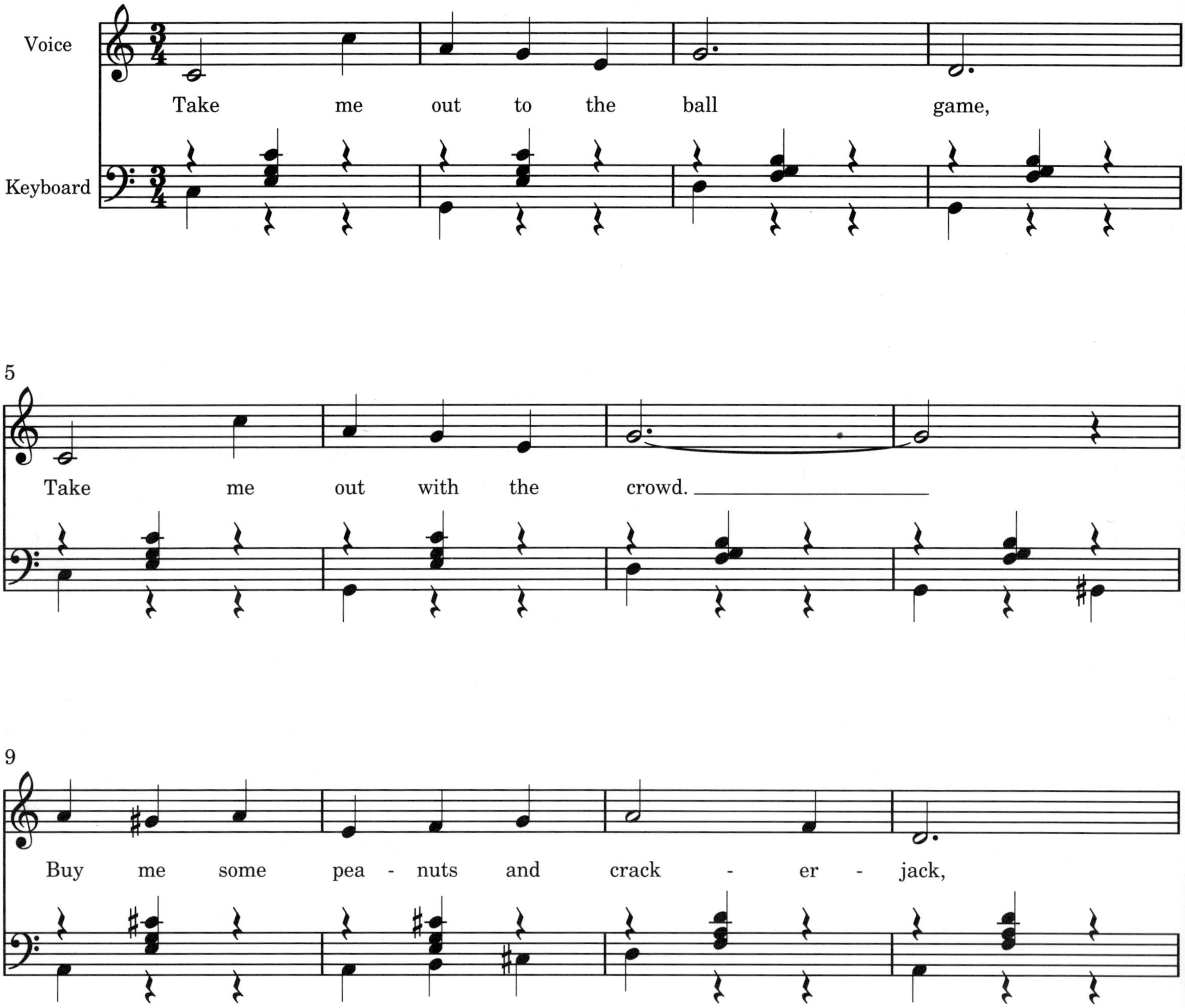
Voice
Keyboard
Take me out to the ball game,
5
Take me out with the crowd.
9
Buy me some pea - nuts and crack - er - jack,

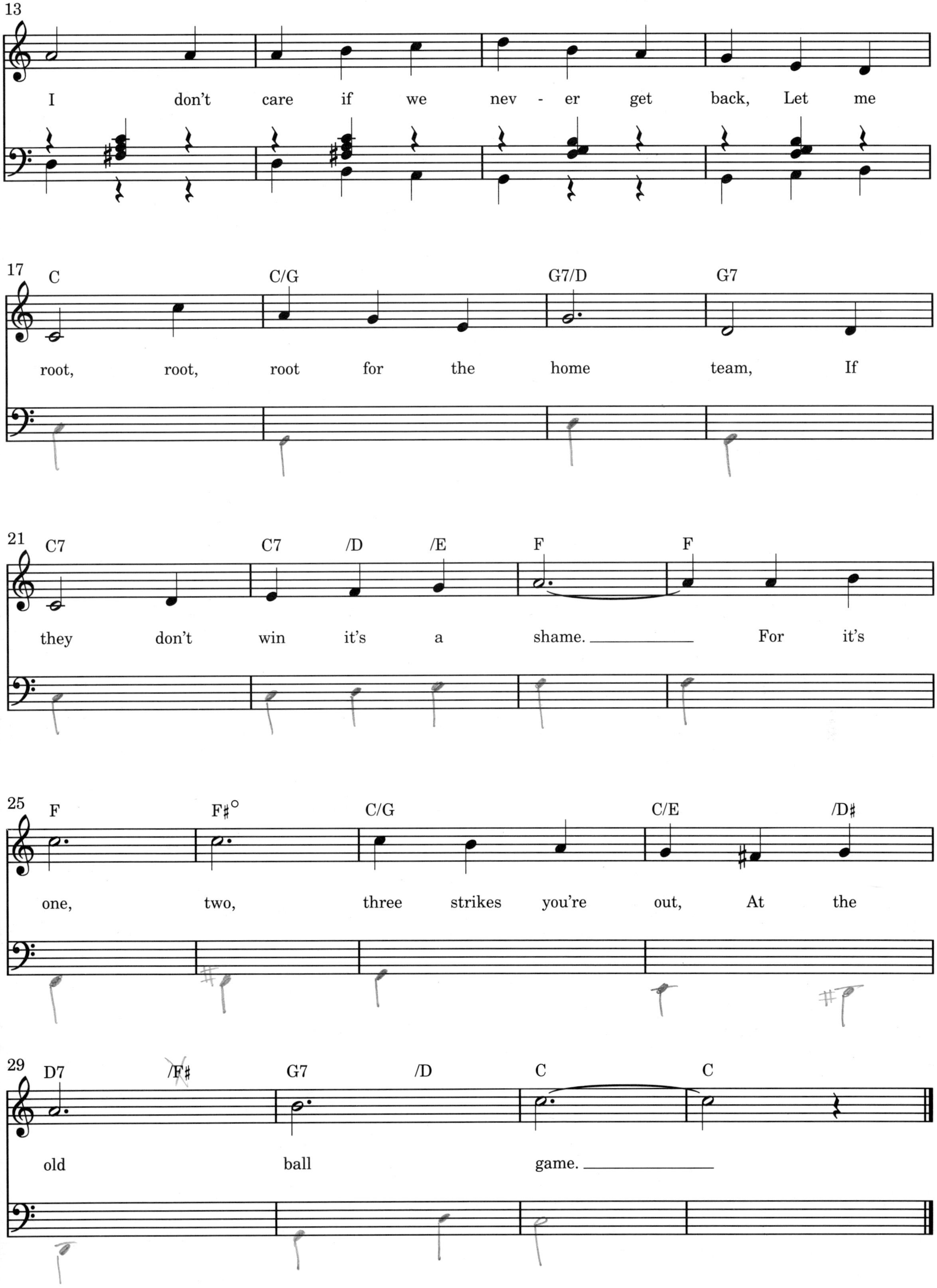
13
I don't care if we nev - er get back, Let me
17
C C/G G7/D G7
root, root, root for the home team, If
21
C7 C7 /D /E F F
they don't win it's a shame. For it's
25
F F♯° C/G C/E /D♯
one, two, three strikes you're out, At the
29
D7 /F♯ G7 /D C C
old ball game.

3. Harmonize in keyboard style.

Let Us Break Bread Together

Spiritua

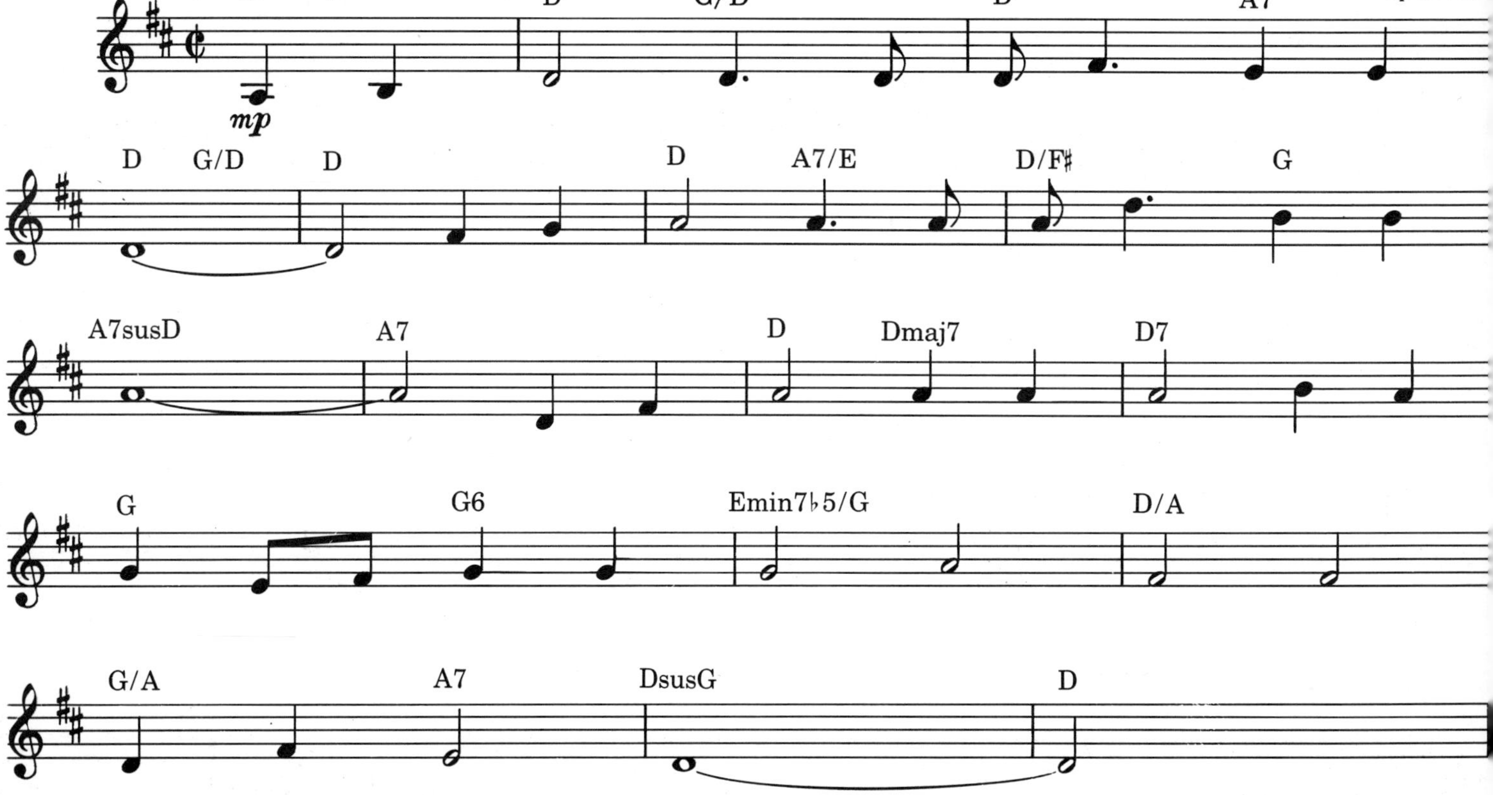

4. Determine harmonies and play in an appropriate style.

I've Been Working on the Railroad

American

A-7 - play c# right? no

5. Harmonize in keyboard style.

5th is dispensable - 3rd has to be there

Comin' Through the Rye

Scottish

In a relaxed manner

G/D (?)

TRANSPOSITION

1. Your singer has a cold—play this down a fourth in the key of D major.

Salti di terza

NICOLA VACCAJ
(1790–1848)

Andantino

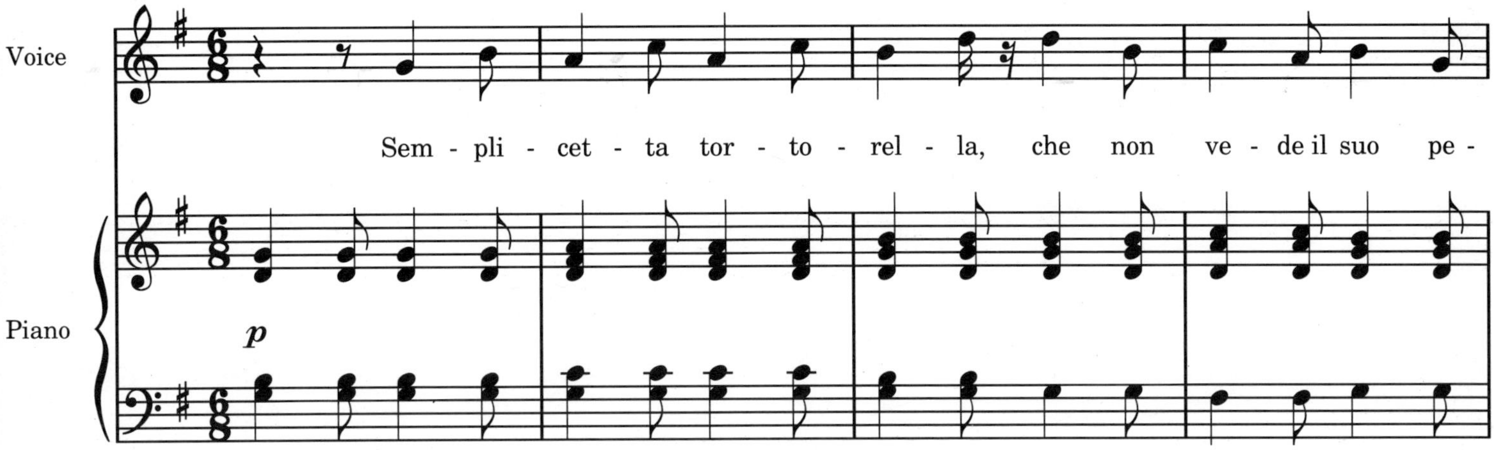

5
ri - glio, per fug - gir dal cru - do ar - ti - glio vo - la in grem - bo al cac - cia -

9
tor per fug - gir dal cru - do ar - ti - glio, per fug - gir dal cru - do ar-

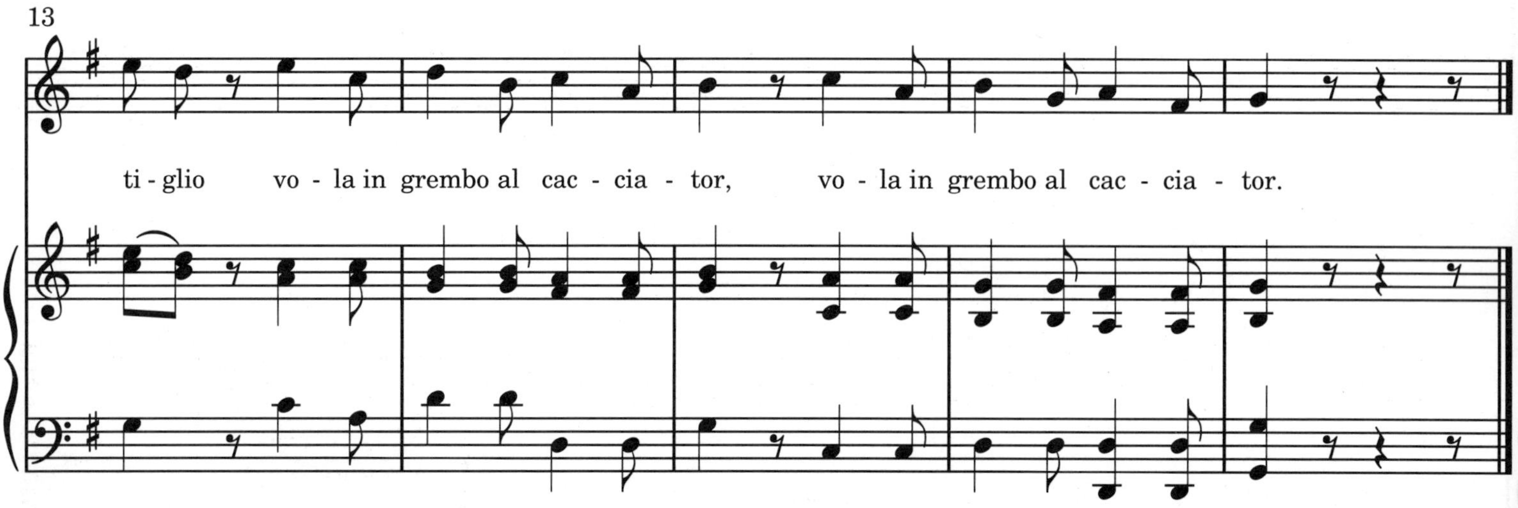
13
ti - glio vo - la in grembo al cac - cia - tor, vo - la in grembo al cac - cia - tor.

2. Play in the key written, then modulate as indicated in the final bar and play again.

Study in D-Flat Major

CARL CZERNY, Op. 139, No. 6
(1791–1857)

3. Play the trumpet part as your teacher or partner plays the accompaniment. Switch parts and perform again.

Sonatina

(Excerpts)

II

WOLFGANG AMADEUS MOZART
(1756–1791)
Arranged by Jay Ernst

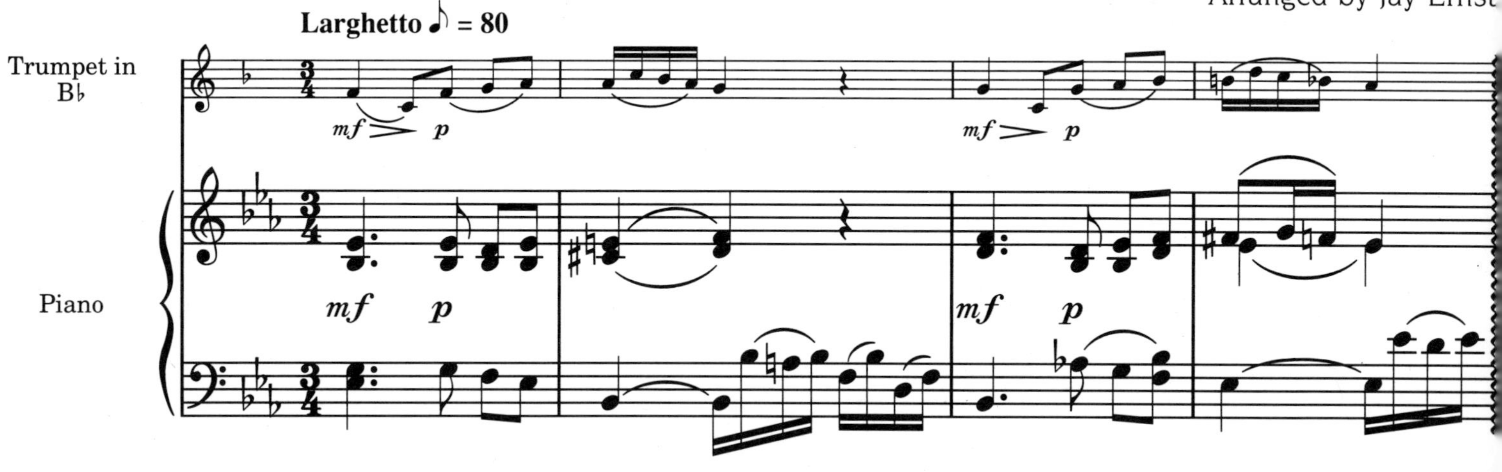

III

IMPROVISATION

1. Return to the Pachelbel *Sarabande* (p. 43). Improvise a countermelody as your teacher or a partner plays the printed score. Use the following plan:

Bars 1–8 Based on chord tones only. Countermelody should move in contrary motion to upper voice of printed score.

Bars 9–12 Add passing tones and lower and/or upper neighbor tones.

Bars 13–16 You are "on your own."

2. Using the following harmonic progression, improvise a sixteen-bar piece in the style of the Pachelbel *Sarabande* (p. 43).

$$\begin{array}{llll} 1 & 2 & 3 & 4 \\ \frac{3}{4}\,|\,\text{I} & |\,\text{V} & |\,\text{vi} & |\,\text{iii} \quad | \end{array}$$

$$\begin{array}{llll} 5 & 6 & 7 & 8 \\ |\,\text{ii6} & |\,\text{vi7} & |\,\text{ii7 V7} & |\,\text{I} \quad | \end{array}$$

$$\begin{array}{llll} 9 & 10 & 11 & 12 \\ |\,\text{IV} & |\,\text{I} & |\,\text{ii7 V7} & |\,\text{I} \quad | \end{array}$$

$$\begin{array}{llll} 13 & 14 & 15 & 16 \\ |\,\text{vii}^{\varnothing}\text{7 V7/vi} & |\,\text{vi ii6} & |\,\text{iii6 V7} & |\,\text{I} \quad \| \end{array}$$

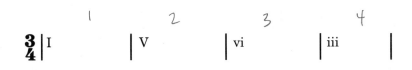

ENSEMBLE

1. Trade parts at the "Con moto" section. There should be no break in pulse when you switch parts.

Moderato

ALEXANDER GRETCHANINOV
(1864–1956)

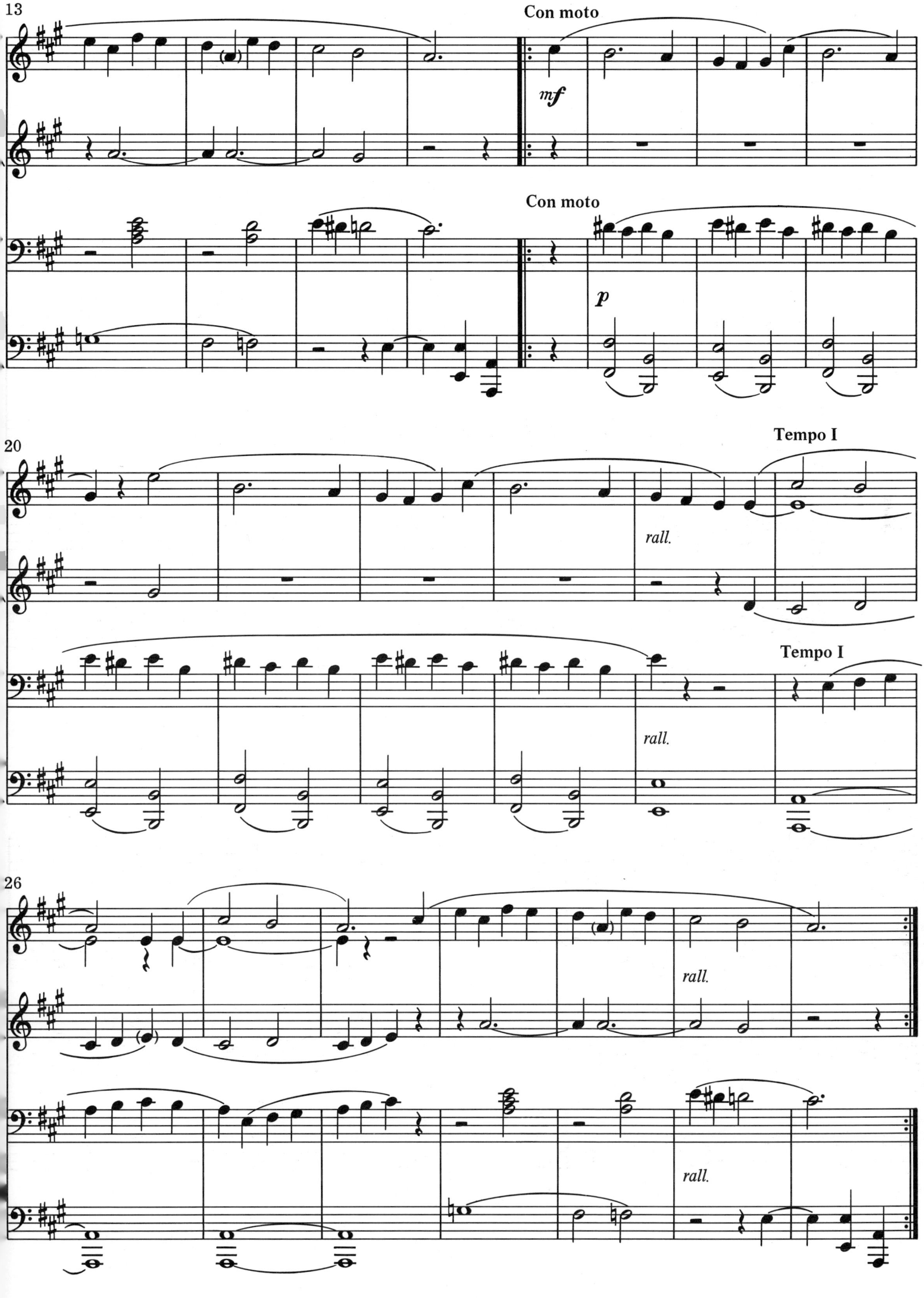
13
Con moto
mf
Con moto
p
20
Tempo I
rall.
Tempo I
rall.
26
rall.
rall.

Jingle Bells

JAMES PIERPONT
(1785–1866)
Arranged by Jerry Ray

13
17
f
21

24
3
mf
4
mp
28
32

36
3
40
f
mf
44

48
52
f
56
f

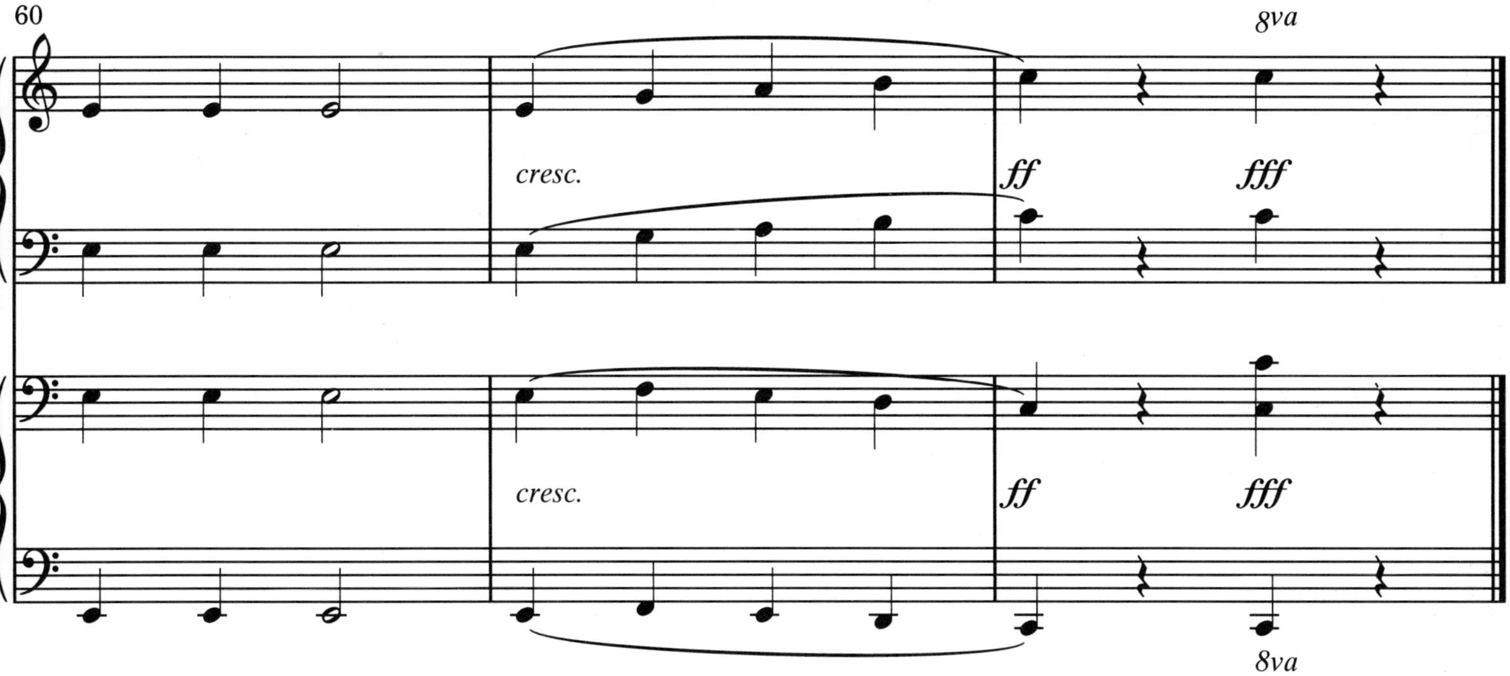

SUBSEQUENT REPERTOIRE

Summer Shadows

Flowing

MARJORIE BURGESS

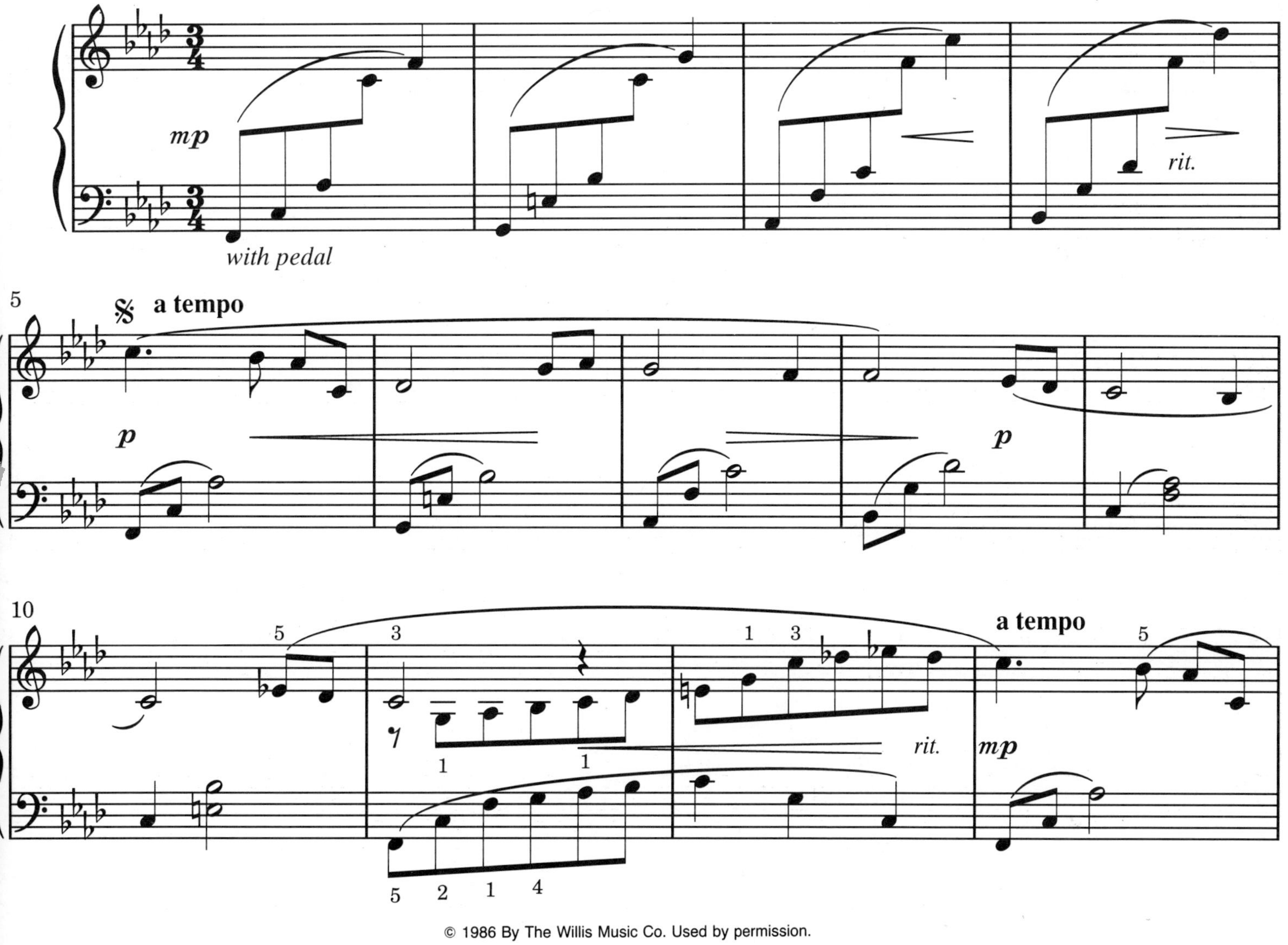

14
2nd time to
19
a tempo
rit.
mf
23
28
33
D.S. al Coda
p
rit.
Coda
rit.
p

Prelude in C Major

from *The Well-Tempered Clavier*, Book 1

JOHANN SEBASTIAN BACH
(1685–1750)

[Moderato]

18
21
24
27
30
33

5.

EXEMPLARY REPERTOIRE

RELATED SKILLS AND ACTIVITIES

SUBSEQUENT REPERTOIRE

Altered/Borrowed Triads

EXEMPLARY REPERTOIRE **Adagio** Daniel Steibelt

INQUIRY

1. Scan the piece. Observe:

- Form
- Nonpivot modulation
- ♯iv$^6_3$—Italian augmented sixth chord

This triad is built on the raised fourth scale degree of the key. It consists of ♯4, ♭6, and an unaltered tonic. The triad usually occurs in first inversion, forming the augmented sixth between the bass and another voice. This interval resolves outward to the dominant octave.

♯iv It6 V

- Use of appoggiaturas

PERFORMANCE

1. Play the melodic line of the A section. Pay particular attention to the use of two-note slurs for appoggiaturas and notes of resolution.
2. Play A section as written.
3. Play B section. Listen carefully for proper voicing.
4. Play *Adagio* as written.

Adagio

DANIEL STEIBELT
(1765–1823)

RELATED SKILLS AND ACTIVITIES

TECHNIQUE

1. Play the following scale in rhythm. Then play the scale in the key of B major.

2. Tap the rhythm before playing. Then play the scale in the key of G♭ major.

3. Analyze and then play.

Prelude in E-Flat Major

MUZIO CLEMENTI, Op. 43
(1752–1832)

READING

1. The tenor clef positions middle C on the fourth line of the staff. Play the following violoncello excerpt.

2. Play the following violoncello excerpt as your teacher plays the accompaniment.

Sicilienne

(Excerpt)

GABRIEL FAURÉ, Op. 78
(1845–1924)

3. Play the clarinet solo from each Mozart excerpt. Choose a partner to play the accompaniment.

Concerto in A Major for Clarinet and Orchestra

(Excerpt)

I

WOLFGANG AMADEUS MOZART, K. 622
(1756–1791)

II

III

4. Fingerings are indicated for performance of violin I and II in the right hand. There are times when intervals dictate that violin II is played with the left hand.

Play:

- Violin I and II, viola
- Violin II, viola, cello

Menuetto and Trio

FRANZ JOSEPH HAYDN
(1732–1809)

5. Play all parts of Trio.

The rest of this page has been left blank to avoid difficult page turns.

6. Play all three parts of the Haydn *Psalm 31*.

Psalm 31

FRANZ JOSEPH HAYDN
(1732–1809)

Andante
mp
Soprano
Alto
Bass
Mein Gott, ich hab auf dich ge - baut. Du
5
bist mit mei - ner Not ver - traut. Du bist die
10
Kraft, die mei - nen Geist aus Äng - sten und Ge -
cresc.
mf
15
fah - ren reisst, aus Äng - sten und Ge - fah - ren reisst.

7. Refer to the reading suggestions for chorale style on pages 25–26 and apply to the following hymn.

L'Omnipotent

Genevan Psalter
(1551)

8. Read the following accompaniment. Then choose a partner and play as an ensemble.

Rondo

(Excerpt)

from *Sonata for Violin and Piano*

JOHANN BAPTIST WANHAL
(1739–1813)

15
mf
18
f
f
22
dolce
p dolce
25
p

9. Practice RH as blocked intervals with LH as written, bars 1–11. For bars 13–18, reverse process. Then accompany a singer, playing as written.

Das Kinderspiel

(Overbeck)

WOLFGANG AMADEUS MOZART
(1756–1791)

Munter
mf
Soprano
Piano
Wir Kin - der, wir schme - cken der Freu - den recht viel, wir
5
schä - kern und ne - cken, ver - steht sich im Spiel; wir lär - men und
10
sin - gen und ren - nen rund - um, und hü - pfen und sprin - gen im

15

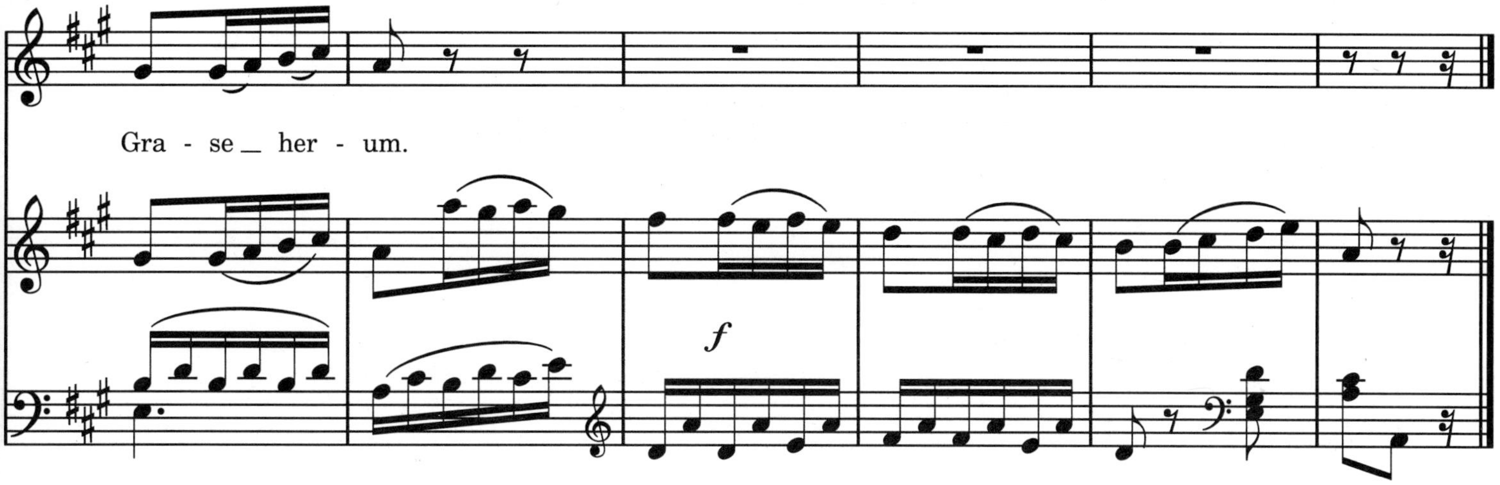
Gra - se _ her - um.
f

KEYBOARD THEORY

1. Borrowed chords use notes that are accidentals in the major key but would be diatonic in a minor key. The following example shows the borrowed triads most often used in a major key.

D major

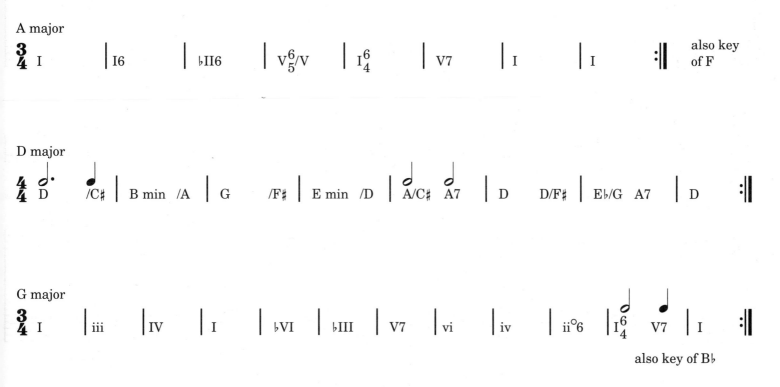

ii° | III (built on ♭3) | iv | VI (built on ♭6) | ♭II | ♭II6 (N6) Neapolitan Six

2. Play the following progressions using borrowed triads.

A major

3/4 I | I6 | ♭II6 | V^6_5/V | I^6_4 | V7 | I | I :‖ also key of F

D major

4/4 D /C♯ | B min /A | G /F♯ | E min /D | A/C♯ A7 | D D/F♯ | E♭/G A7 | D :‖

G major

3/4 I | iii | IV | I | ♭VI | ♭III | V7 | vi | iv | ii°6 | I^6_4 V7 | I :‖

also key of B♭

HARMONIZATION

1. Use a two-handed "root-chord" accompaniment for this folk tune.

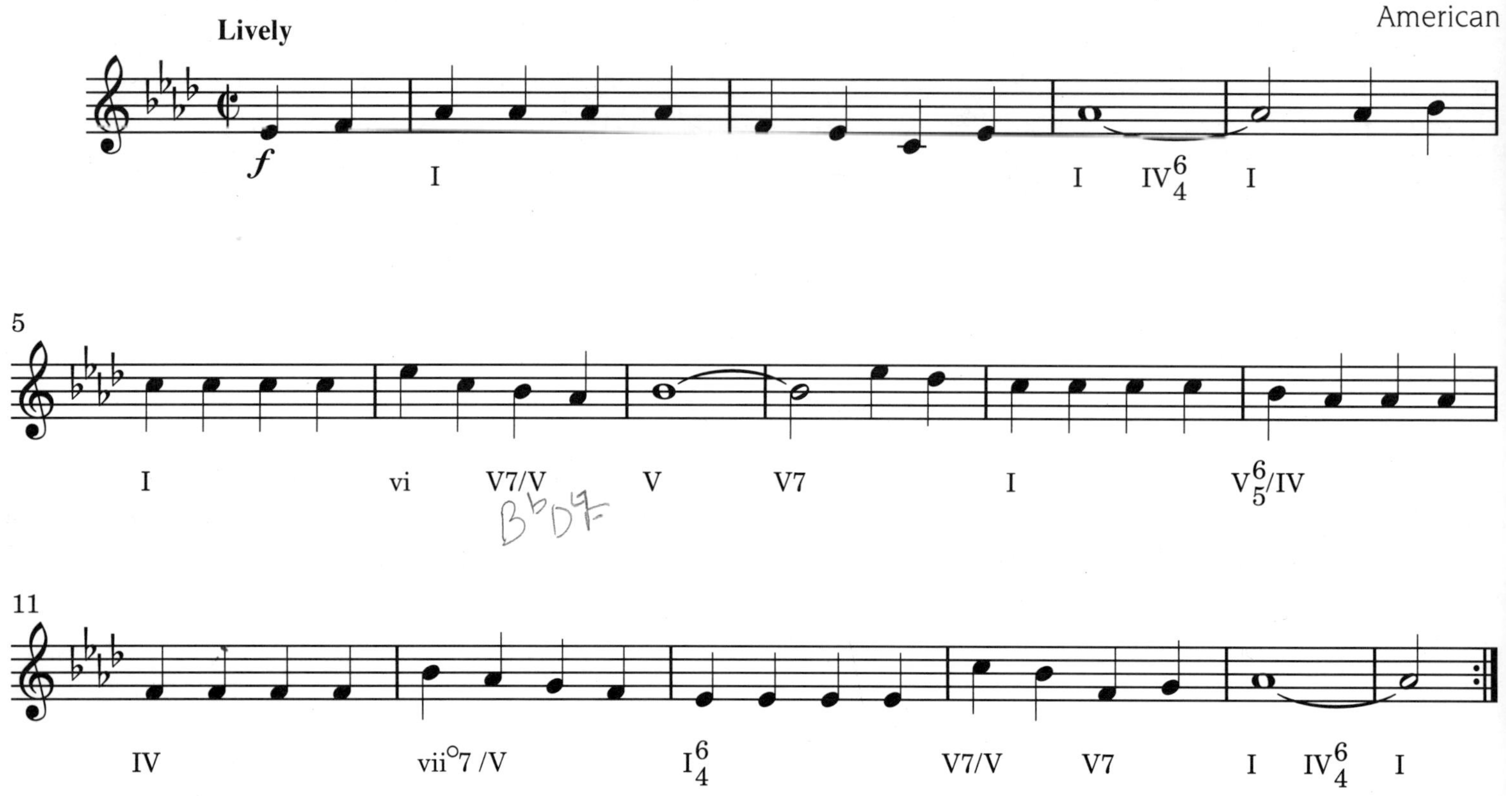

2. Harmonize the following and include vi, V7/IV, V7/V, III. Play the verse by ear. Use keyboard style.

3. Choose an appropriate style and play.

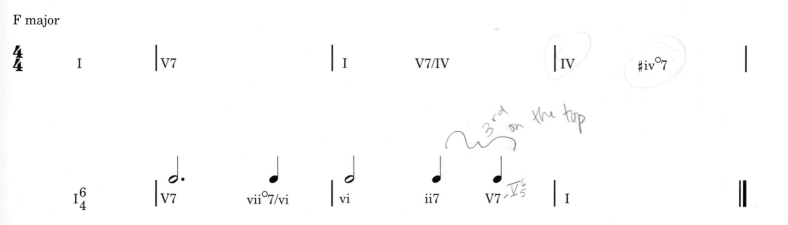

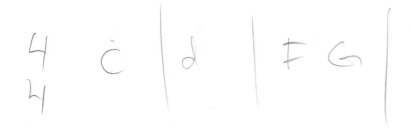

4. Play a two-handed accompaniment using the following progression.

F major

4/4 I | V7 | I V7/IV | IV ♯iv°7 |

I^6_4 | V7 vii°7/vi | vi | ii7 V7 | I ‖

5. Add the melody to *Auld Lang Syne* and play in keyboard style.

TRANSPOSITION

1. Transpose the *Etude in* D to D♭ major, D Dorian, and A♭ major.

Etude in D

LUDVIG SCHYTTE, Op. 108, No. 7
(1848–1909)

Allegro moderato

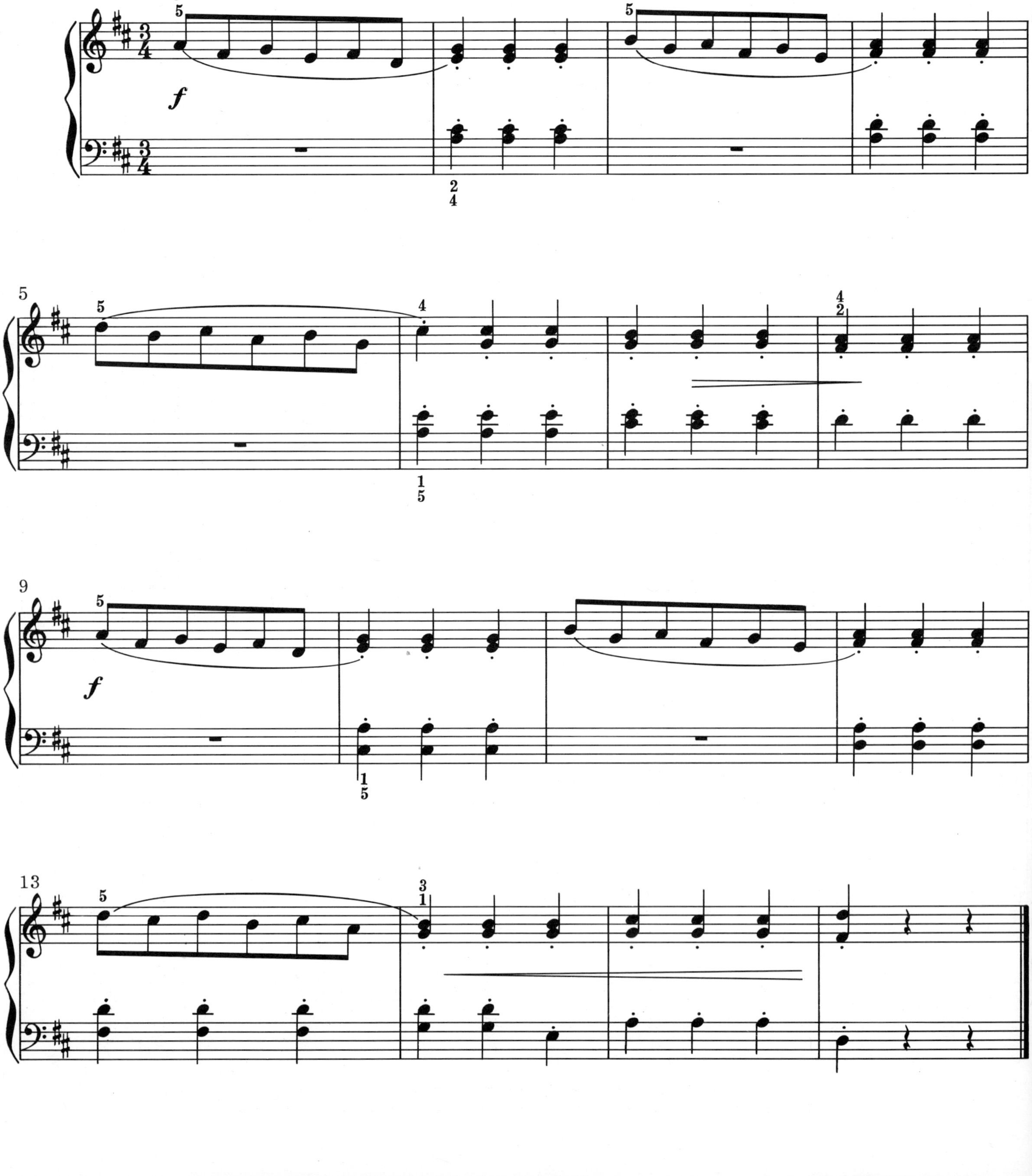

2. Play the solo line of the Saint-Saëns *Romance*. Think in the new key.

Romance

(Excerpt)

CAMILLE SAINT-SAËNS, Op. 36
(1835–1921)

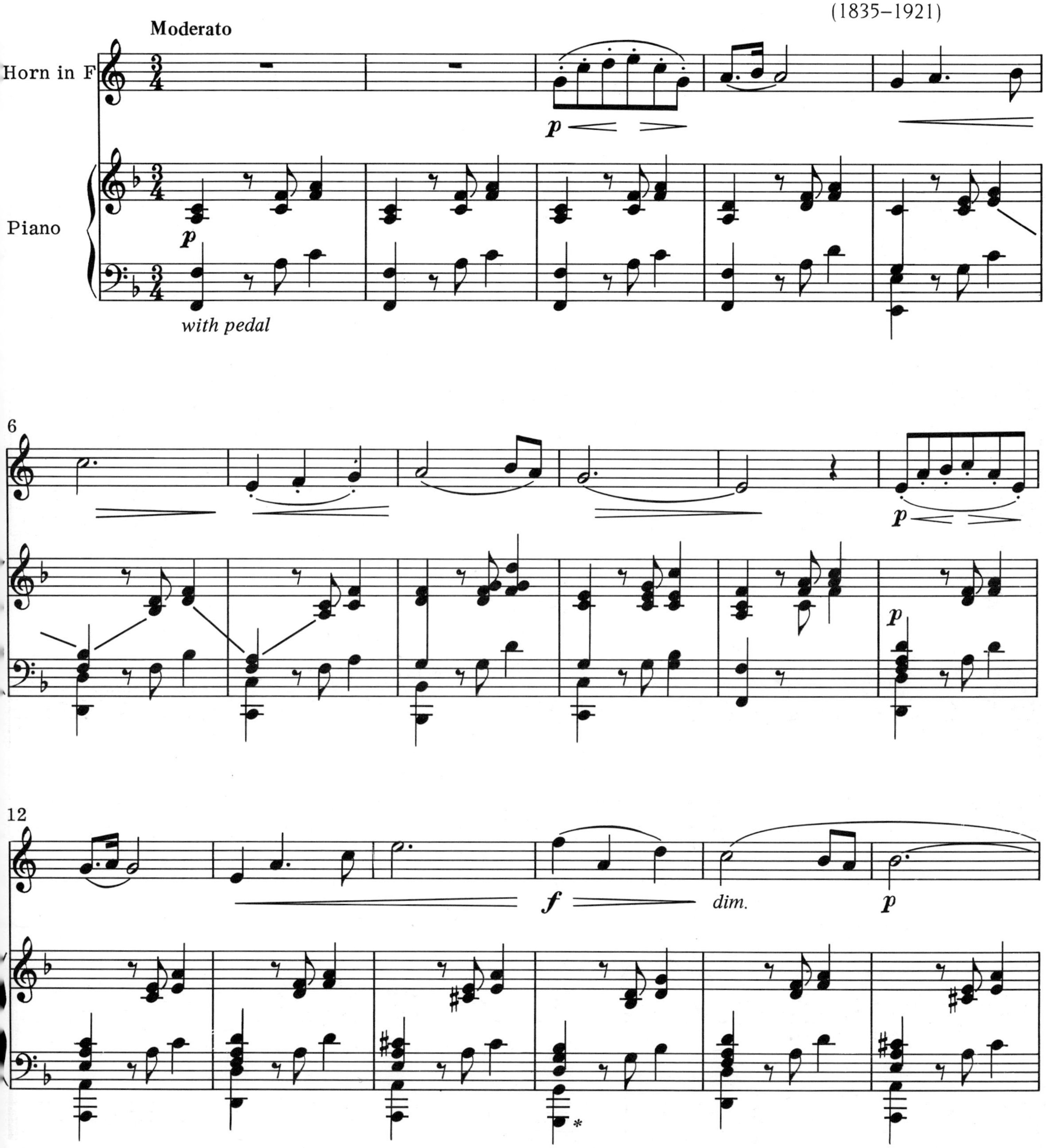

*May be played on full-range keyboards.

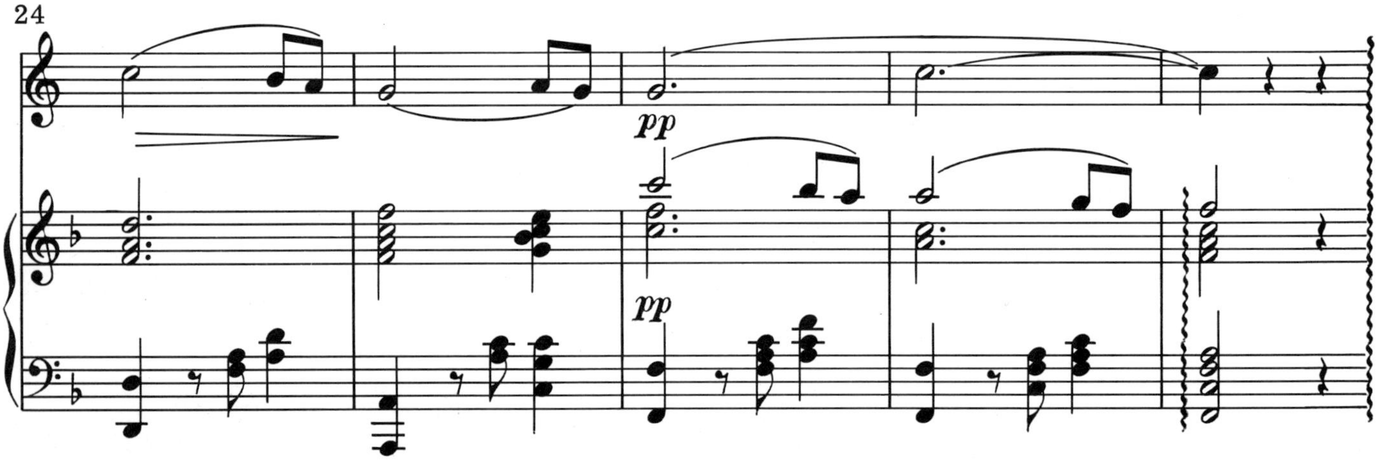

Then play the *Romance* as an ensemble (primo—French horn; secondo—accompaniment). Now trade parts and play again.

3. Play the clarinet solo as your teacher plays the accompaniment.

Sonata for Clarinet and Piano

(Excerpt)

CAMILLE SAINT-SAËNS, Op. 167
(1835–1921)

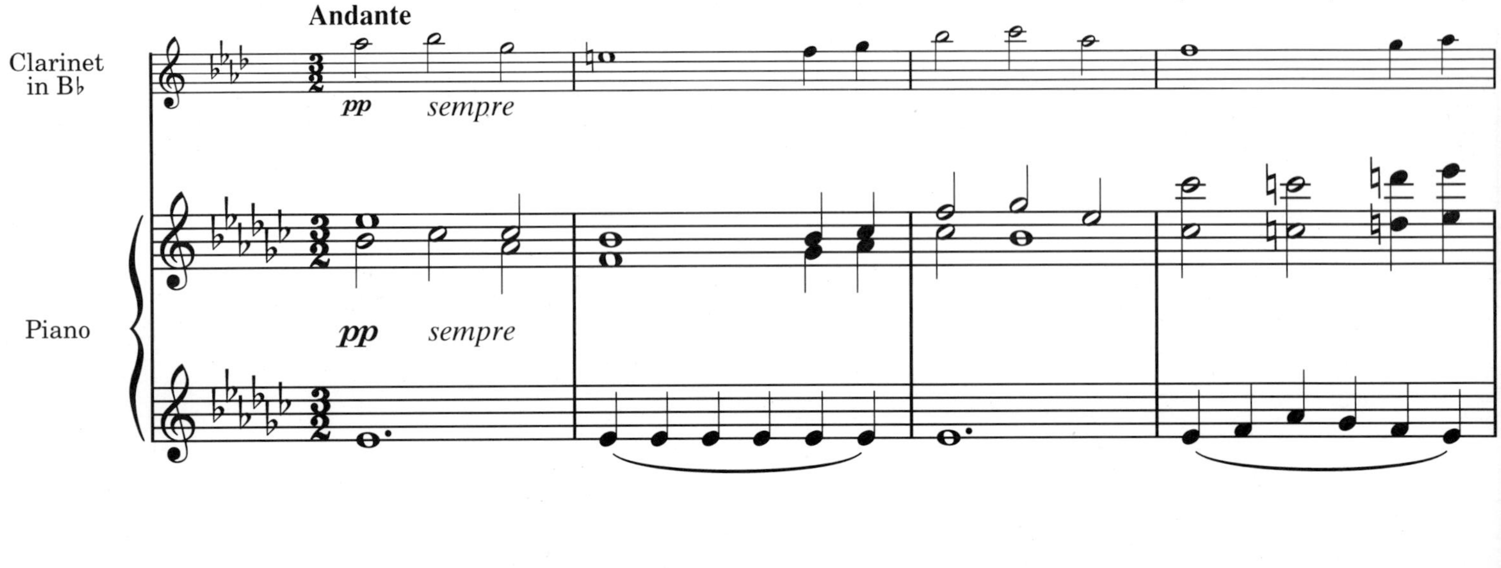

5
9
8va
sempre pp
13
(♭)

4. Play the following: 1) E♭ Alto; 2) 1st, 2nd and 3rd Horns (F); 3) 1st, 2nd and 3rd Trombones and Tuba; 4) 2nd Trombone and Tuba.

Air for Saxophone

(Excerpt)

ALEC WILDER and LOONIS McGLOHON

7
14

IMPROVISATION

Create improvised music for the following technique exercises in classical ballet.

1. At the barre: *Petite battlements sur le cou-de-pied* (moderately fast $\frac{4}{4}$ meter; two-bar introduction and thirty-two bars of exercise).

2. In centre floor: *Port de bras* and *révérence* (slow $\frac{3}{4}$ meter; two-bar introduction and thirty-two bars of exercise with the appropriate *révérence* conclusion).

Use the following form for each:

Intro	–	2 bar
A	–	8 bar
A	–	8 bar
B	–	8 bar
A	–	8 bar
Révérence	–	2 bar

ENSEMBLE

1. Play the Mozart *Menuetto and Trio* as a three-part ensemble (part 1—oboe I and II; part 2—corni in B♭; part 3—bassoon I and II).

Menuetto and Trio

from *Divertimento* No. 9

WOLFGANG AMADEUS MOZART, K. 240
(1756–1791)

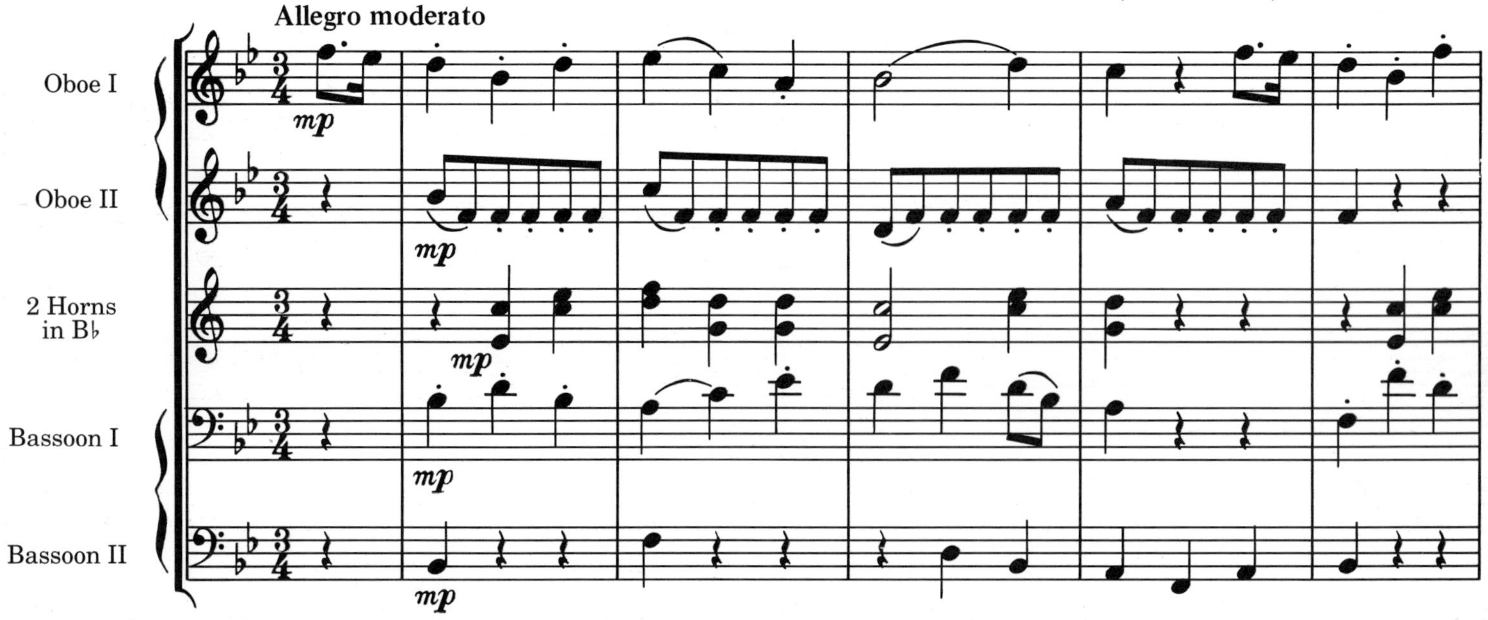

6
p
p
p
p
11
f
f
17
f
f
f

Menuetto da capo

2. Play as an ensemble: part I—corno I and II; part 2—oboe I and II; part 3—clarinet I and II; part 4—bassoon I and II.

Minuetto and Trio

from *Serenade* No. 12 WOLFGANG AMADEUS MOZART, K. 388
(1756–1791)

37
43
Fine
Trio in canone al rovescio
49
Oboe I
mezza voce
Oboe II
mezza voce
Bassoon I
mezza voce
Bassoon II
mezza voce

56
63
69

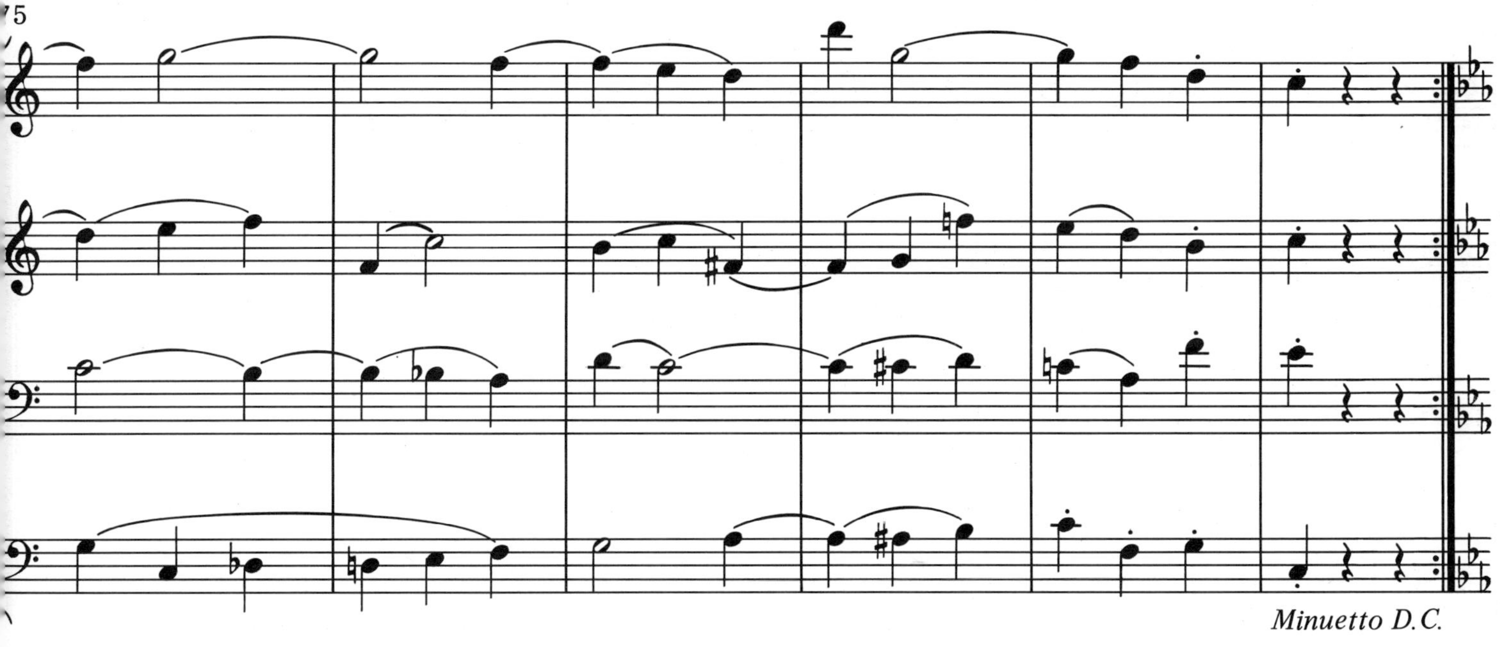

Rondeau

from *First Suite*, first movement
(The PBS "Masterpiece Theatre" Theme)

JEAN JOSEPH MOURET
(1682–1738)

Arranged by Weekley and Arganbright

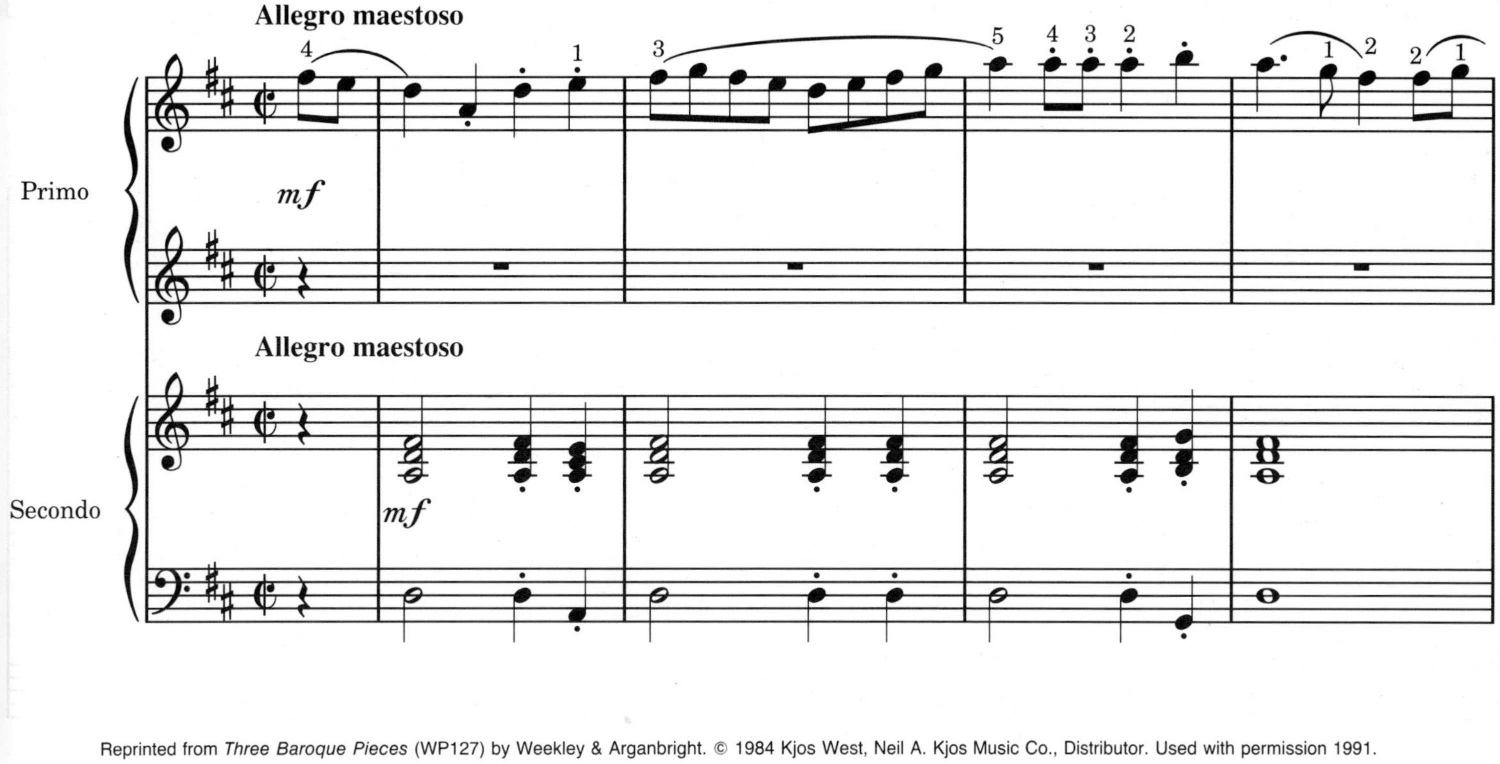

8va
(8va)
(8va)
mp

17
mp
21
mf
25
mf

Meno mosso
8va
ff
Meno mosso

(8va)
41
ff
(8va)
45
rit.
rit.

1. Play twice. On the repeat, sing as you play.

The Water Is Wide

British Isles Folksong
Arranged by Lynn Freeman Olson

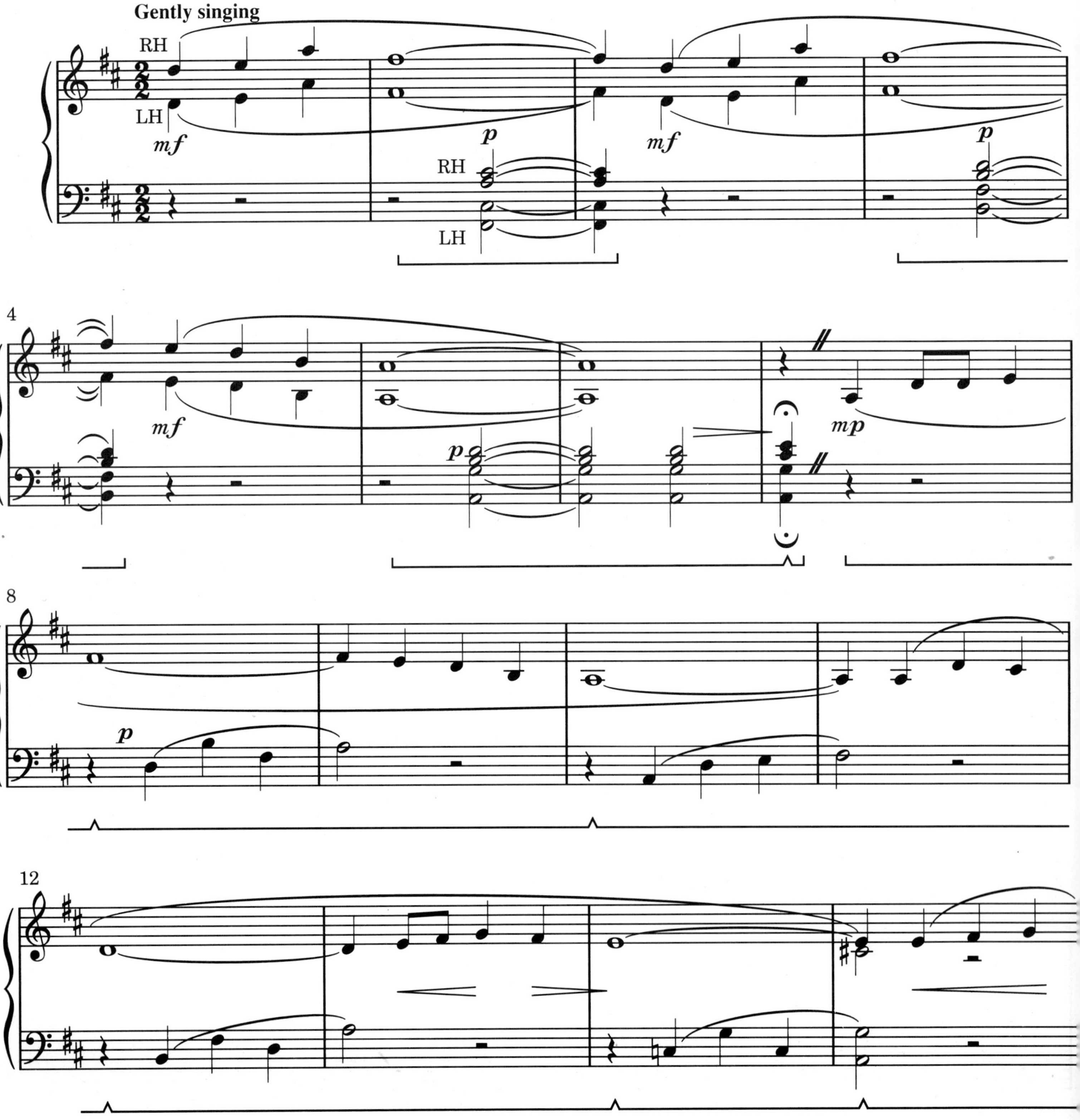

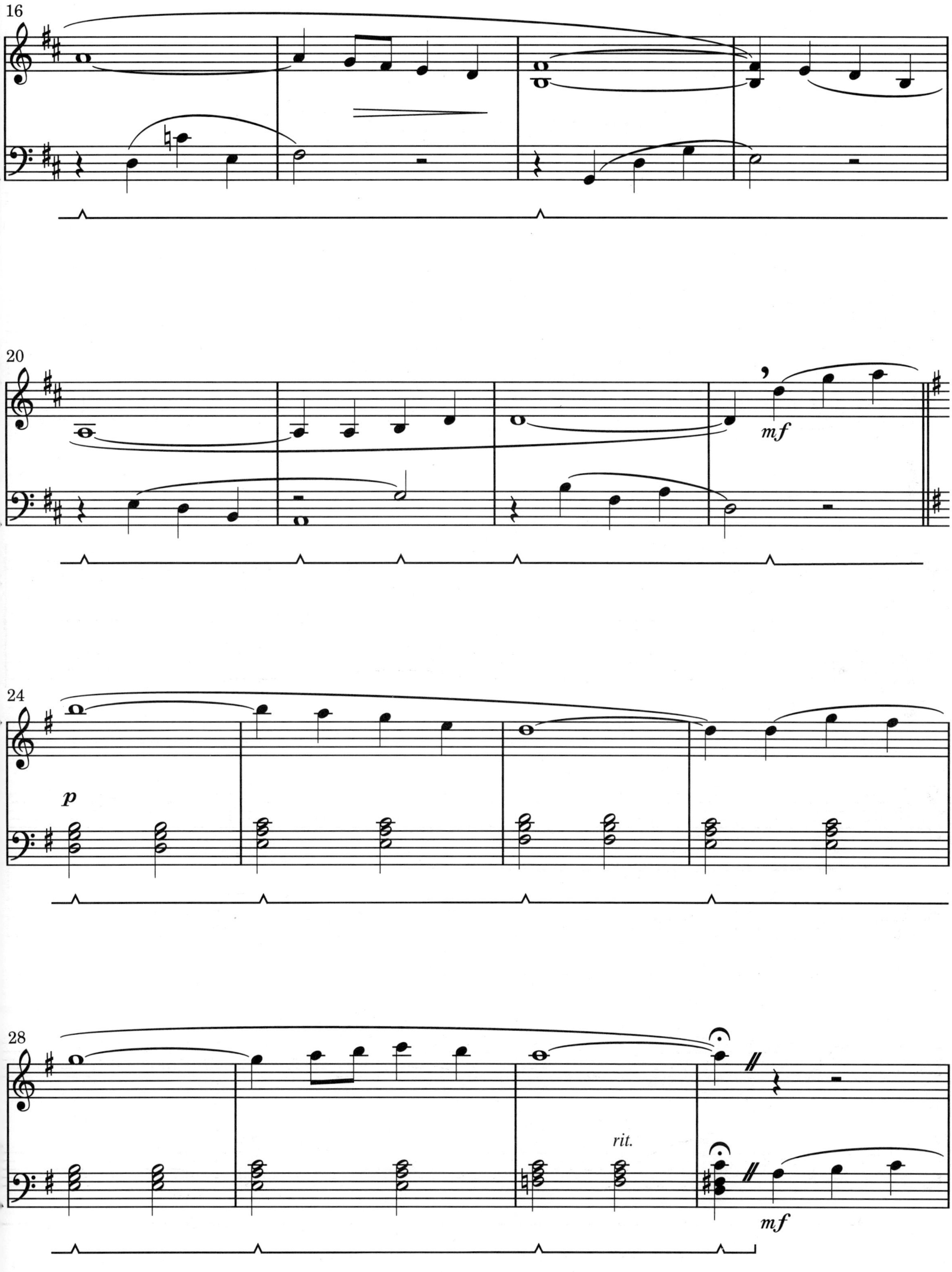
16
20
mf
24
p
28
rit.
mf

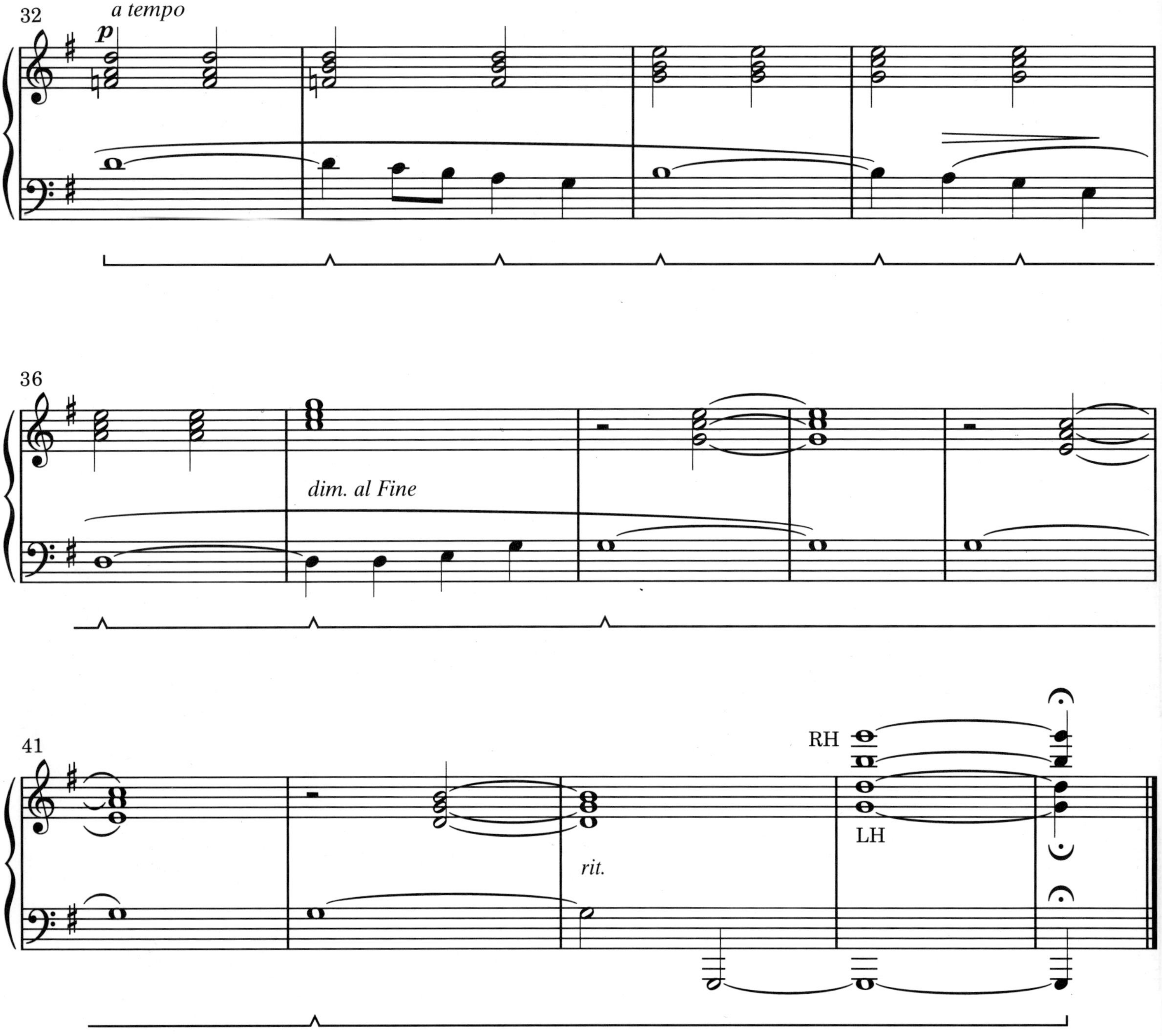

The water is wide, yet I must go.
Oh, would that I had wings to fly!
Is there a boat that will carry two?
Then both may go, my love and I.

A ship that sails out on the sea
Is loaded deep, deep as she can be,
Yet not so deep as the love I'm in—
I know not if I sink or swim.

2. Plan chord shapes silently. Note that pedal is generally used throughout when performing this piece.

II

from *Three-Score Set*

WILLIAM SCHUMAN
(1910–   )

6.

EXEMPLARY REPERTOIRE

RELATED SKILLS AND ACTIVITIES

SUBSEQUENT REPERTOIRE

Altered Seventh Chords/ Extended Harmonies (Ninth, Thirteenth)

EXEMPLARY REPERTOIRE	**Castanetta**	John Chagy
	Three Segment Blues	Alan Swain

INQUIRY (*Castanetta*)

1. Scan the piece. Observe:

   - Static rhythm of sections
   - Chord shapes
   - Repetition
   - Hemiola
   - Augmented sixth chord

PERFORMANCE

1. Block chords throughout:

A Section

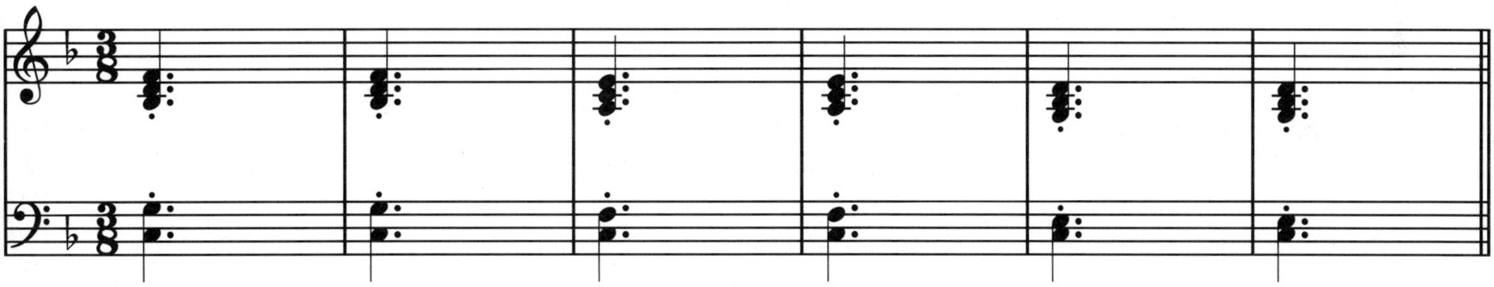

B Section

2. Practice cadential measures.

3. Play as written.

Castanetta

JOHN CHAGY

Allegro con spirito

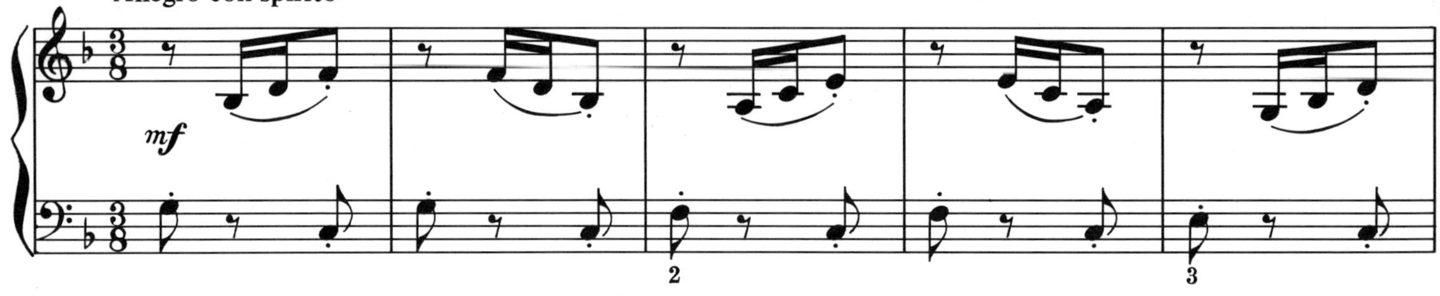

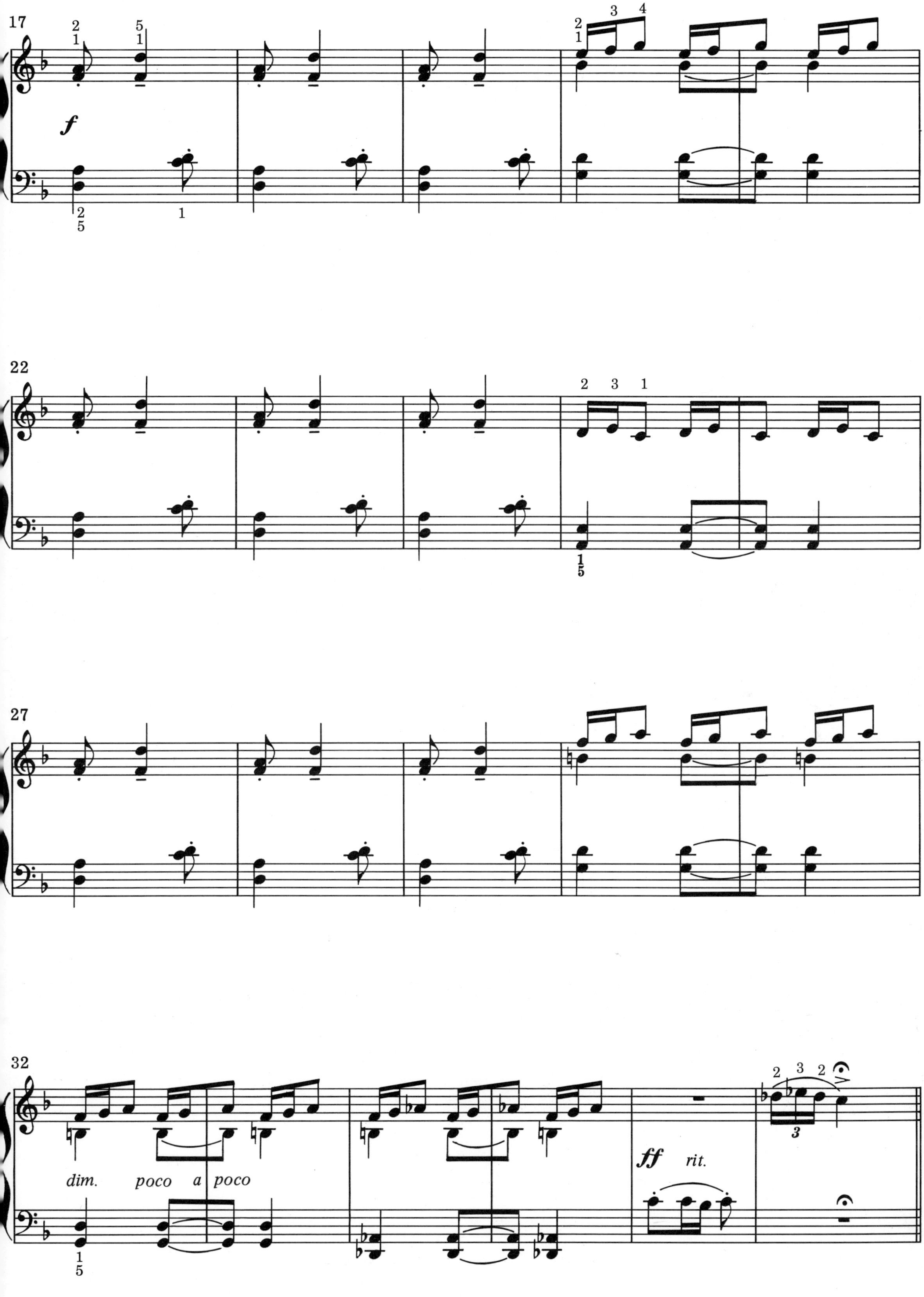
17
f
22
27
32
dim. poco a poco
ff rit.

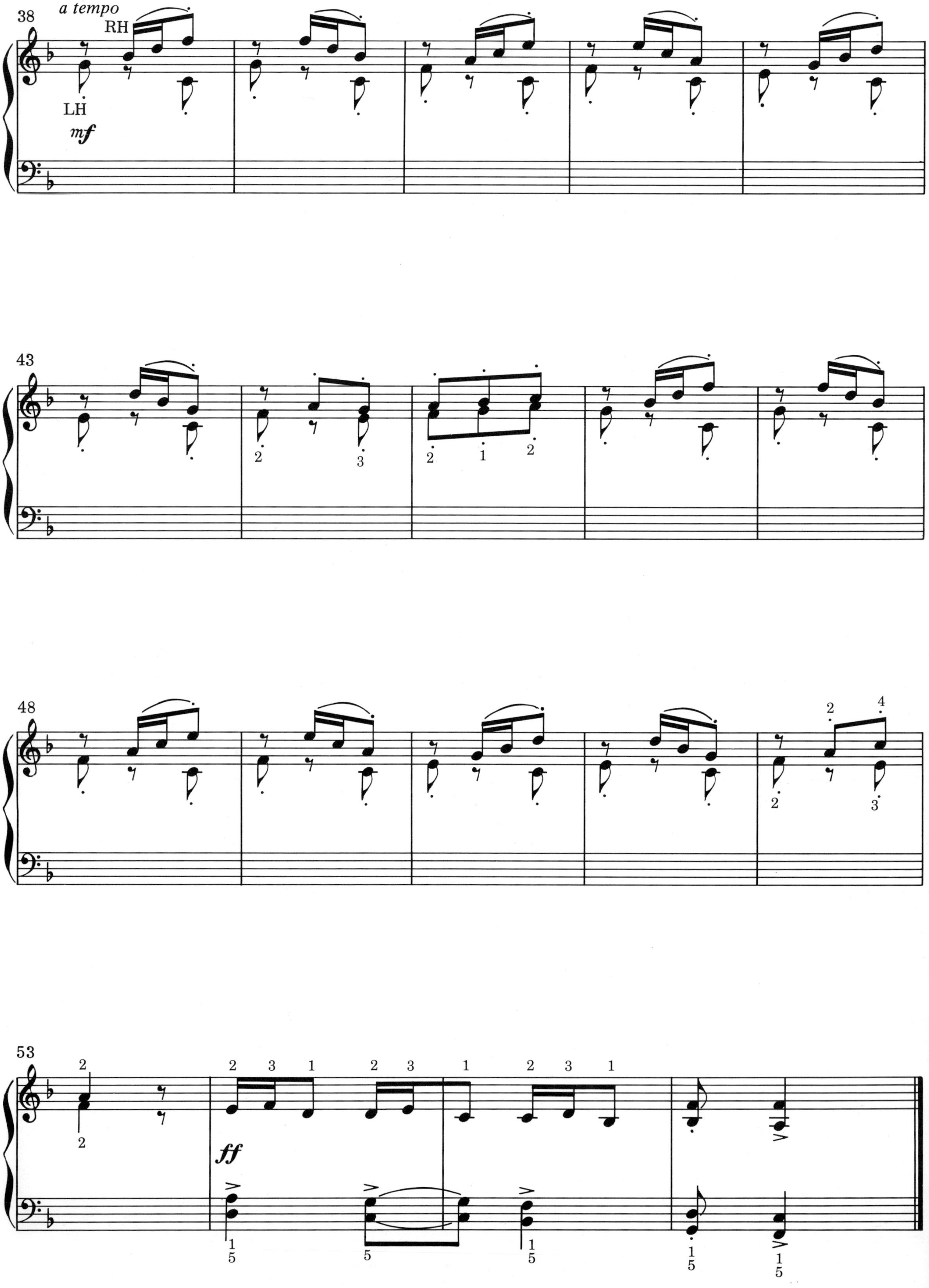
a tempo
RH
LH
mf
ff

INQUIRY

1. Scan the piece *Three Segment Blues*. Observe:

    - LH non-root chords
    - Accents

PERFORMANCE

1. Remember that eighth notes in blues ARE NOT played as straight rhythms. They have a triplet feel to them. Accents will also fall *off the beat* for the most part.

2. HAVE FUN!

Three Segment Blues

ALAN SWAIN

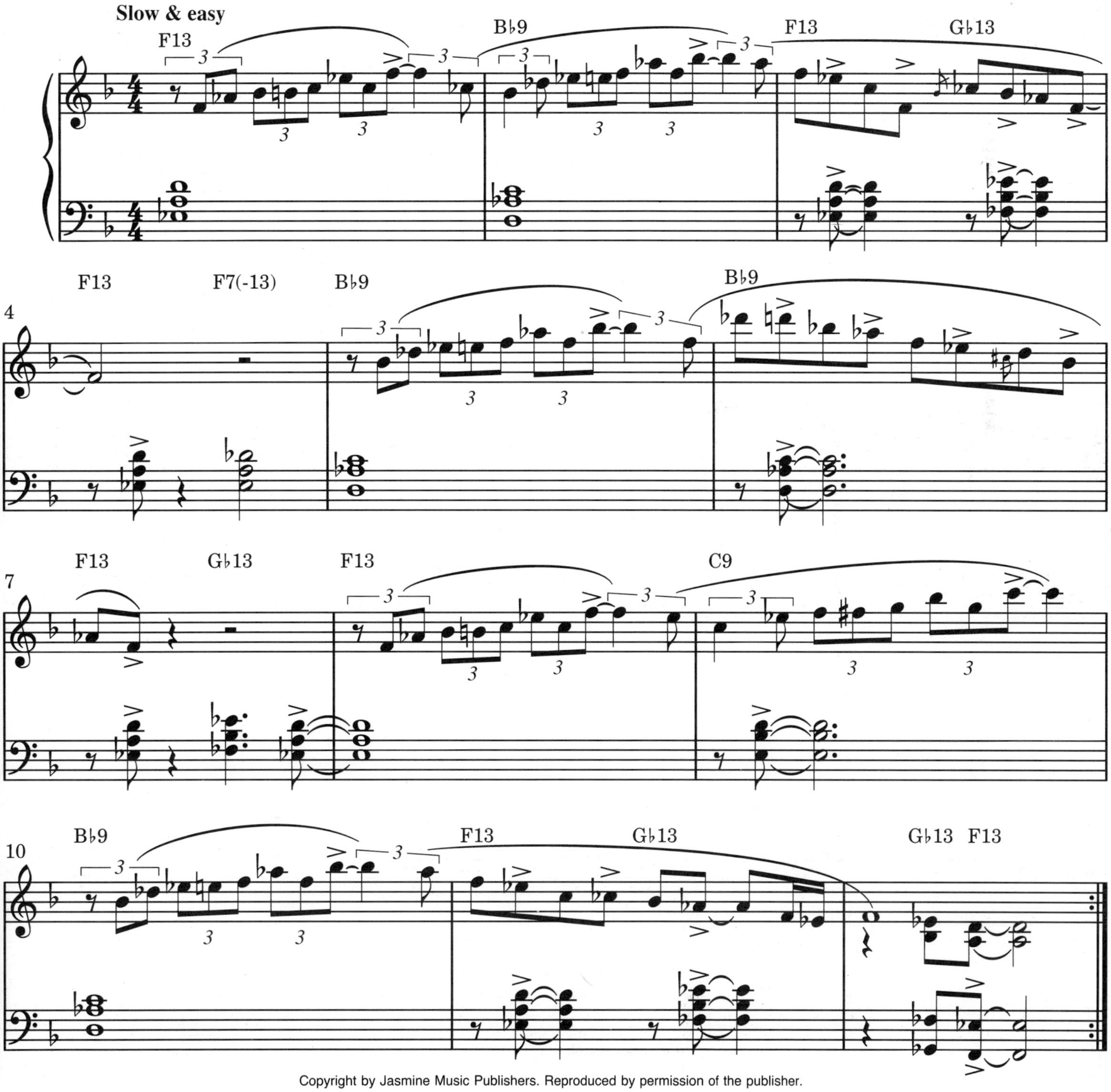

RELATED SKILLS AND ACTIVITIES

TECHNIQUE

1. Review the white-key major scales. Start with C and repeat in the keys of D, E, F, G, A, and B major.

2. Play the Clementi *Prelude* in the key of C minor also.

Prelude in G Minor

MUZIO CLEMENTI, Op. 43
(1752–1832)

Allegro ma non troppo

3. Play in the key of C♯ major as well.

Study in C

JEAN BAPTISTE DUVERNOY, Op. 176
(1800–1880)

READING

1. Play this piece as an ensemble: part I—clarinet; part 2—violins I and II; and part 3—viola and cello.

Quintet in A Major

(Excerpt)

WOLFGANG AMADEUS MOZART, K. 581
(1756–1791)

18
arco
arco
arco
23
28
fp
fp
p

Try other combinations of parts: part 1—violin I and cello; part 2—violin II and viola; part 3—clarinet; and so on.

2. Play the following parts: tenor I and tenor II; baritone and bass; tenor I and bass; all four.

Lonesome Road

(Excerpt)

Traditional
Arranged by Robert W. Thygerson

Slowly, with expression – rubato style

3. Choose a partner and play accompaniment as partner sings. Omit doublings in chords if necessary for ease of playing.

Joshua Fit da Battle of Jericho

(Excerpt)

Spiritual

Arranged by Margaret Bonds

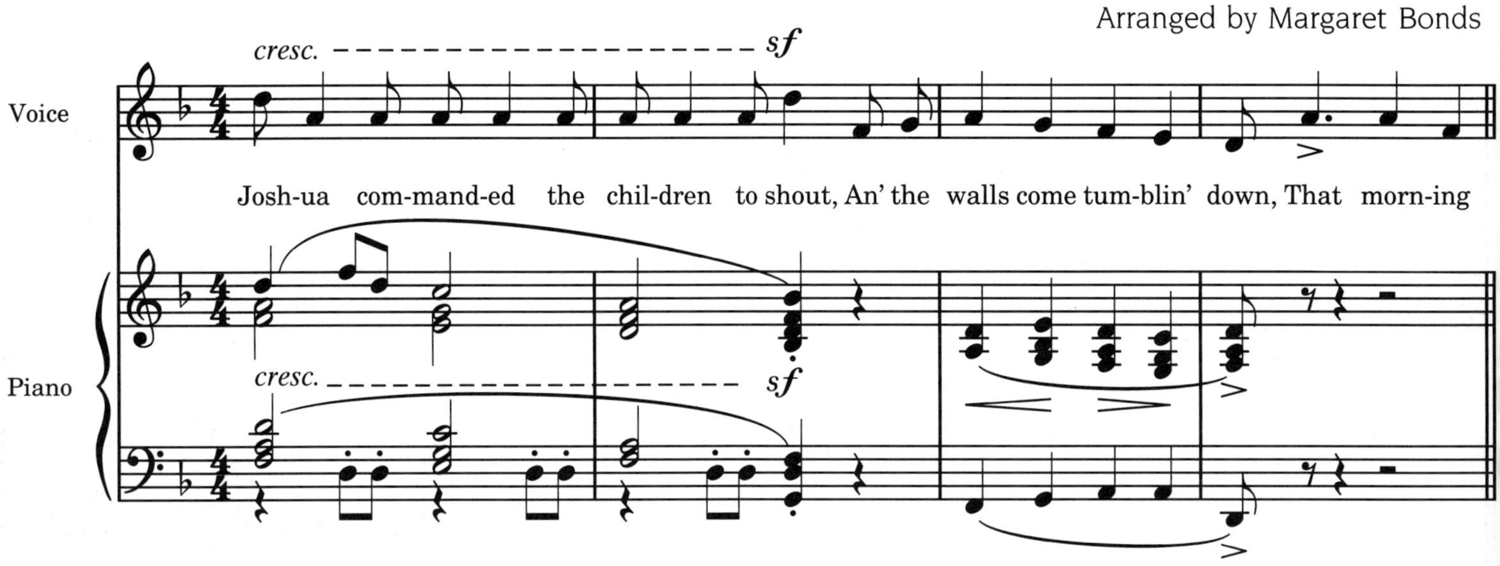
cresc.
sf
Voice
Josh-ua com-mand-ed the chil-dren to shout, An' the walls come tum-blin' down, That morn-ing
Piano
cresc.
sf

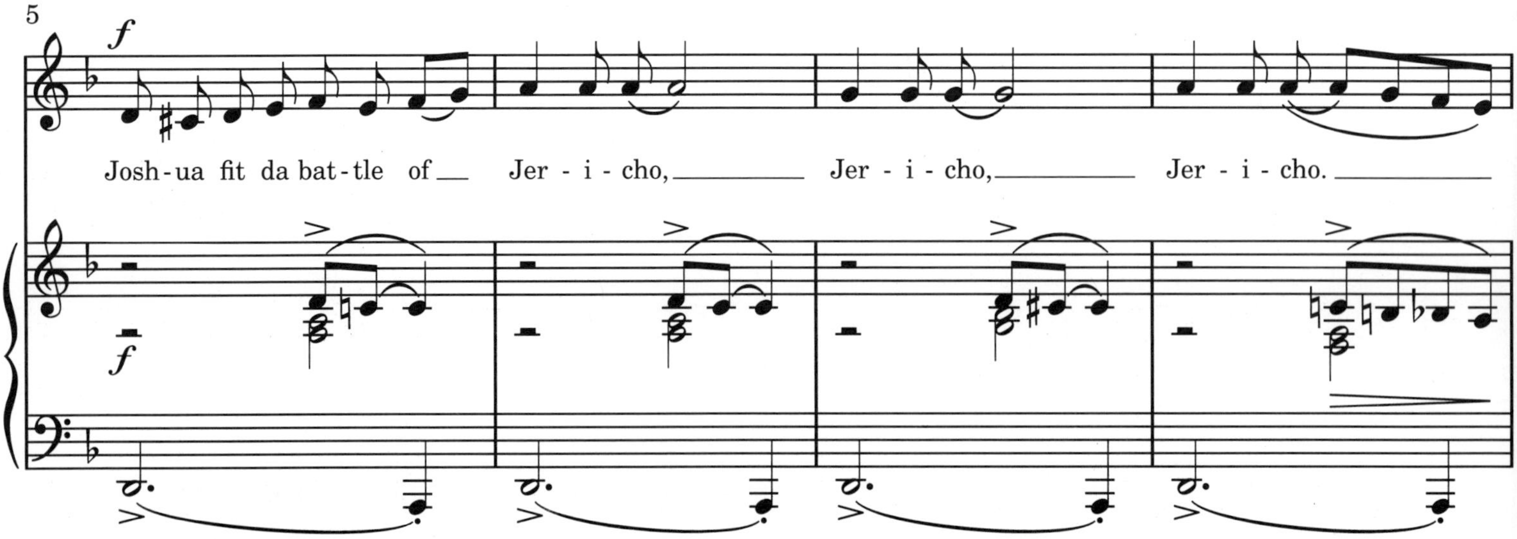
5
f
Josh-ua fit da bat-tle of Jer - i - cho, Jer - i - cho, Jer - i - cho.
f

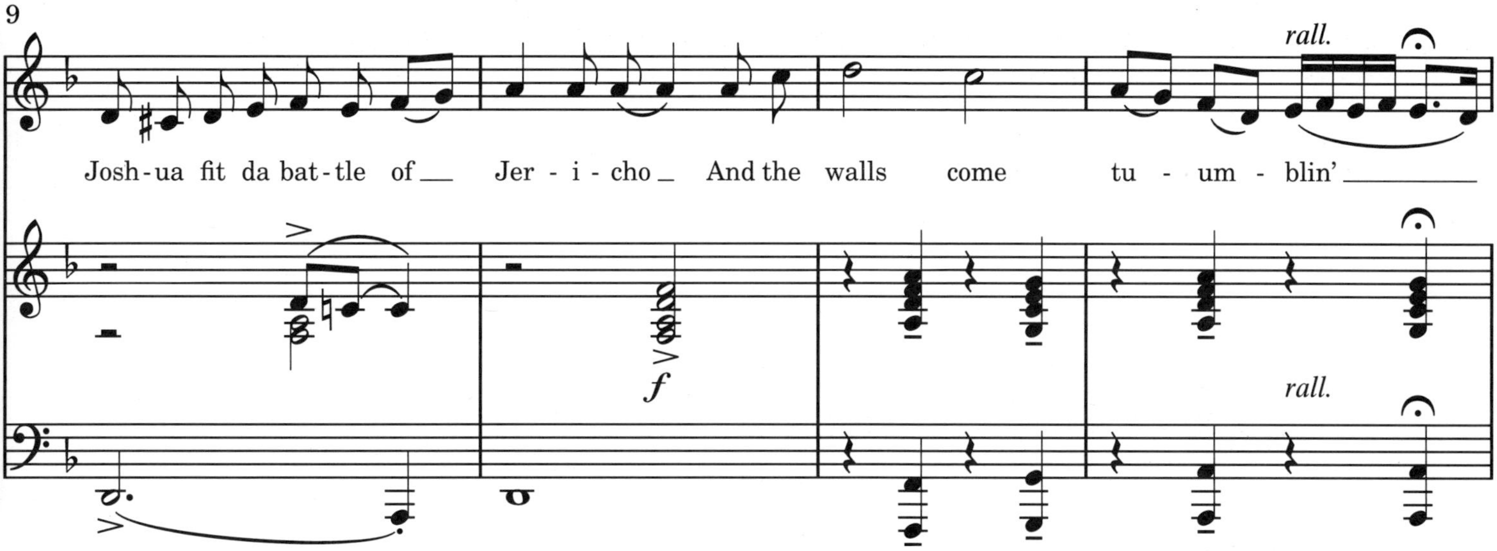

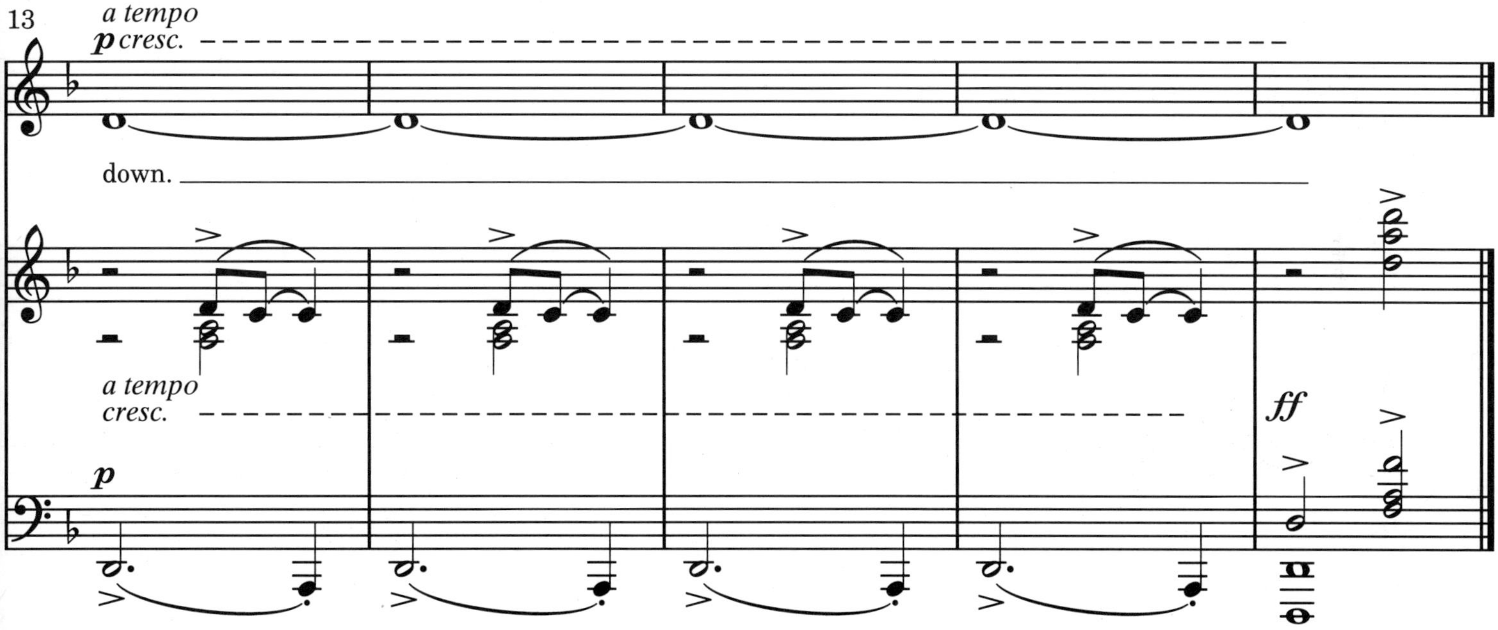

4. Choose a partner and play *Sarabande* as a duet (primo—viola; secondo—accompaniment).

Sarabande

JOHN ERNST GALLIARD
(1680–1749)

5
9
f
f
13
p
f
p
f
1.
2.
1.
2.

5. Play the accompaniment as the class sings parts.

Sure on This Shining Night

(Excerpt)

SAMUEL BARBER
(1910–1981)

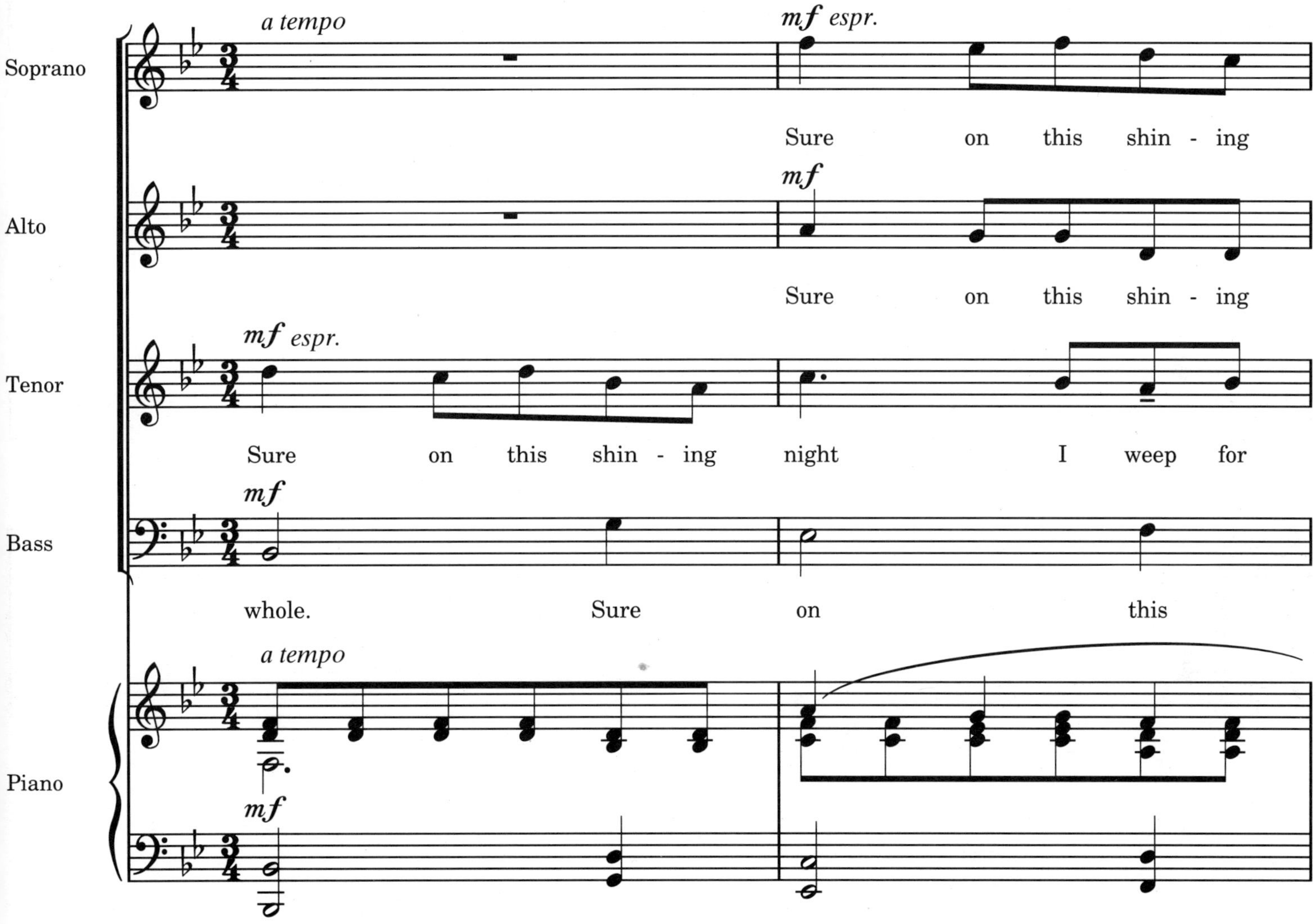
Soprano
Alto
Tenor
Bass
Piano
a tempo
mf espr.
Sure on this shin - ing
mf
Sure on this shin - ing
mf espr.
Sure on this shin - ing night I weep for
mf
whole. Sure on this
a tempo
mf

3
p
night I weep for won - der wan - d'ring far a -
p espr.
night I weep for won - der wan - d'ring far a - lone Of
p pp
won - der wan - d'ring far a -
p
shin - ing night wan - d'ring far a -

7
dim. poco a poco
rall.
a tempo
lone Of shad - ows on the stars.
p sempre marc.
shad - ows on the stars.
dim. poco a poco
lone Of shad - ows on the stars.
dim. poco a poco
lone Of shad - ows on the stars.
dim. poco a poco
rall.
a tempo

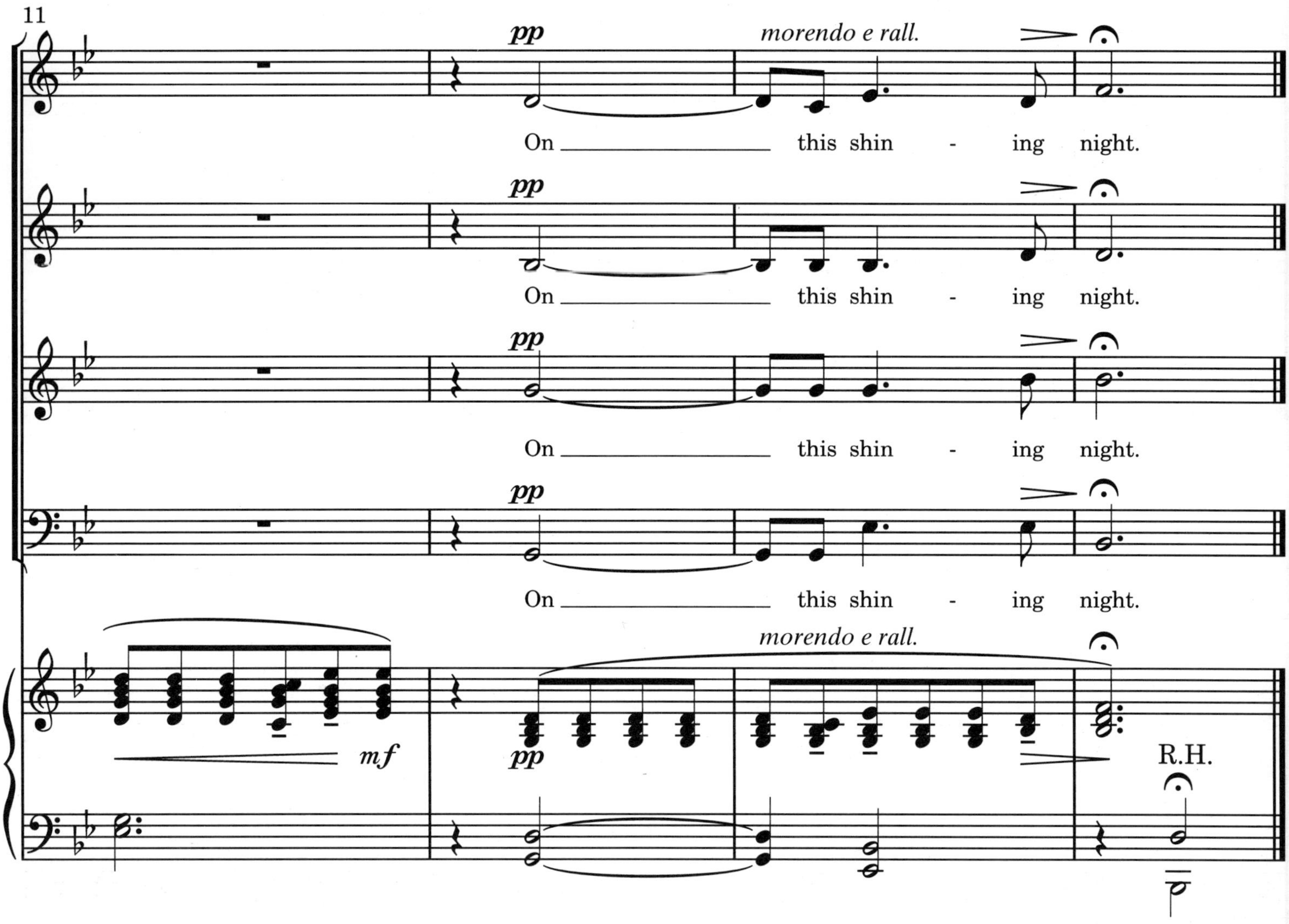

6. Play the accompaniment as you sing or accompany a classmate.

Der Tod und das Mädchen

FRANZ SCHUBERT, Op. 7, No. 3
(1797–1828)

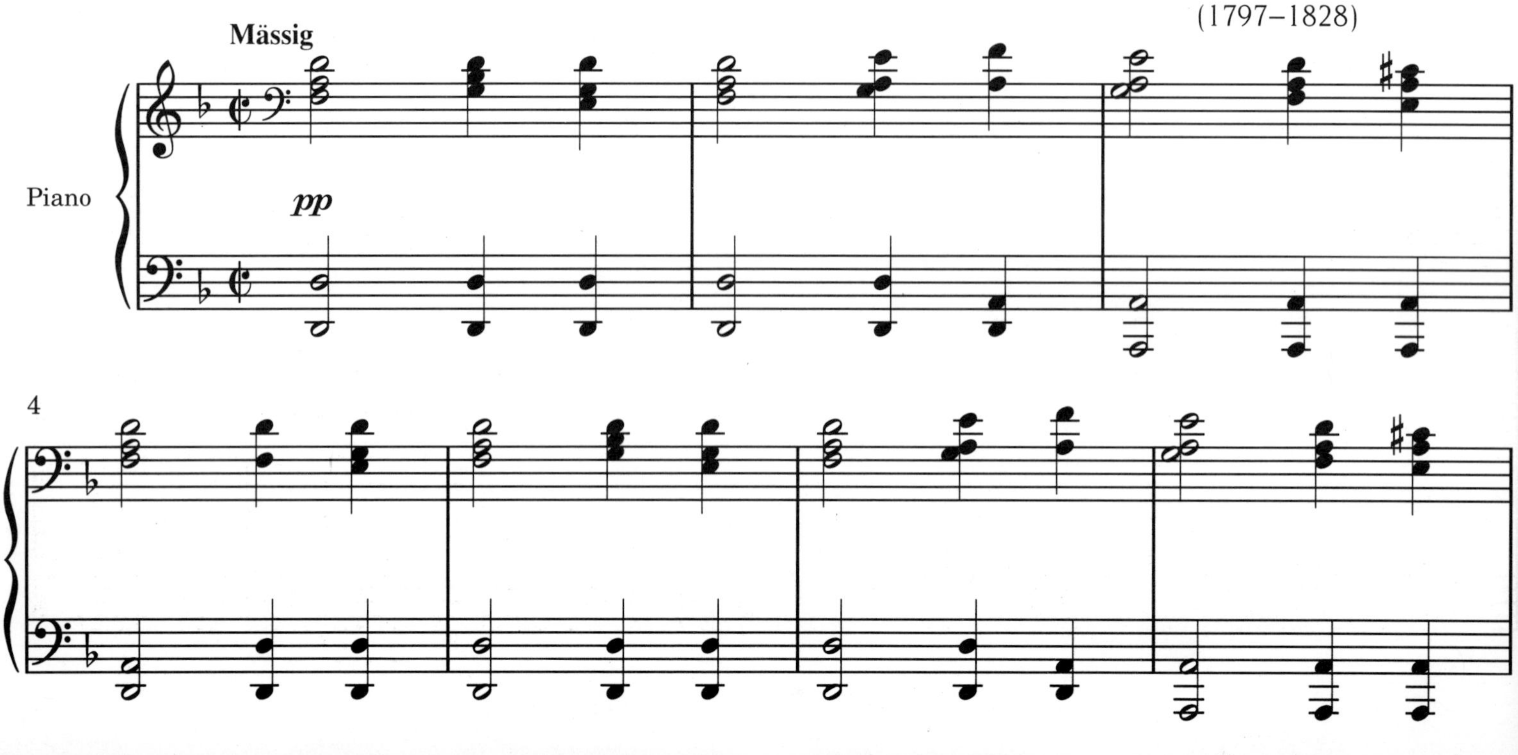

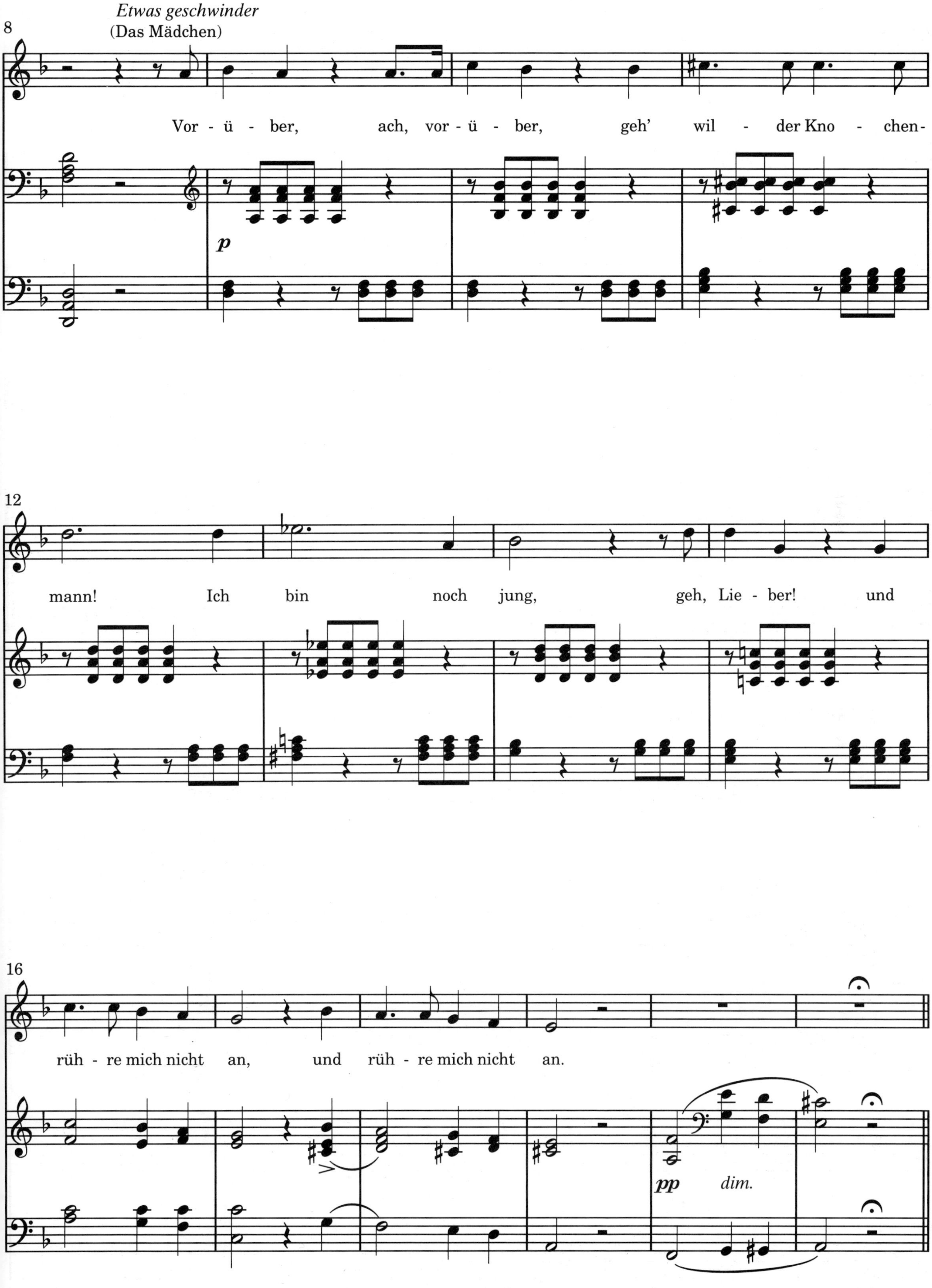
Etwas geschwinder
(Das Mädchen)
8
Vor - ü - ber, ach, vor - ü - ber, geh' wil - der Kno - chen-
p
12
mann! Ich bin noch jung, geh, Lie - ber! und
16
rüh - re mich nicht an, und rüh - re mich nicht an.
pp
dim.

22
Das erste Zeitmass
(Der Tod)
Gib dei - ne Hand, du schön und zart Ge - bild! bin
pp
26
Freund, und kom - me nicht, zu ___ stra - fen.
30
Sei gu - tes Muts! ich bin nicht wild, sollst

KEYBOARD THEORY

1. Altered seventh chords fall into one of two categories—those that are borrowed from the parallel minor and those that tonicize a chord diatonic to the key (secondary dominants—V7 of iii and so on). The following example shows both types.

Play the following progressions in the keys indicated. Move to the closest chord possible.

D major

3/4 I | V7/IV | iv | $ii^{ø}7$ | I^{6}_{4} | V7 | $vii^{o}7$ | I ||

E♭ major

4/4 – V7 | I | I7 | vii7 | $ii^{ø}7$ V7 | I ||

2. Augmented sixth chords fall into a category of altered sevenths. The Italian is actually a triad, but in first inversion the sound is that of a dominant seventh chord. The German, Italian, and French augmented sixths all contain a ♯4 of the key, and this tone acts as leading tone to the dominant.

♯iv	It	(♯6)	contains ♯4, ♭6, tonic
♯iv7	Ger	($^{♯6}_{5}$)	contains ♯4, ♭6, tonic, ♭3
ii7	Fr	($^{♯6}_{4}$ 3)	contains 2, ♯4, ♭6, tonic
♯ii7	Ger	($^{♯6}_{♯4}$ 3)	contains ♯2, ♯4, ♭6, tonic

(doubly augmented resolves to I^{6}_{4})

Spell augmented sixth chords in the keys given; then play in the proper inversion and resolve. The doubly augmented sixth is the only one resolving to I^{6}_{4}; the others resolve to V.

Example: Key of F, German

Spell: B♮ D♭ F A♭ /Play:

Spell: G♯ B♮ D♭ F /Play:

or

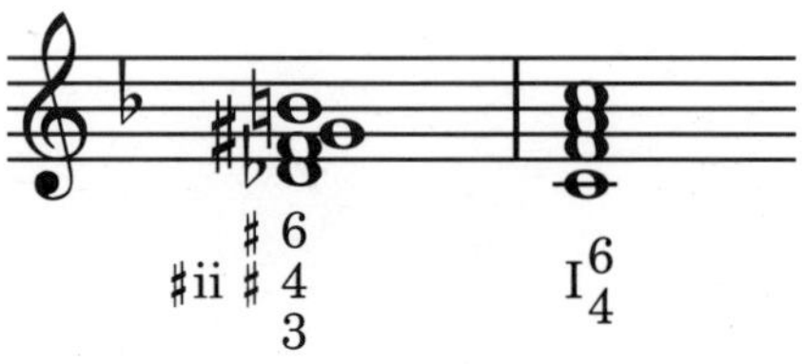

The sound is identical until the chord of resolution.

Spell and play the following. Include the chord of resolution.

Key of A major—German

Key of B♭ major—Italian

Key of D major—French

Key of E♭ major—German

Key of G major—French

Key of A♭ major—Italian

Key of C major—German

Key of D♭ major—French

Rh blues scale
1 b3 4 #4 5 b7

3. Extended harmonies add a new dimension to blues improvisation. In the example below, notice which chord members are included with each harmony. This voicing is standard for blues when using harmonies that go beyond triads and sevenths.

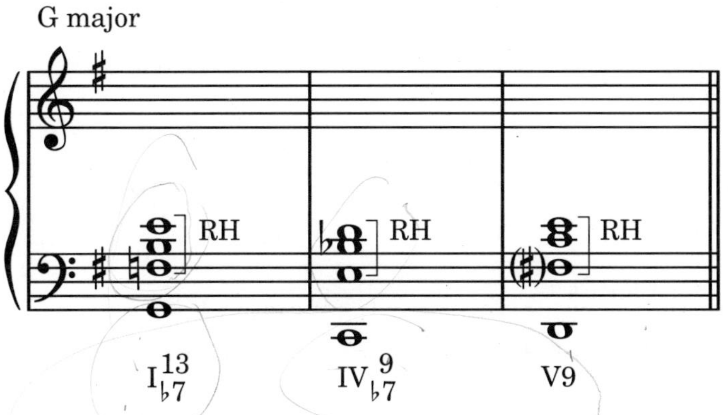

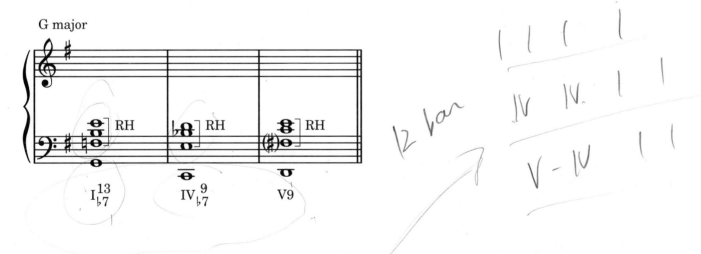

12 bar
I I I I
IV IV I I
V - IV I I

Keyboard players often omit roots of chords when improvising in a blues style. The following chords are referred to as "non-root" voicing.

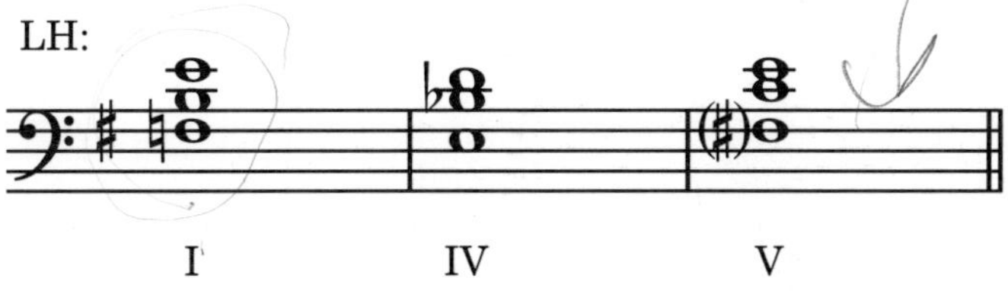

apply to St Louie on next page

then rh free improv

HARMONIZATION

1. Use non-root chords to harmonize.

St. Louie Blues

W. C. HANDY
(1873–1958)

2. Use a two-handed accompaniment as you sing.

My Wild Irish Rose

CHAUNCEY OLCOTT
(1858–1932)

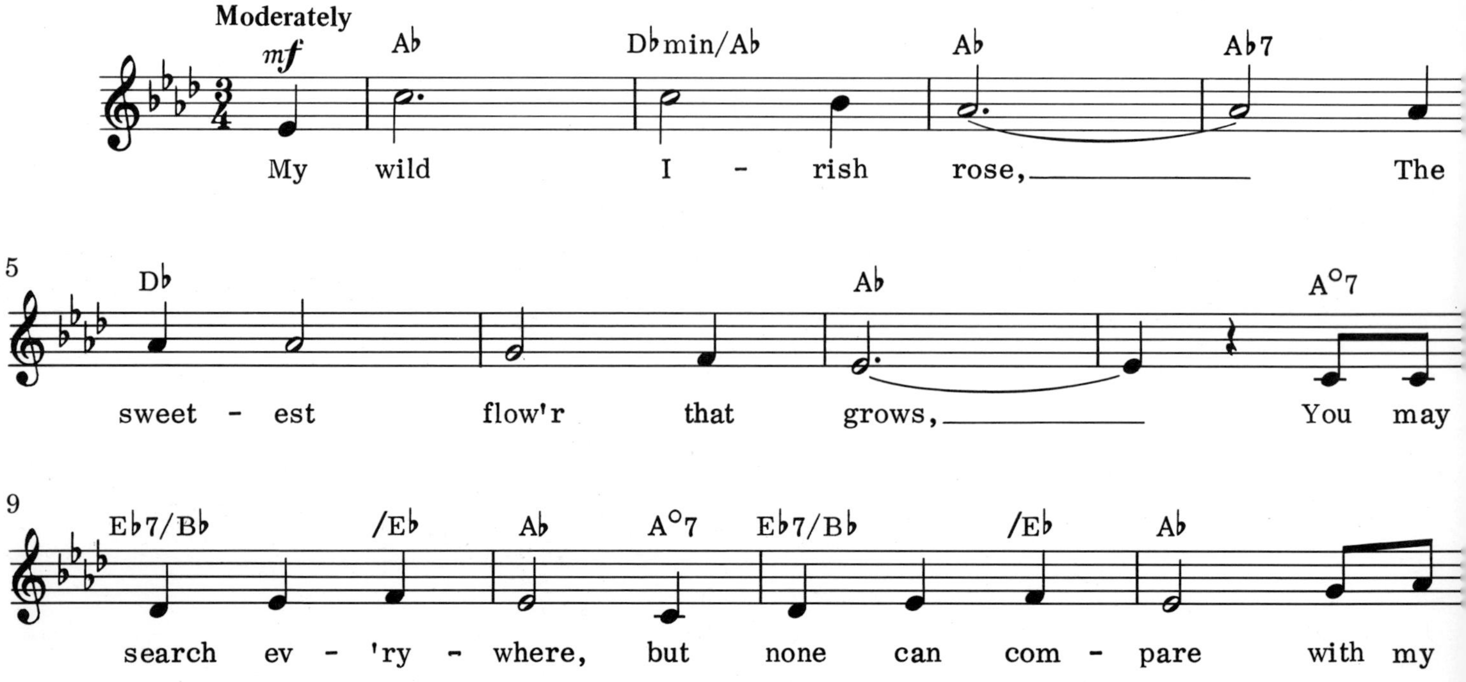

3. Accompany in keyboard style.

Eddie's Tune

MARTHA HILLEY

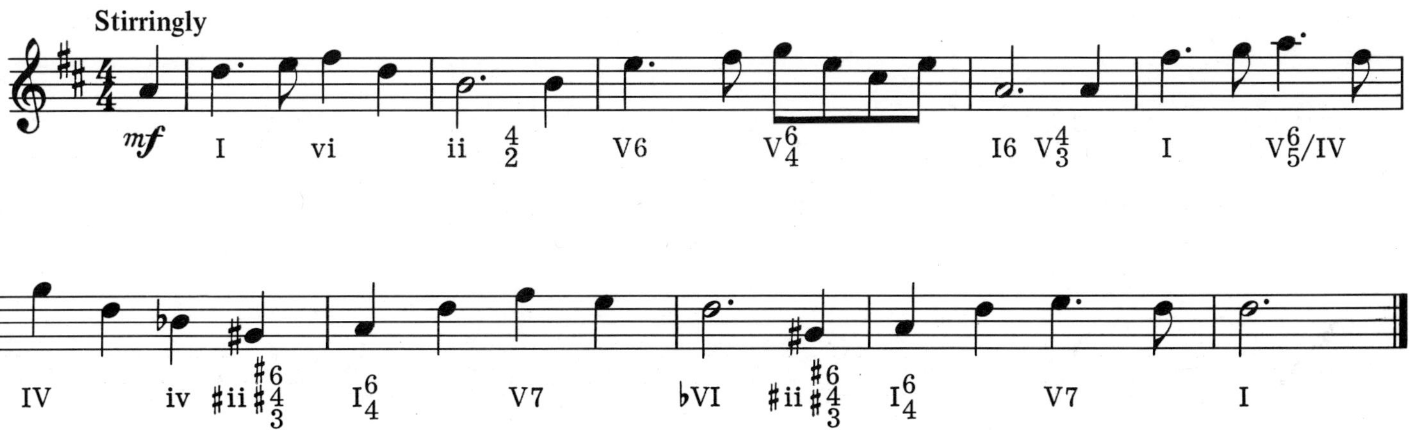

4. Play first with only two voices—melody and indicated bass. What do you notice about the first bar-and-a-half of each line? Now play with full harmonies.

Seymour

Traditional Hymn Tune
Adapted from Carl Maria von Weber

TRANSPOSITION

1. Play in the key of E♭ major.

My Country, 'Tis of Thee

ANONYMOUS

2. Play the horn part as a partner accompanies you.

Panis Angelicus
(Excerpt)

CÉSAR FRANCK
(1822–1890)

3. Determine the transposed key for both pairs of instruments. Perform as an ensemble. Think in the new key.

Trio I

(Excerpt)
from *Serenade* No. 10

WOLFGANG AMADEUS MOZART, K. 361
(1756–1791)

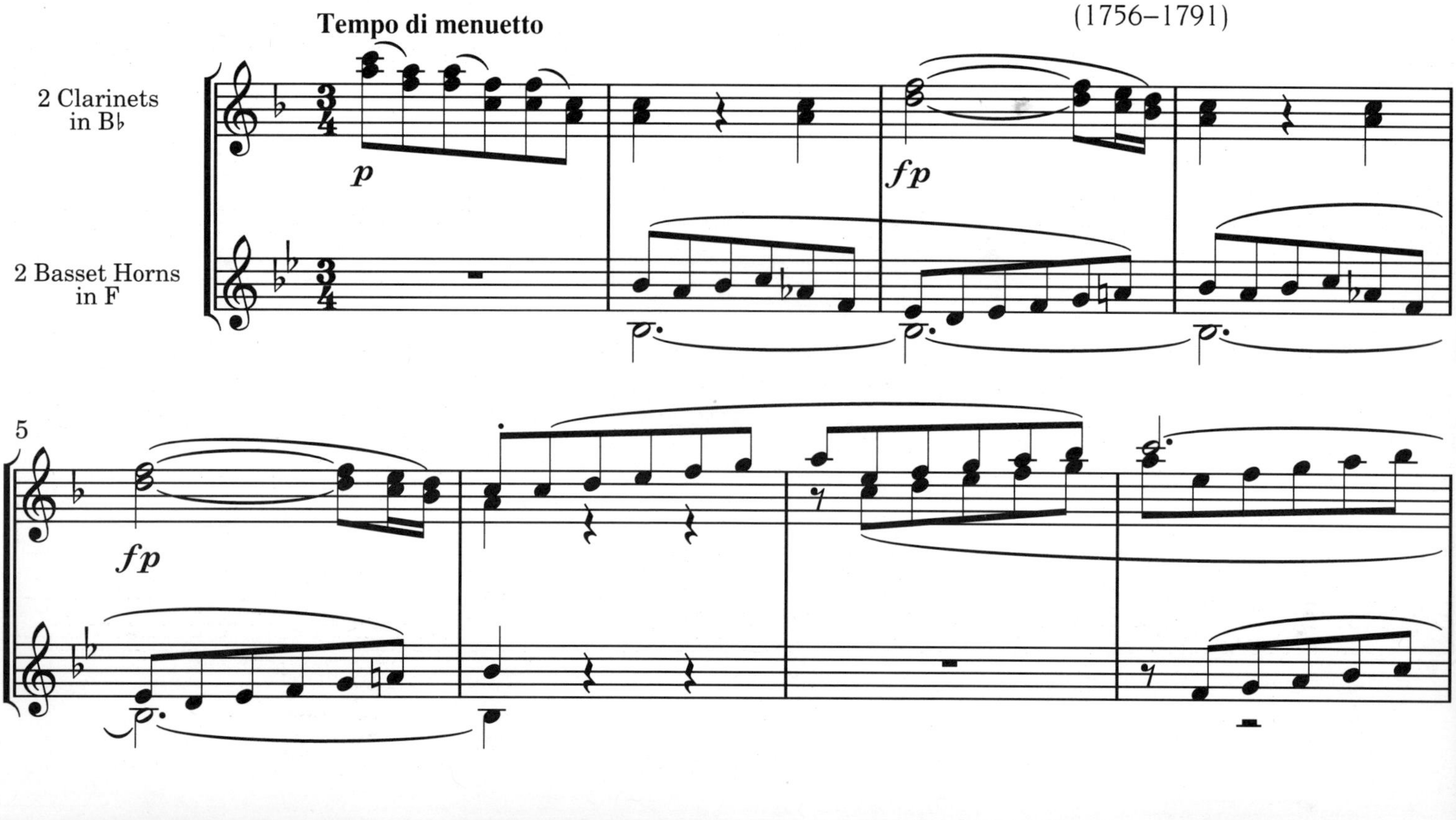

9
fp
13
fp
18
sf
p
24
29

4. Transpose Türk's *Zur ersten übung der Terzen und Sexten* to C major, E major, and F♯ major.

Zur ersten übung der Terzen und Sexten

DANIEL GOTTLOB TÜRK
(1756–1813)

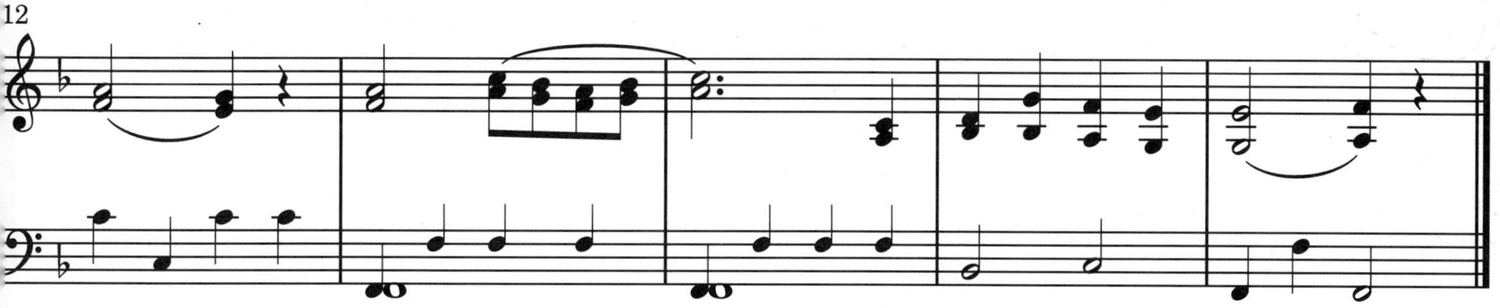

IMPROVISATION

1. Improvise three choruses of blues in F:

- Chorus 1—RH 13th and 9th chords with LH walking bass
- Chorus 2—LH non-root 13th and 9th chords with RH blues scale melody
- Chorus 3—RH 13th and 9th chords with LH walking bass

2. Use the following accompaniment as the basis for your melodic improvisation. Play both parts.

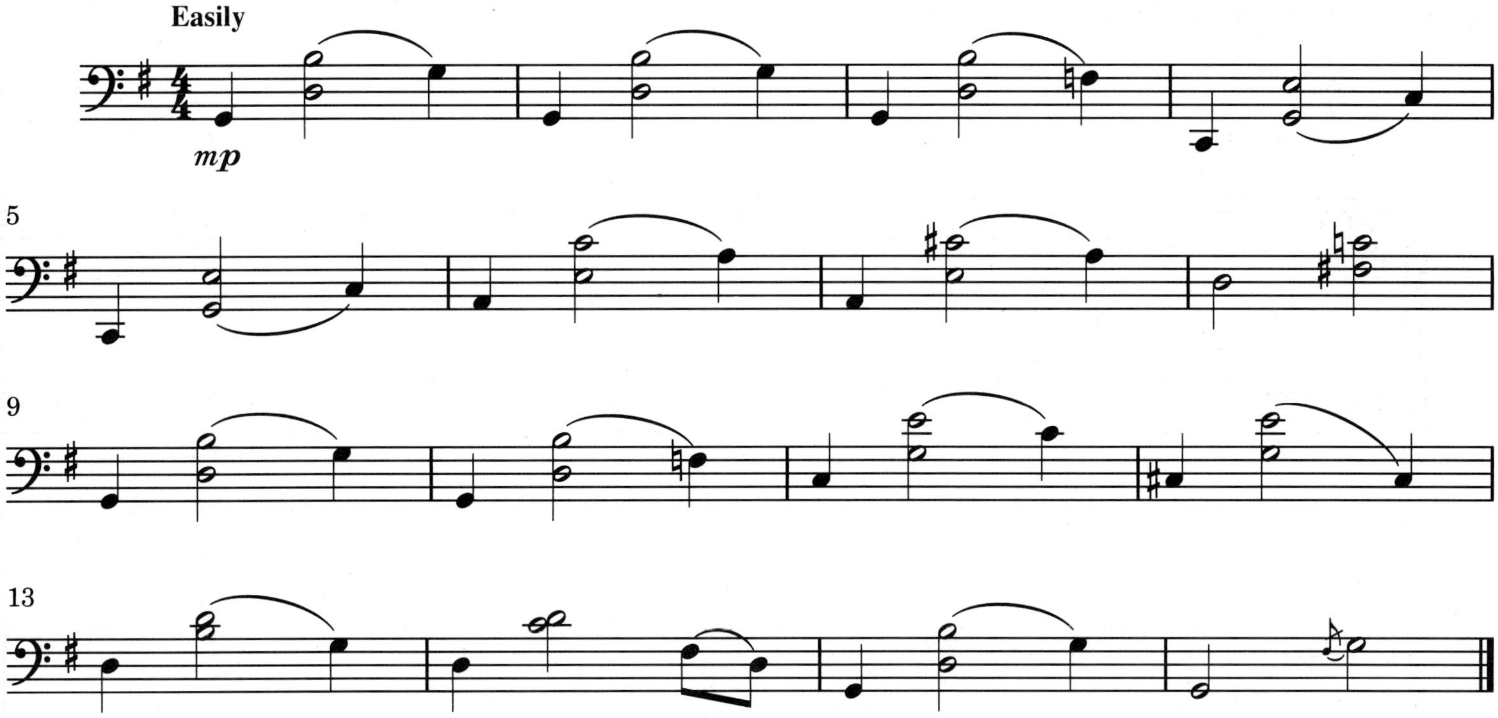

3. Develop the following fragments into sixteen-bar segments to use with basic movement by seven-year-old children.

Walk

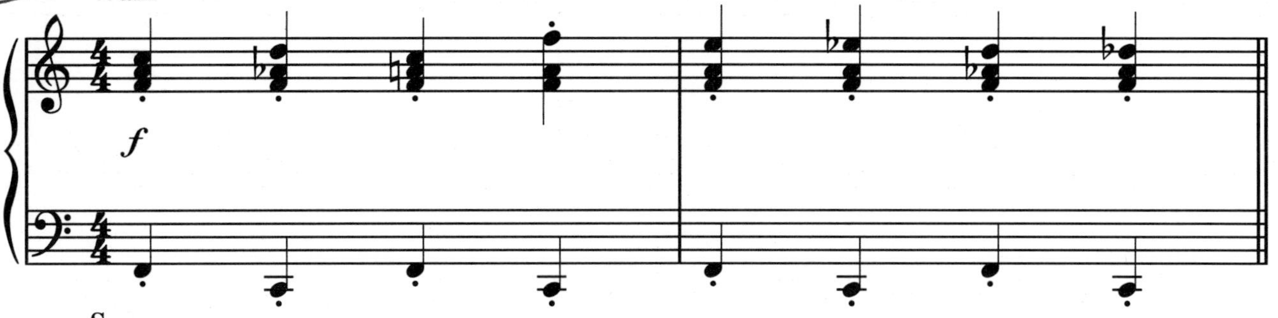

Sway

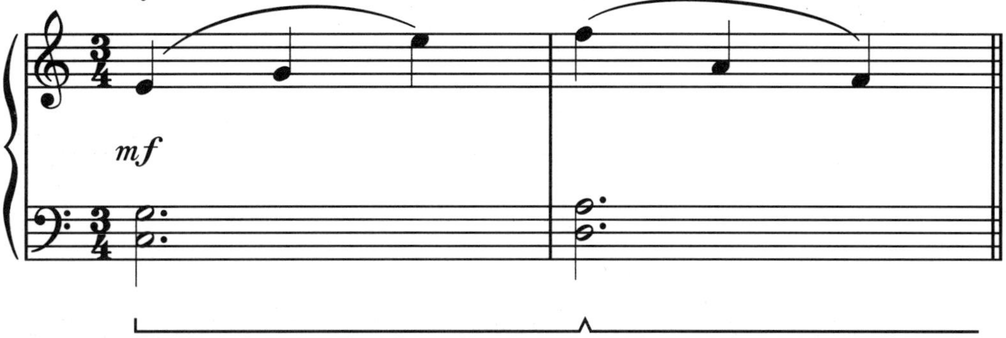

Jog

ENSEMBLE

1. Which part must set tempo? Discuss as a class before playing.

Allegro Moderato

from *On the Green Meadow*

ALEXANDER GRETCHANINOV
(1864–1956)

19
p
p
23
f
come sopra
mf
28
f
Meno mosso
p
rit.
Meno mosso
rubato
p
rit.

2. You will notice that part 1 is blank—improvisation on B♭ blues scale is part 1. There are several ways to perform this ensemble:

- Trio: part 1 improvises; part 2; part 3
- Duet: part 1 improvises; parts 2 and 3 played as one
- Duet: part 1 improvises; part 2 omitted; part 3
- Solo: part 1 improvises and plays part 2 as written
- Tradin' 12s: play as trio and on each repeat move to next part

Red Rover, It's Over!

M. HILLEY

Low down ♫ = ♩♪ (triplet)

1. Practice left-hand chord movement. A light touch is appropriate. Practice right hand alone with special care in phrasing.

Waltz

FRANZ SCHUBERT, Op. 18a, No. 5
(1797–1828)

17
mf
p
21
mf
p
25
pp
28
31
mf
1.
2.

2. Perform *Gospel Song* in the following ways.

- Play as written
- Sing, on loo, as you play your part (SATB)
- Do guitar symbol chord analysis and perform as ensemble—part 1: as written; part 2: one student improvises high obligato based on chord tones for first half with added passing tones for second half

Gospel Song

EUGENIE R. ROCHEROLLE

3. The following solo demonstrates some possibilities for using the major third. Learn this solo well so that you understand how to use this important note when improvising the blues.

A Natural for Blues

ALAN SWAIN

7.

Supplementary Materials

READING

1. Play all four parts.

Quartet in B-Flat Major

(Excerpt)

FRANZ SCHUBERT, Op. 168
(1797–1828)

2. Determine logical fingering before playing.

Bist du bei mir

(Excerpt)

JOHANN SEBASTIAN BACH
(1685–1750)

Andante
Voice
Piano
p
Bist du bei mir, geh ich mit Freu - den zum Ster - ben
6
und zu mei - ner Ruh, zum Ster - ben und zu mei - ner Ruh.

10
Bist du bei mir. geh ich mit Freu - den zum Ster - ben
tr
p
15
und zu mei - ner Ruh, zum Ster - ben und zu mei - ner Ruh.
Fine

3. Play while paying close attention to tied notes.

Chorale

LYNN FREEMAN OLSON

con ped.

4. Play different combinations.

String Quartet
(Excerpt)

WOLFGANG AMADEUS MOZART, K. 80
(1756–1791)

16
23
Trio
30
f
p

5. Play several combinations of voices: soprano and bass; alto and tenor; soprano, alto, and tenor; alto, tenor, and bass; soprano, alto, tenor, and bass.

Green Grow the Lilacs

(Excerpt)

Irish

Arranged by Paul Montan

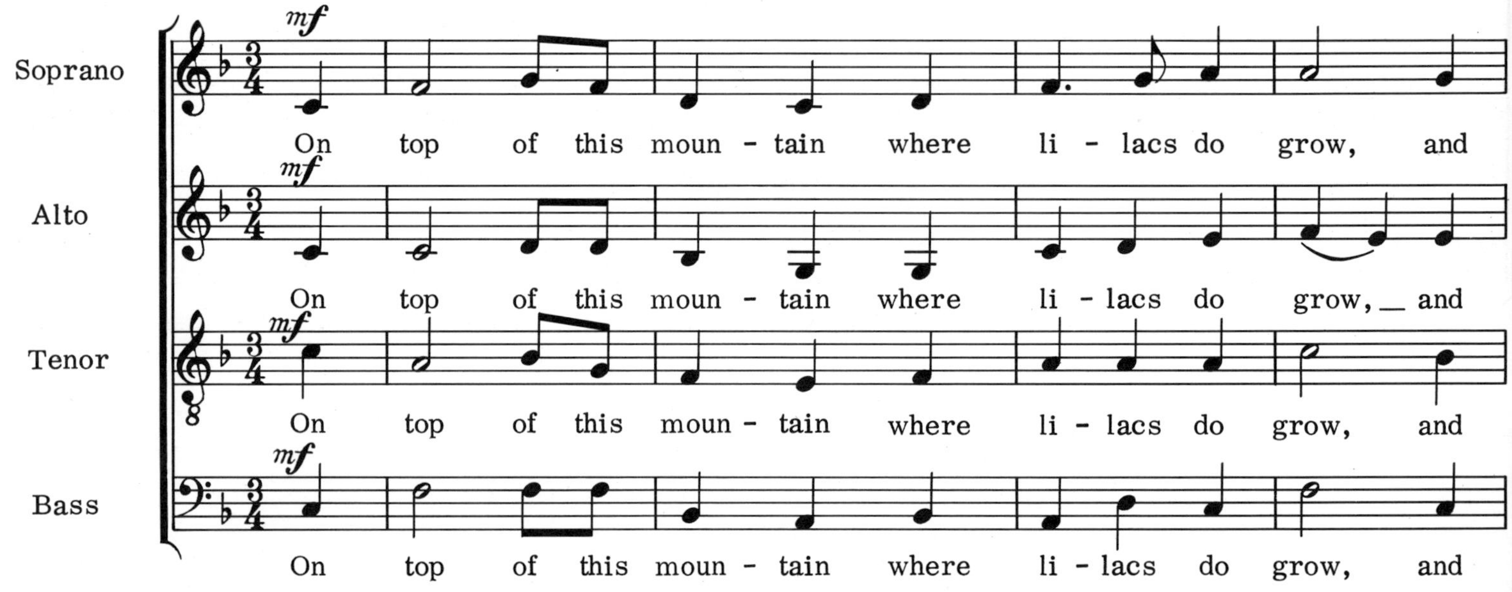
Soprano
Alto
Tenor
Bass
mf
On top of this moun - tain where li - lacs do grow, and
On top of this moun - tain where li - lacs do grow, and
On top of this moun - tain where li - lacs do grow, and
On top of this moun - tain where li - lacs do grow, and

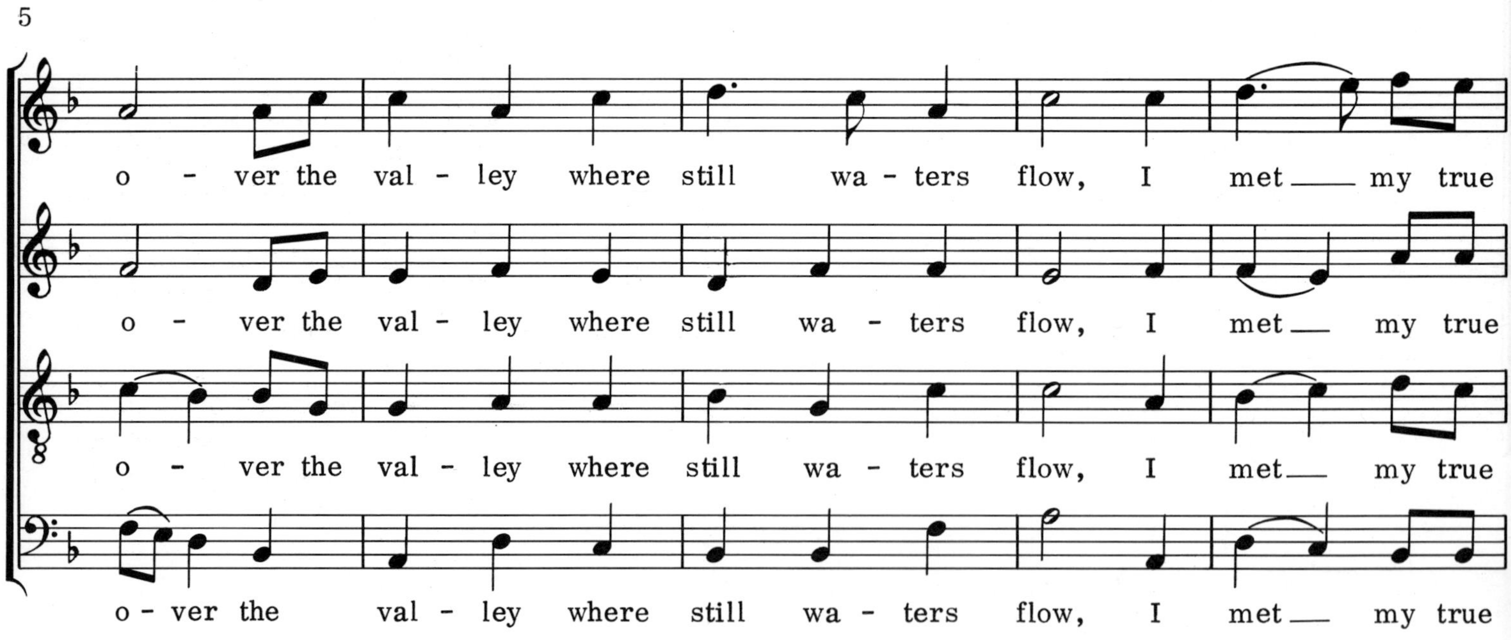
5
o - ver the val - ley where still wa - ters flow, I met my true
o - ver the val - ley where still wa - ters flow, I met my true
o - ver the val - ley where still wa - ters flow, I met my true
o - ver the val - ley where still wa - ters flow, I met my true

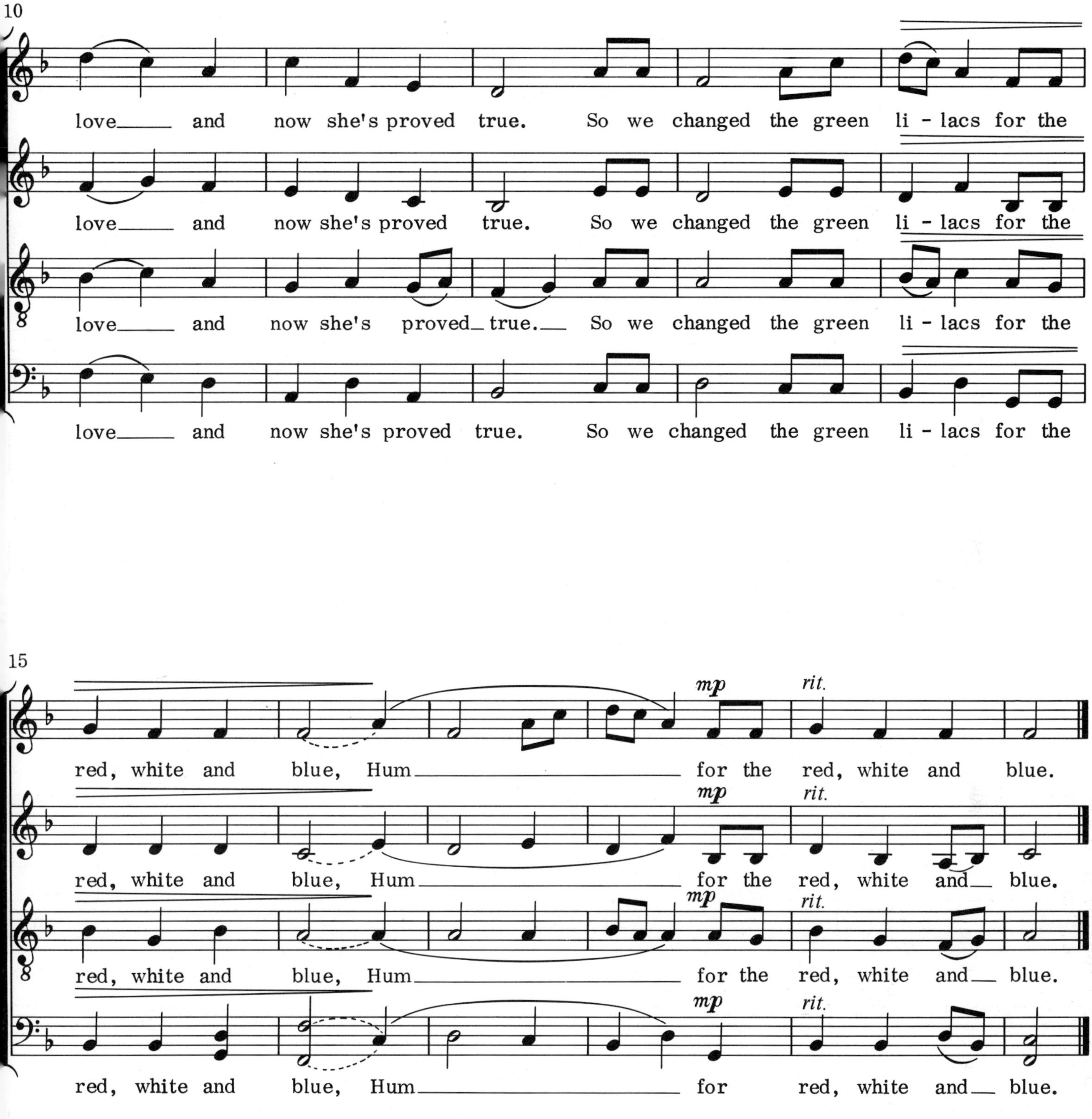
10
love and now she's proved true. So we changed the green li - lacs for the
love and now she's proved true. So we changed the green li - lacs for the
love and now she's proved true. So we changed the green li - lacs for the
love and now she's proved true. So we changed the green li - lacs for the
15
mp
rit.
red, white and blue, Hum for the red, white and blue.
red, white and blue, Hum for the red, white and blue.
red, white and blue, Hum for the red, white and blue.
red, white and blue, Hum for red, white and blue.

6. This solo has several harmonic variations for you to study.

- In the second measure the chord remains F7. This is one of the many harmonic options when using the blues form.
- Circle of fifth chord progressions are substituted for the usual blues changes.

Practice each hand separately. Scat sing the way you want the right-hand ideas to sound when you put both hands together.

Walkin' and Talkin' Blues

ALAN SWAIN

7. Choose a partner and perform.

I Wonder as I Wander

Appalachian Carol
Adapted and arranged by John Jacob Niles
and Lewis Henry Horton

Espressivo ♩. = 60
Voice
Piano
mp
p
Cm Fm Cm7 Fm
I won-der as I wan-der, out un-der the sky, How
5
Cm Fm Cm7 Cm Fm
Je - sus the Sav - ior did come for to die For poor on - 'ry peo - ple like
8
Cm7 C7 Fm Cm7 Fm
f
rit.
piú lento
you and like I... I won - der as I wan - der, out un - der the sky.

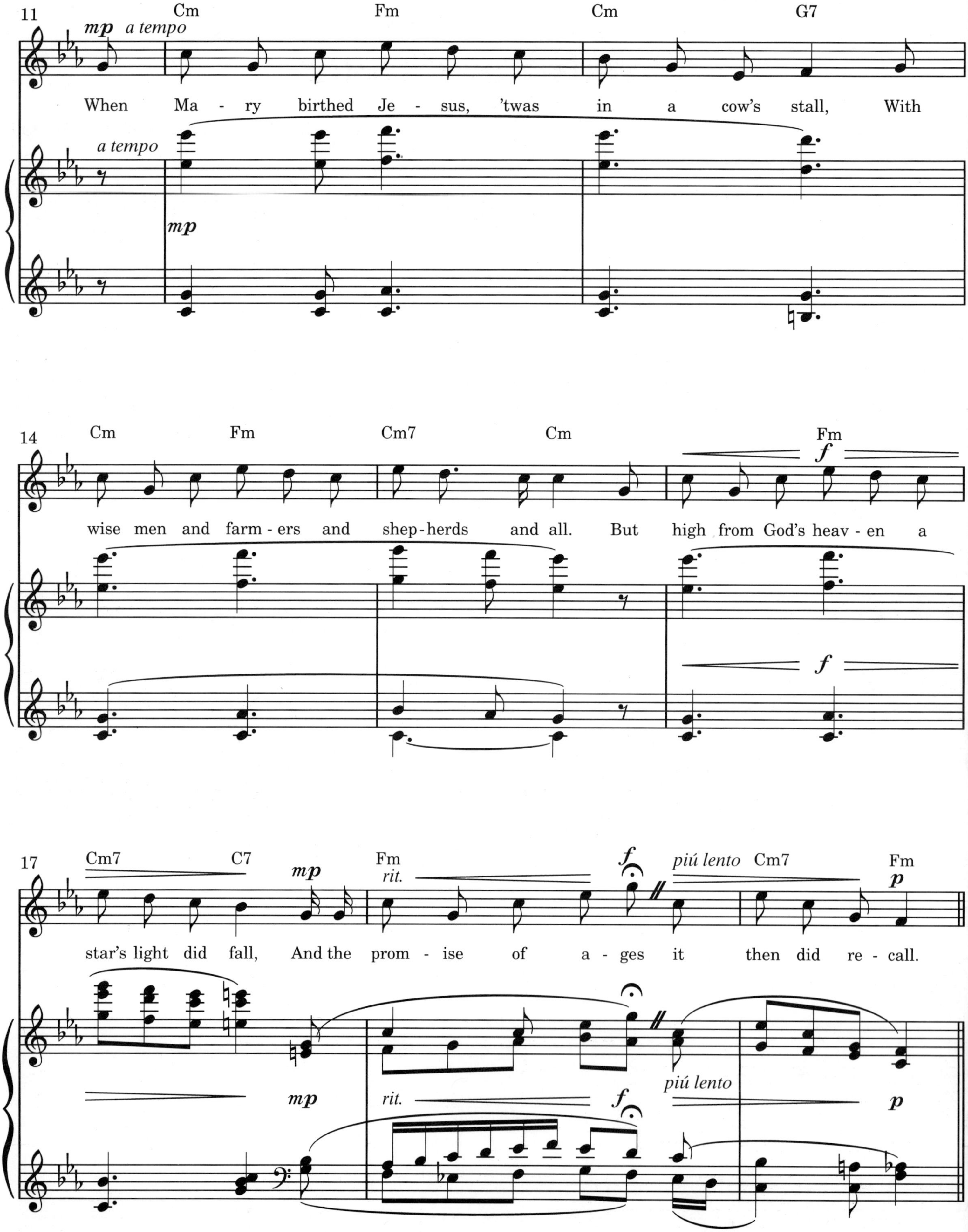

11
mp a tempo
Cm Fm Cm G7
When Ma - ry birthed Je - sus, ’twas in a cow’s stall, With
a tempo
mp
14
Cm Fm Cm7 Cm Fm
f
wise men and farm - ers and shep - herds and all. But high from God’s heav - en a
f
17
Cm7 C7 Fm piú lento Cm7 Fm
mp rit. f p
star’s light did fall, And the prom - ise of a - ges it then did re - call.
mp rit. f piú lento p

8. Simplify and accompany a partner.

Variations sérieuses

ARCANGELO CORELLI
(1653–1713)

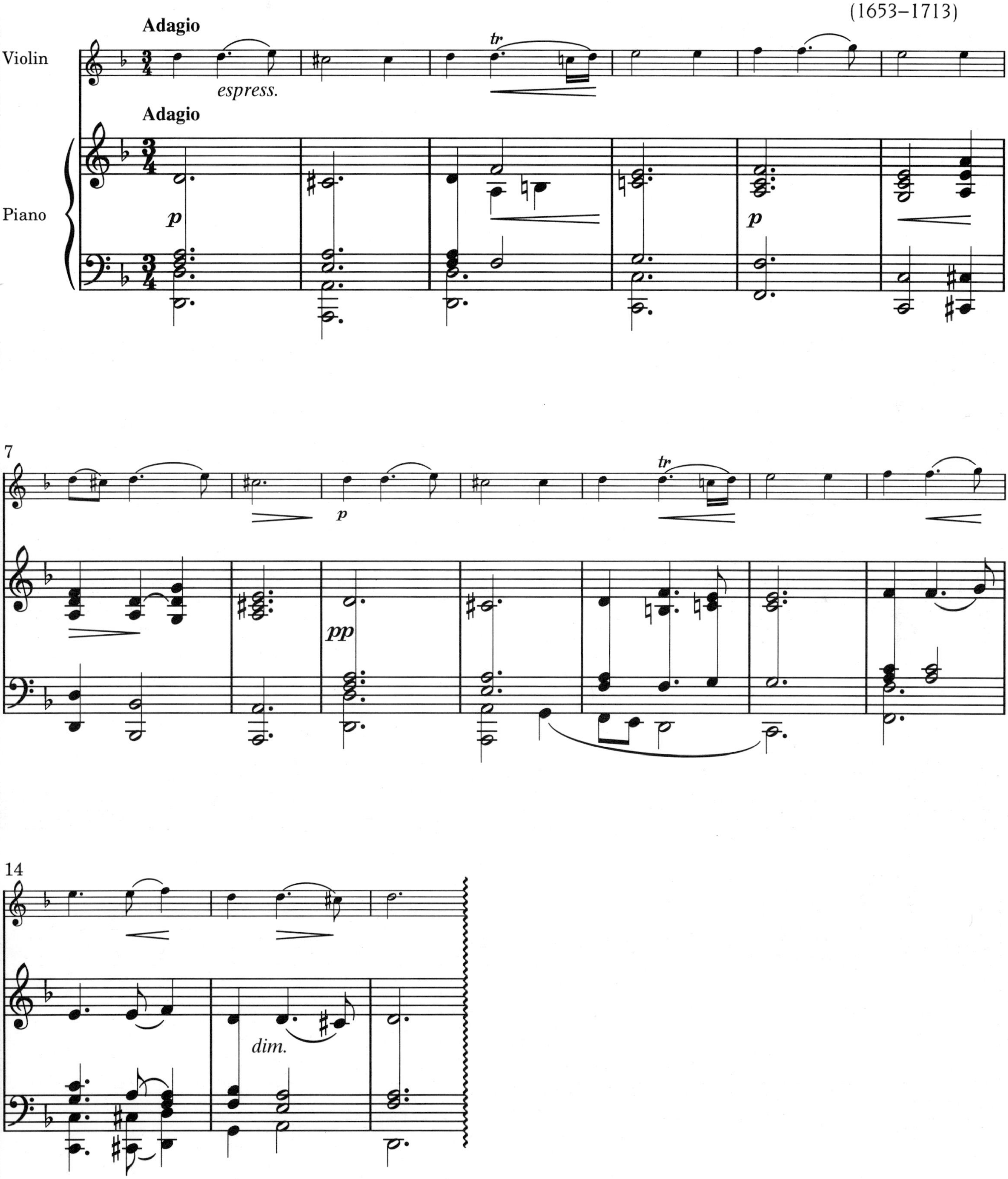

Allegretto
Violin
p
Allegretto
Piano
p
p
Andante
sosten.
espressivo
p
Andante
Clar.
mf
Bassi
stacc.
p
Adagio
Adagio
f

9. Look for parallel motion.

String Quartet in D Minor

(Excerpt)

WOLFGANG AMADEUS MOZART, K. 421
(1756–1791)

Andantino

Violin I
Violin II
Viola
Violoncello

11
16
22
cresc.
cresc.
cresc.
cresc.

28
pp
f

34

10. Play the left hand of rehearsal part as you conduct with your right hand.

Alleluia

(Excerpt)

ROBERT MUCZYNSKI

Allegro moderato
Soprano
Alto
Tenor
Bass
(For rehearsal only)
f
Al - le - lu - ia, Al - le - lu - ia, Al - le -
Al - le - lu - ia, Al - le - lu - ia, Al - le -
Al - le - lu - ia, Al - le - lu - ia, Al - le - lu - ia,
Al - le - lu - ia, Al - le - lu - ia, Al - le - lu - ia,

4
lu - ia, Al - le - lu - ia, Al - le - lu - ia, Al - le - lu -
lu - ia, Al - le - lu - ia, Al - le - lu - ia, Al - le - lu -
Al - le - lu - ia, Al - le - lu - ia, Al - le - lu -
Al - le - lu - ia, Al - le - lu - ia, Al - le - lu -
p
8
ia, Al - le - lu - ia,
ia, Al - le - lu - ia,
- ia,
- ia,

11. Determine fingering before playing these accompaniment excerpts.

Caro mio ben

(Excerpts)

GIUSEPPE GIORDANI
(1753–1798)

Moderato
Voice
Piano
mf
13
14
Il tuo fe-del so - spi-ra o-gnor. Ces - sa, cru-del, tan -
18
to ri - gor, ces - sa cru-del, tan - to ri - gor, tan - to ri-gor!

12. Observe parallel motion.

Quartet in A Major

(Excerpt)

LUDWIG van BEETHOVEN, Op. 18, No. 5
(1770–1827)

13. Choose a partner and perform.

Ich grolle nicht

(Excerpt)

from *Die Dichterliebe*

ROBERT SCHUMANN
(1810–1856)

Nicht zu schnell *(not too fast)*

mf
Voice
Ich grol - le nicht, und wenn das Herz auch
Piano
mf
4
bricht, e - wig ver - lor' - nes Lieb,
7
e - wig ver - lor' - nes Lieb! ich grol - le

10
nicht, ich grol - le nicht. Wie du auch
13
strahlst in Di - a - man - ten-pracht, es fällt kein Strahl in dei-nes
16
Her - zens Nacht, das weiss ich längst.
ritard.

14. Play any three parts.

Am Bodensee

(Excerpt)

ROBERT SCHUMANN, Op. 59, No. 2
(1810–1856)

Langsam
Soprano
Alto
Tenor
Bass
p
Wie - der - keh-rend nach dem Va - ter - lan - de, hofft' ich dei-ne Li-lien hand zu
Wie - der - keh-rend nach dem Va - ter - lan - de,
Wie - der - keh-rend nach dem Va - ter - lan - de,
Wie - der - keh-rend nach dem Va - ter - lan - de,

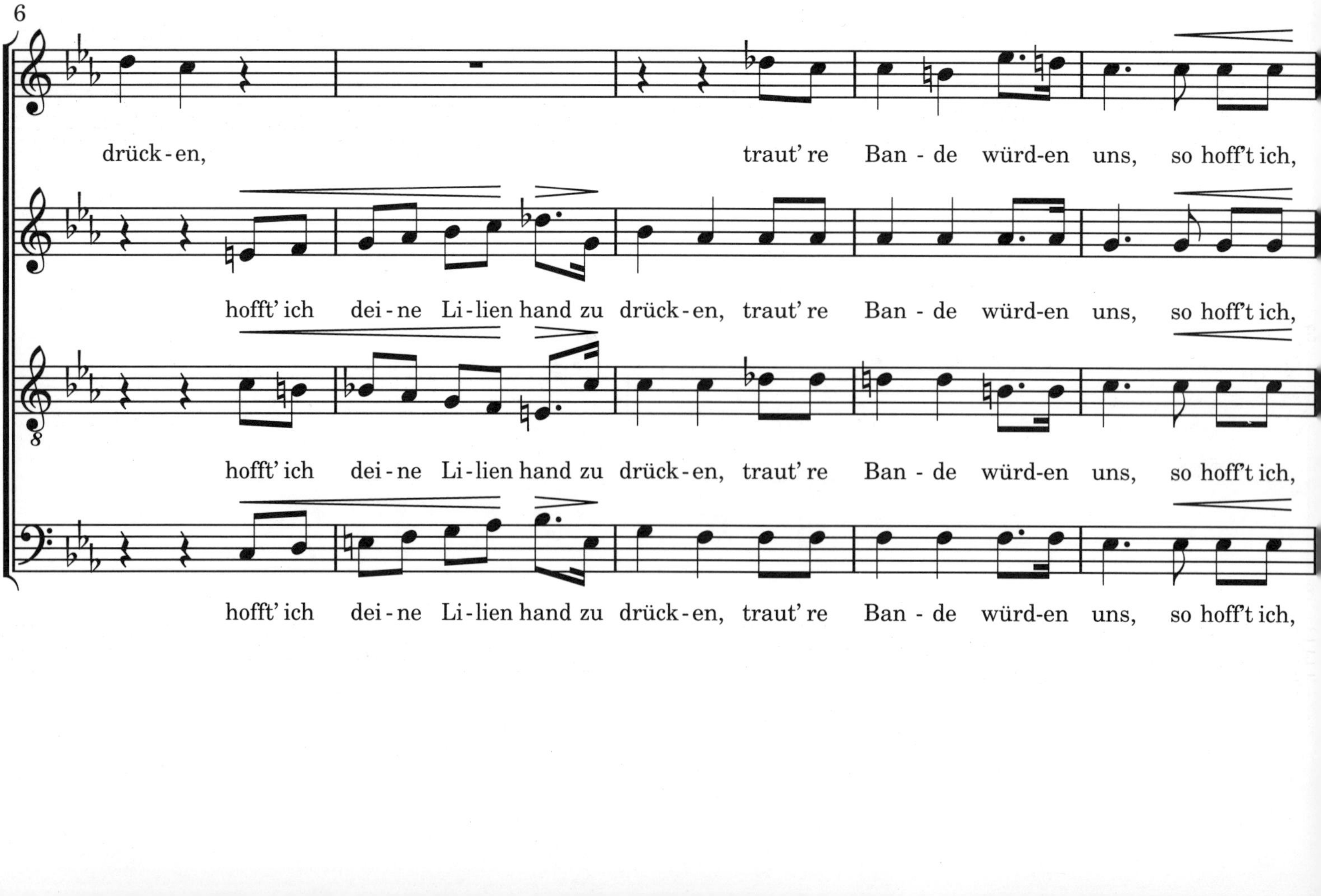
6
drück-en, traut' re Ban - de würd-en uns, so hoff't ich,
hofft' ich dei-ne Li-lien hand zu drück-en, traut' re Ban - de würd-en uns, so hoff't ich,
hofft' ich dei-ne Li-lien hand zu drück-en, traut' re Ban - de würd-en uns, so hoff't ich,
hofft' ich dei-ne Li-lien hand zu drück-en, traut' re Ban - de würd-en uns, so hoff't ich,

11
dann ___ be - glück - en, wie der keh - rend nach dem Va - ter - lan - de!
dann ___ be - glück - en, wie der keh - rend nach dem Va - ter - lan - de!
dann ___ be - glück - en, wie der keh - rend nach dem Va - ter - lan - de!
dann ___ be - glück - en, dann be - glü - cken!

HARMONIZATION

1. Use mostly thirds and sixths in the right hand when accompanying. Play refrain by ear.

Battle Hymn of the Republic

American Camp Meeting Tune

3
6

2. Continue the two-handed accompaniment. Then perform the song with a partner.

Rastlose Liebe

(Excerpt)

CARL FRIEDRICH ZELTER
(1758–1832)

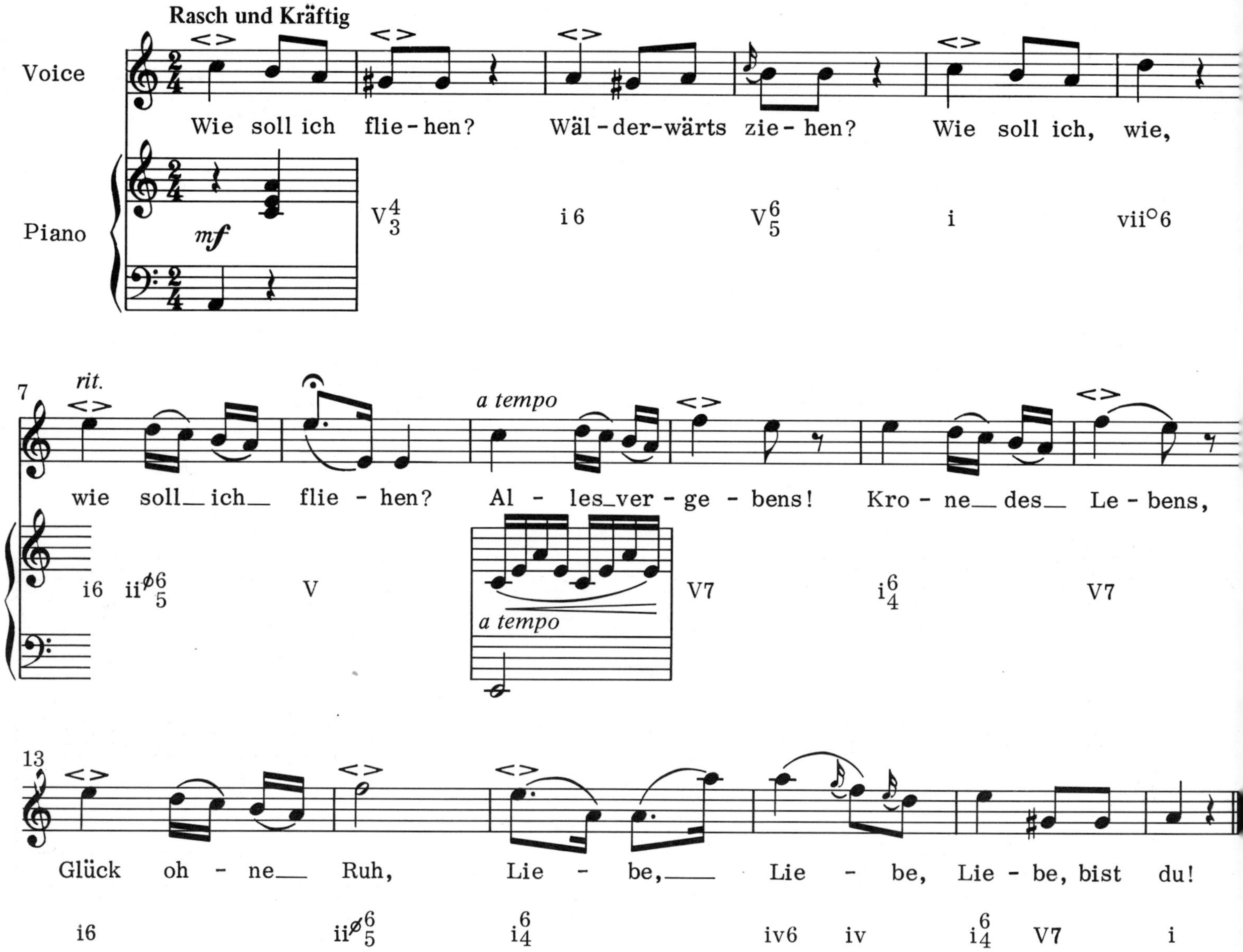
Rasch und Kräftig
Voice
Piano
mf
Wie soll ich flie-hen? Wäl-der-wärts zie-hen? Wie soll ich, wie,
V4 3 i 6 V6 5 i vii°6
rit.
a tempo
wie soll ich flie-hen? Al-les ver-ge-bens! Kro-ne des Le-bens,
i6 ii⌀6 5 V V7 i6 4 V7
a tempo
Glück oh-ne Ruh, Lie-be, Lie-be, Lie-be, bist du!
i6 ii⌀6 5 i6 4 iv6 iv i6 4 V7 i

3. Use keyboard style.

Stodola Pumpa

Czech

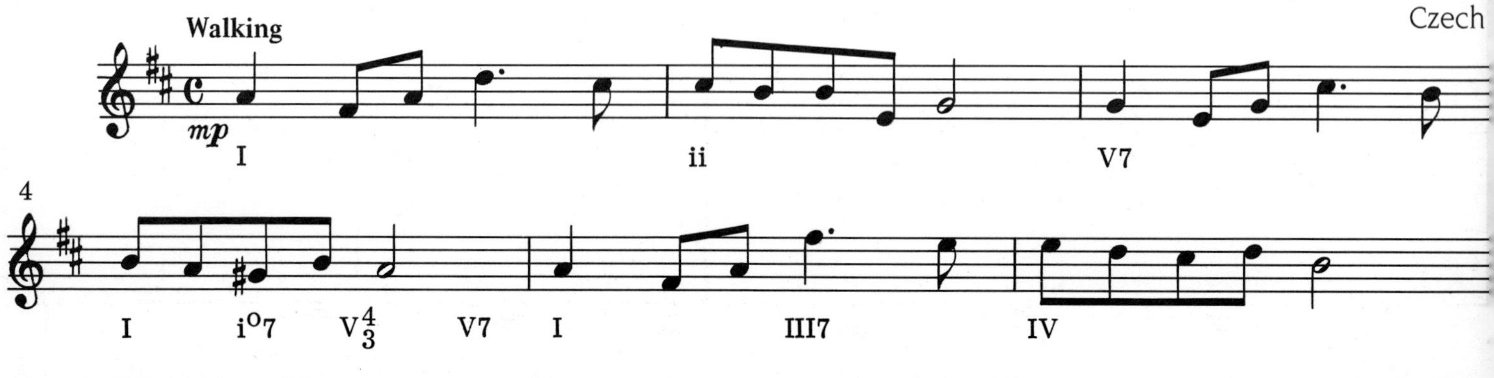
Walking
mp
I ii V7
I i°7 V4 3 V7 I III7 IV

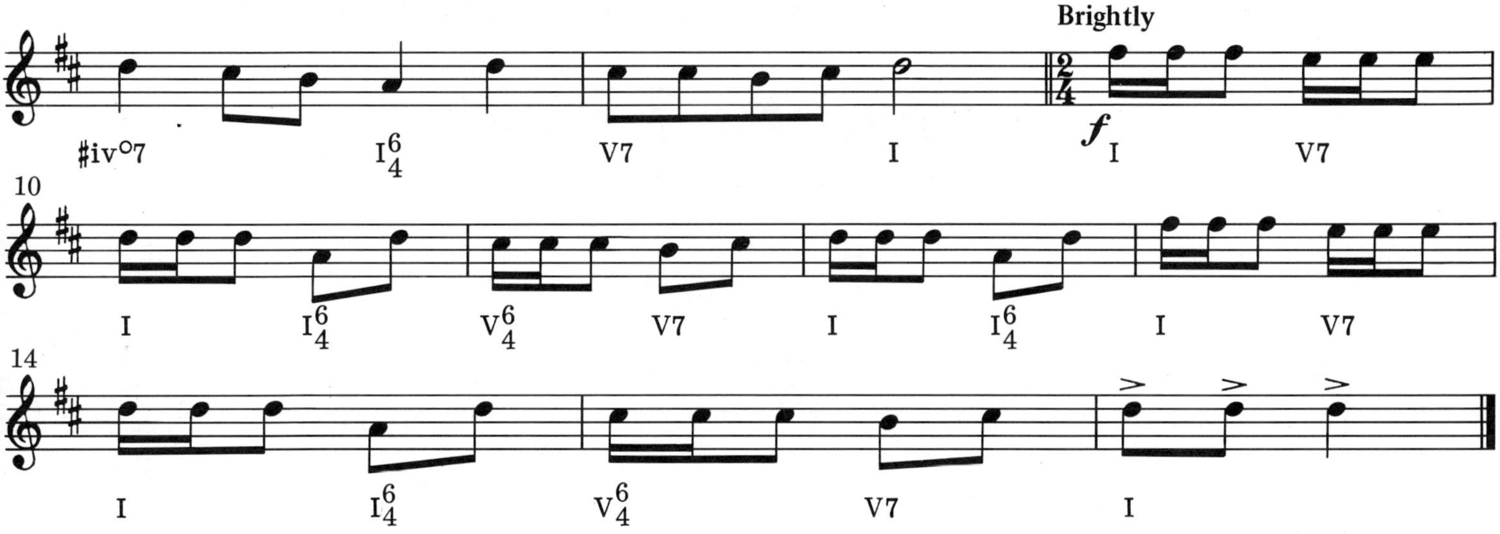

4. Complete in the style.

You're a Grand Old Flag

GEORGE M. COHAN
(1878–1942)

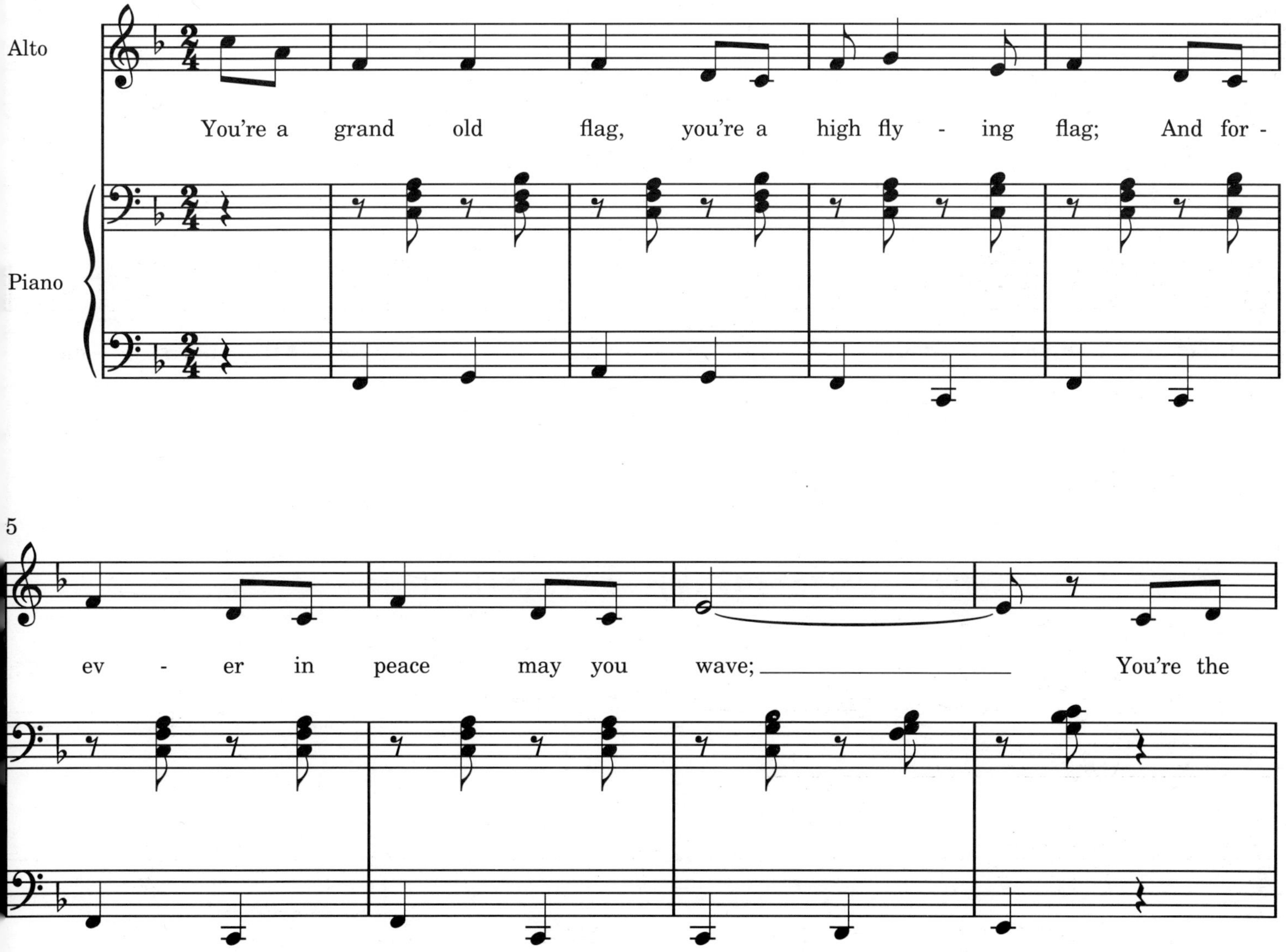

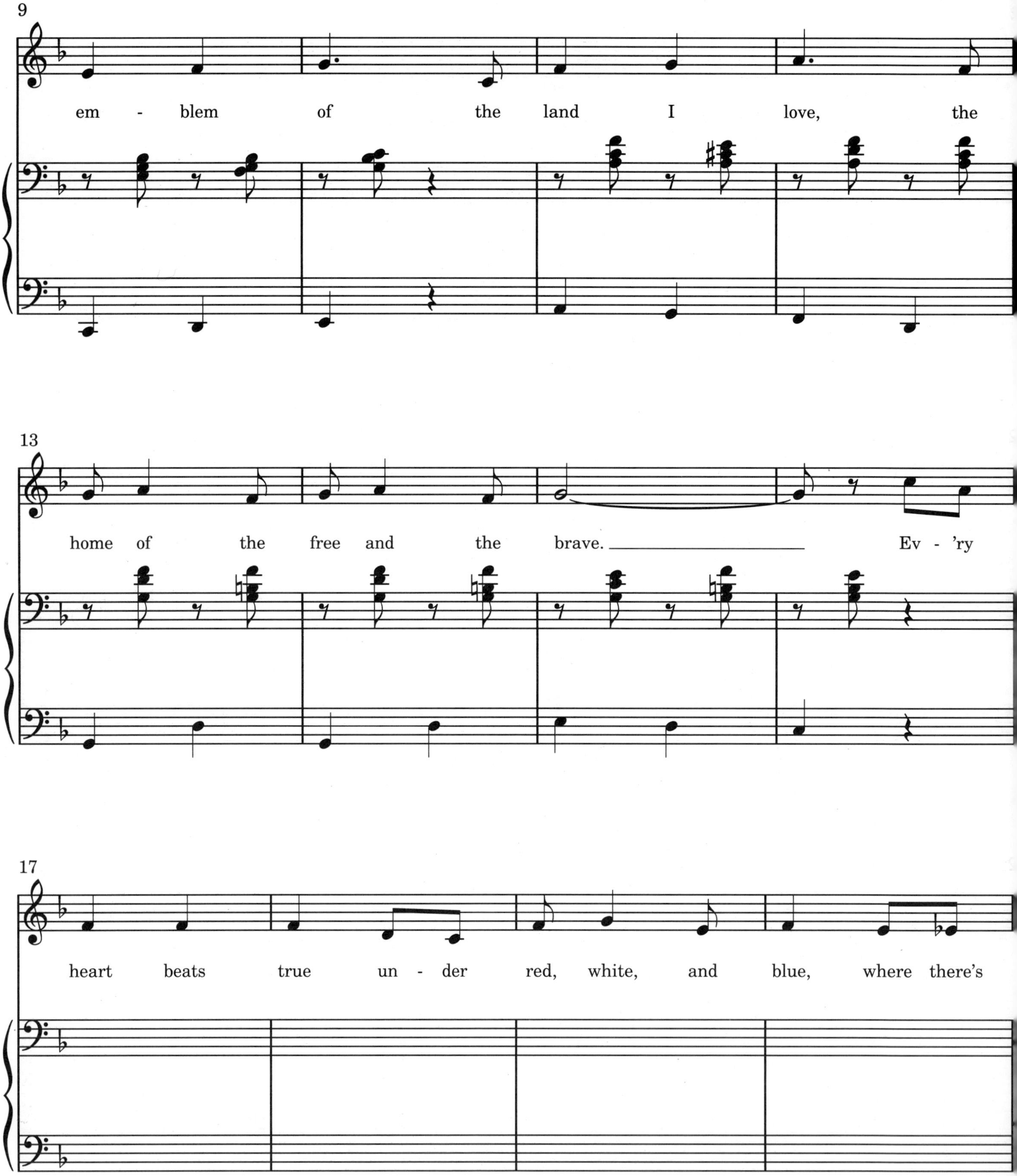
9
em - blem of the land I love, the
13
home of the free and the brave.
Ev - 'ry
17
heart beats true un - der red, white, and blue, where there's

21
nev - er a boast or brag; ___ But should
25
auld ac - quaint - ance be for - got, Keep your
29
eye on the grand old flag. ___

5. Accompany with two-hand keyboard part as you sing.

Meet Me in St. Louis, Louis

KERRY B. MILLS
Words by ANDREW B. STERLING

Valse moderato
B♭
Meet me in St. Lou - is, Lou - is,
5 E♭ B♭ F7
Meet me at the fair,
9 B♭
Don't tell me the lights are shin - ing
13 C7 F7 F A7♭5/E♭
an - y place but there. We will
17 D7 G7
dance the Hooch - ee Kooch - ee, I will
21 C7 F7
be your toots - ie woots - ie;
25 B♭
Meet me in St. Lou - is, Lou - is,
29 C7 F7 B♭
Meet me at the fair.

6. Play a two-handed accompaniment as the class sings.

Give My Regards to Broadway

GEORGE M. COHAN
(1878–1942)

Lively
G /D Bmin7 G G°/B♭ Am7 Cmin6 D7
f
Give my re - gards to Broad - way, Re -
5
Amin7 D7/A D+ G6 G♯° D7/A D7
mem - ber me to Her - ald Square,
9
G Bmin7 G E min7♭5/B♭ D/A A7 D D/A A♯° Bmin
Tell all the gang at For - ty Sec - ond Street that
13
Emin Emin7♭5/B♭ A A7 D7 A min7♭5/E♭ D7
I will soon be there.
17
G /D B min7 G G°/B♭ A min7 C min6 D7
Whis - per of how I'm yearn - ing to
21
Amin7 D7/A D+ G G maj7/F♯ G7/F
min - gle with the old time throng;
25
E7 E7/B E7 /F♯ /G♯ Amin E7/B A min7/C /E E♭7
Give my re - gards to old Broad - way and say that
29
G/D E min A7 D7 G
I'll be there, ere long.

7. Work out a simplification of the accompaniment. Harmonic analysis will help.

An die Hoffnung

LUDWIG van BEETHOVEN, Op. 32
(1770–1827)

Poco Adagio
p
4
Die du so gern in heil-gen Näch - ten fei - erst, und sanft und
8
weich den Gram ver-schlei-erst, der ei - ne zar - te See - le

12
quält, ___
o
15
Hoff - nung, laß, durch dich ___ em - por - ge - ho - ben, den Dul - der
cresc.
18
ah - nen, daß dort o - ben ein En - gel sei - ne
f
f
p
21
Trä - nen zählt.
O ___

24
Hoff - nung, laß, durch dich em - por - ge - ho - ben, den Dul - der ah - nen, daß dort
cresc.
f
28
o - ben ein En - gel sei - ne Trä - nen
f
pp
31
zählt.
tr
tr
D.S.

TRANSPOSITION

1. Determine harmonies to be used and play in A major, B♭ major, and B major. Use the V7 transition chord of the new key.

Flute Tune

JAMES SCHNARS

2. Transpose to the key of A major.

Hush, Little Baby

Traditional

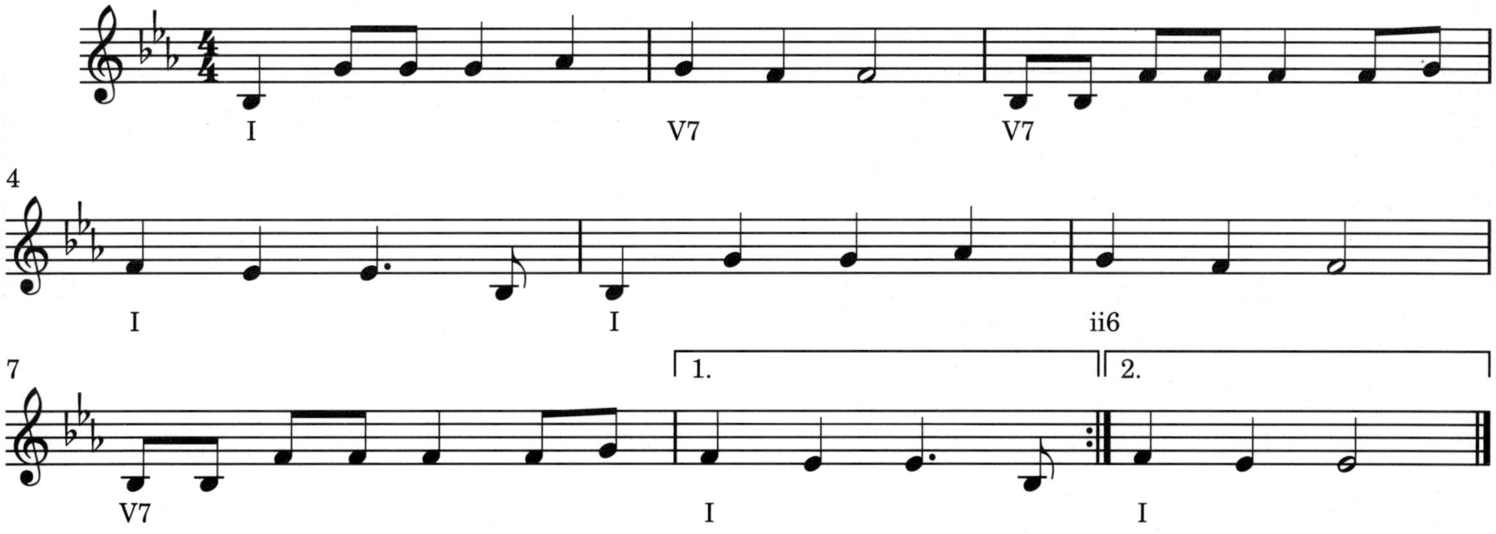

3. Play up a half step.

Du bist die Ruh

(Excerpt)

FRANZ SCHUBERT, Op. 59
(1797–1828)

Larghetto (Langsam)
Piano
pp
5
Du bist die
pp
9
Ruh, der Frie - de mild, die Sehn - sucht

du, und was sie stillt. Ich wei - he
dir roll Lust und Schmerz zur Woh - nung
hier mein Aug' und Herz, mein Aug' und
Herz.

4. Complete in the style indicated. Piano "melody" should double that of the trumpet.

Now the Day Is Over

JOSEPH BARNBY
(1820–1886)

Appendix A—Major Scales

The following major scales use "black-key-group" fingering.

D♭ major

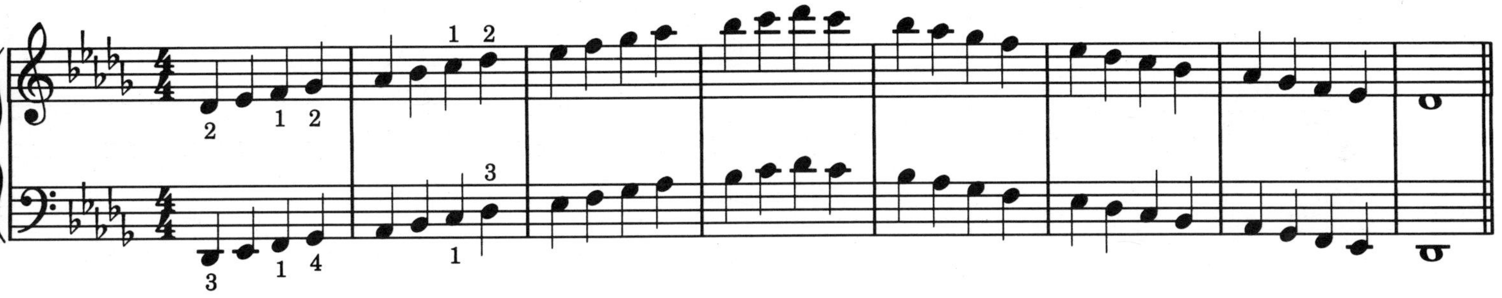

G♭ major

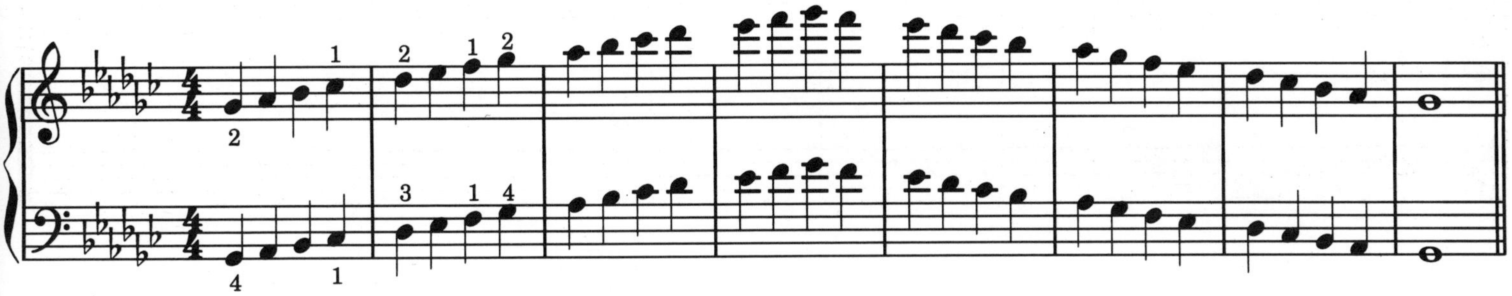

C♭ major

The following enharmonic scales use the same fingerings as above.

C♯ major

F♯ major

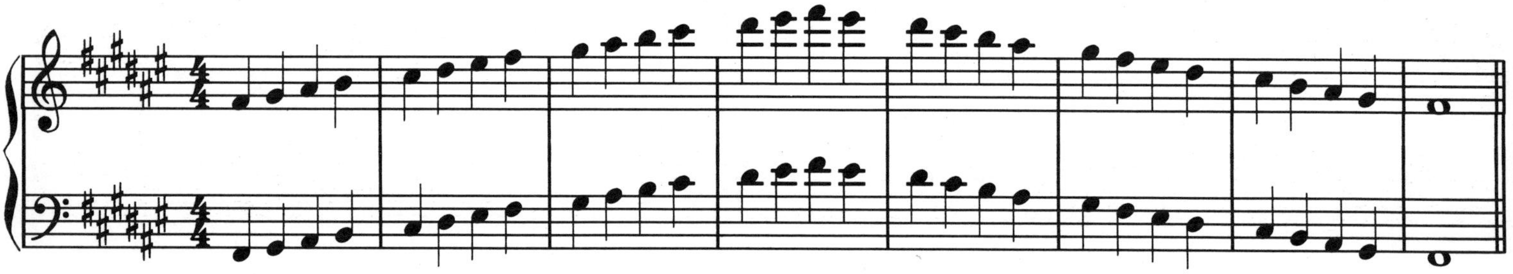

B major

The following major scales use "C major" fingering.

C major

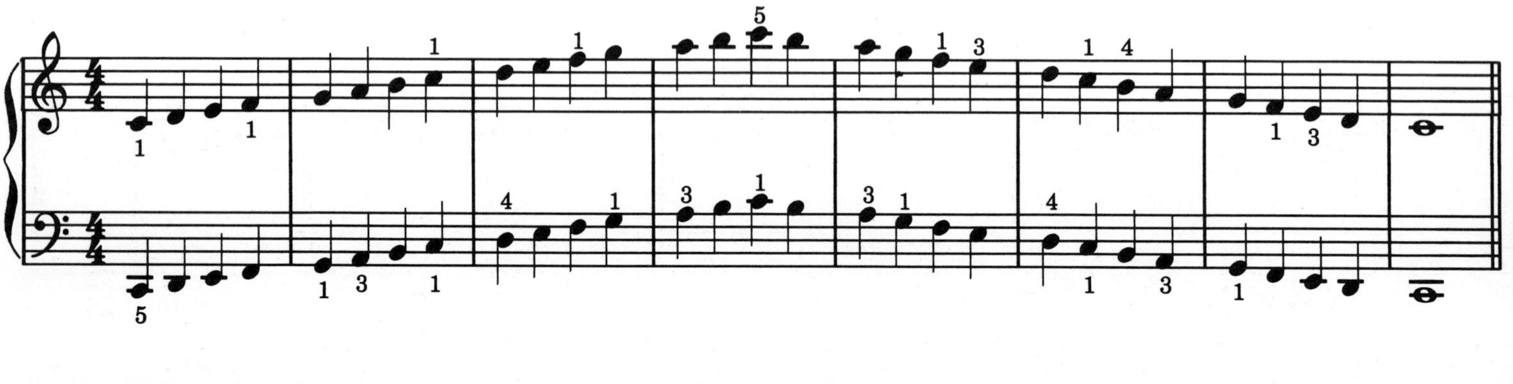

Appendix A

D major

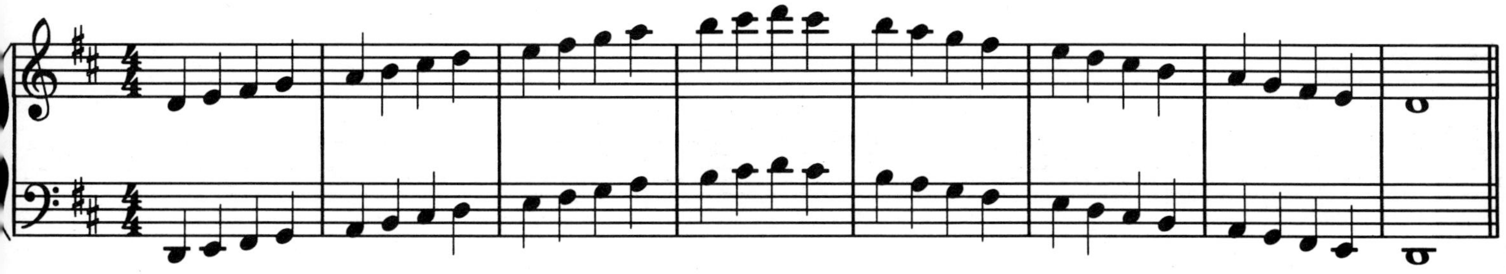

E major

G major

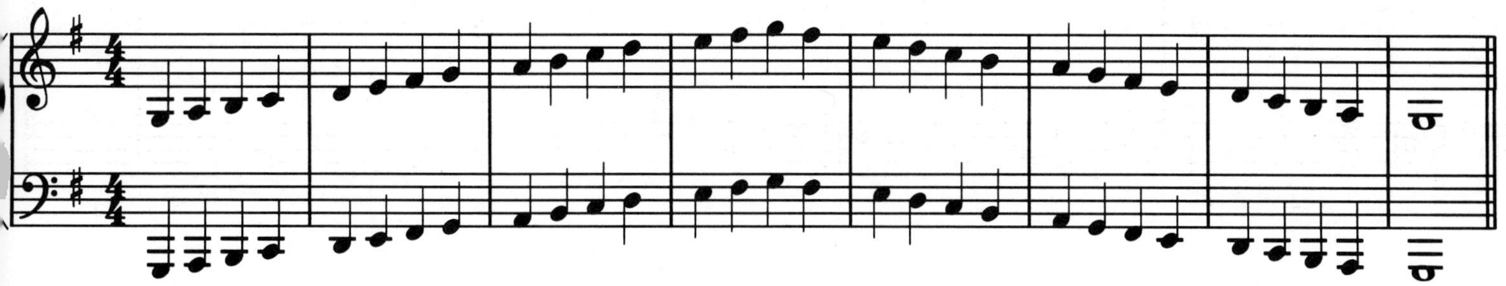

A major

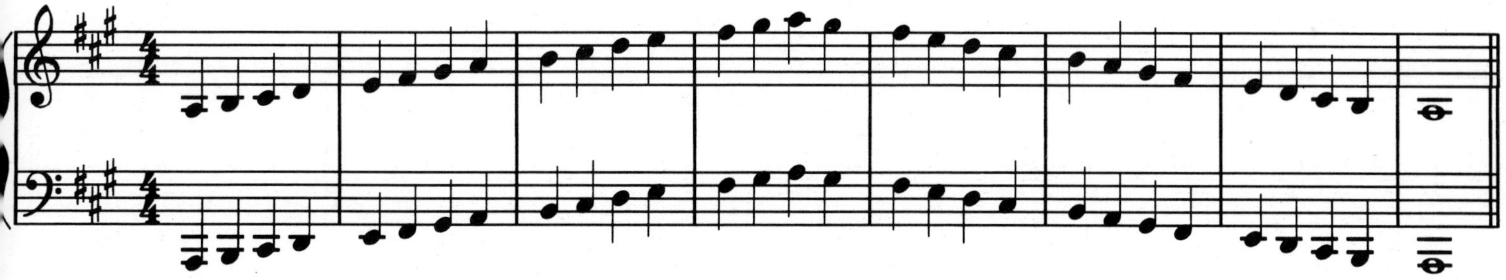

A♭ major uses the same fingering "combination" as C major.

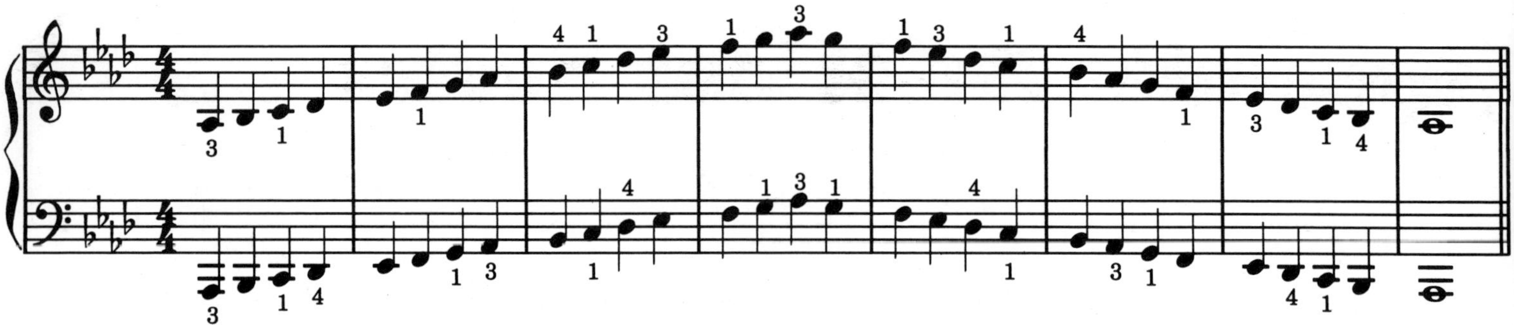

The following major scales are often called "the other majors"!

F major

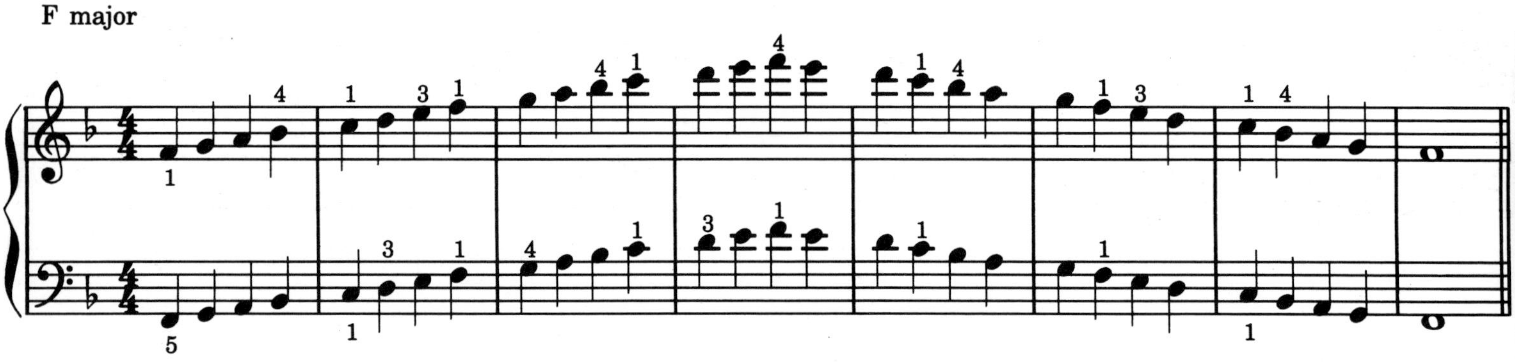

B♭ major

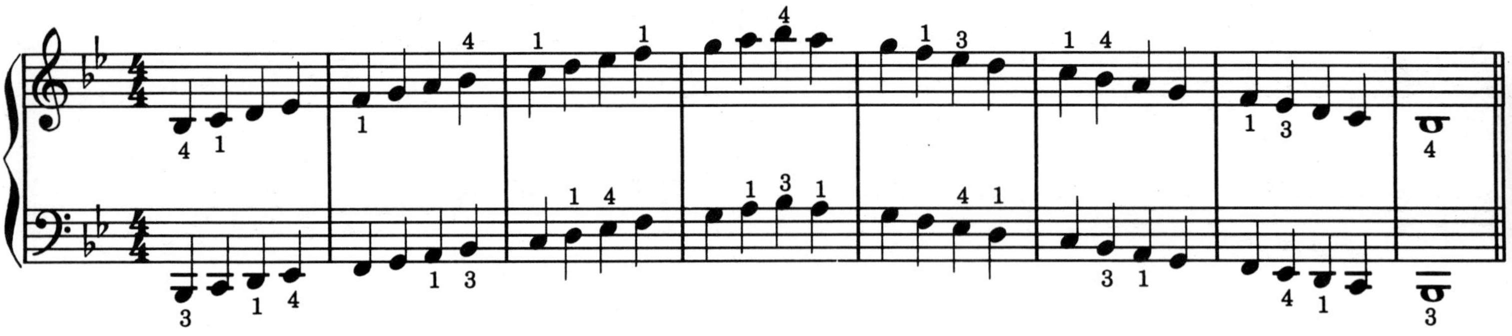

E♭ major

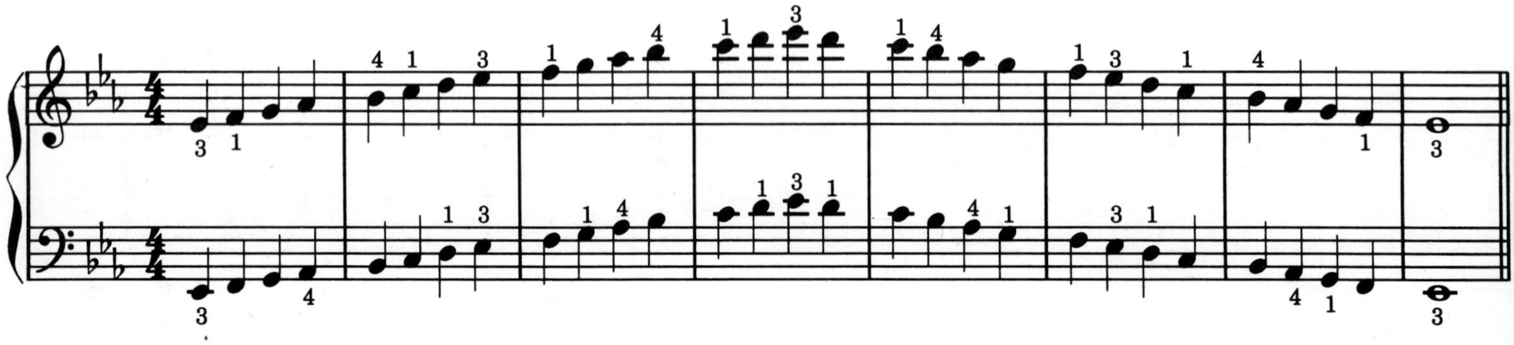

Appendix B—Minor Scales

These "harmonic" minor scales use C major fingering *or* the same fingering combinations as C major.

C minor

D minor

E minor

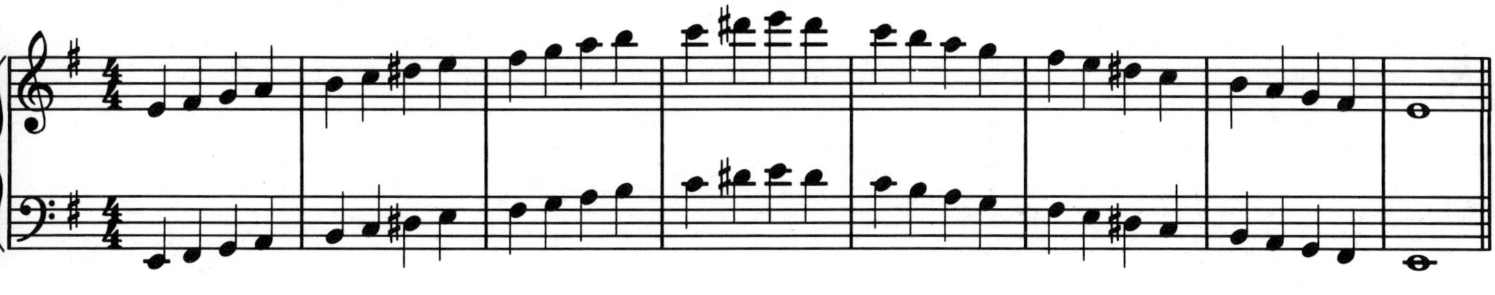

G minor

A minor

A♭ minor

Appendix B

F♯ minor

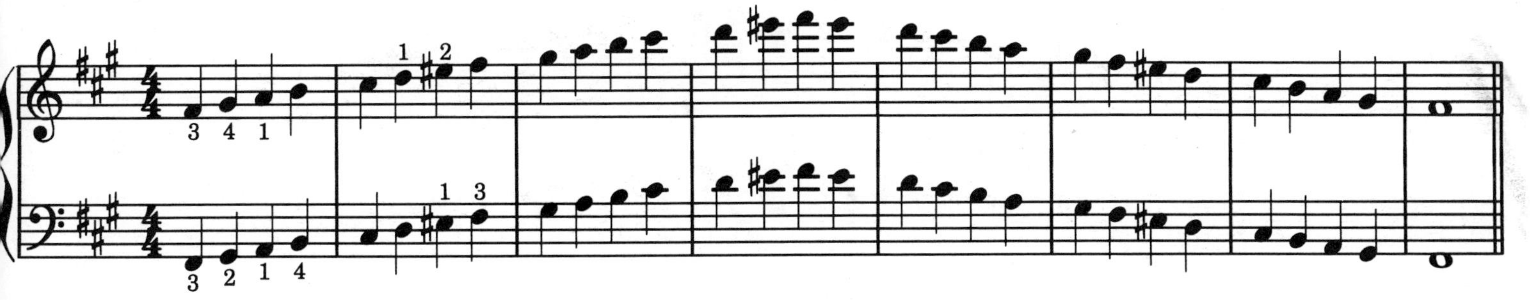

C♯ minor

The black-key-group minors use the same fingering combinations as the black-key-group majors.

B♭ minor

E♭ minor

G♯ minor

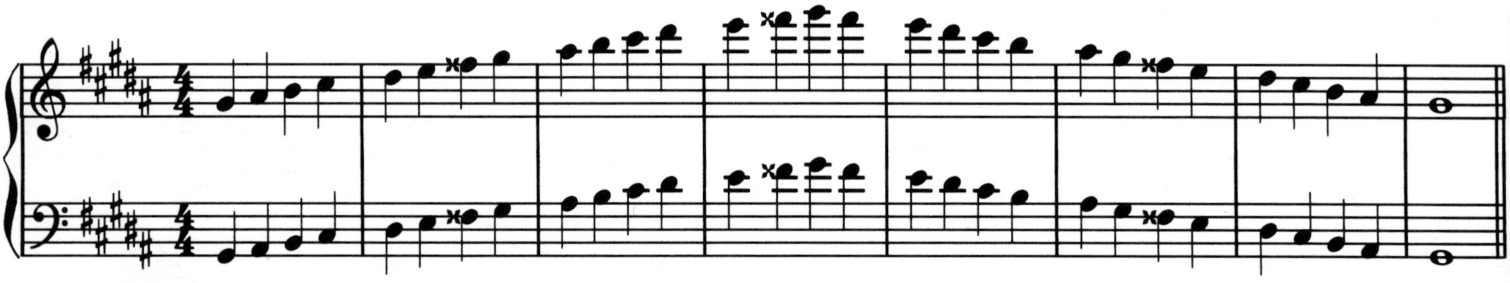

Use the same fingering as F major!

F minor

Appendix C—Chord Types

Major	C M or C	
Minor	C m or C-	
Diminished	C♯° or C♯ dim	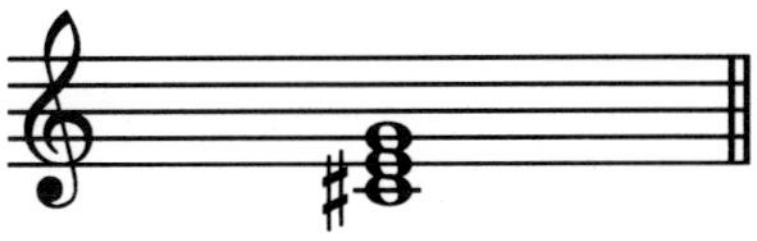
Augmented	C Aug or C + or C (♯5)	
Major-Minor Seventh	C7	
Major-Major Seventh	C M 7 or C Δ 7 or C maj 7	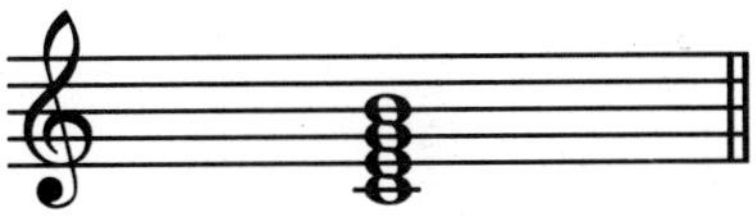
Minor-Minor Seventh	C m 7 or C - 7 or C min 7	
Minor-Major Seventh	C min (maj 7) or C - (Δ 7)	
Diminished-Minor Seventh	C♯ø7 or C♯ - 7♭5 or C♯ min 7♭5	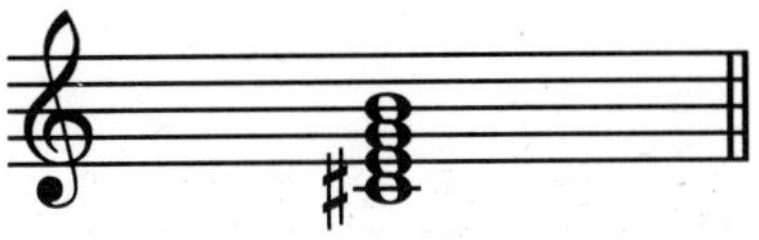

Diminished-Diminished Seventh — C♯° 7 or C♯ (dim 7)

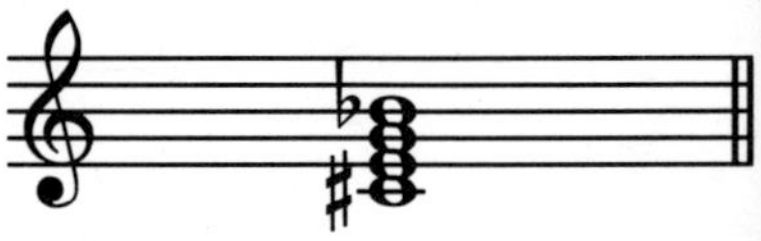

Augmented-Major Seventh — C + (7) or C Aug (7)

Augmented-Minor Seventh — C + (maj 7) or C Aug (maj 7)

Ninth — C 9

Minor Ninth — C 7 (♭9)

Eleventh — C 11

Sharp Eleventh — C 7 (♯11)

Thirteenth — C 13

To reduce the extended harmonies from their five- to seven-note composition, certain tones are usually omitted:

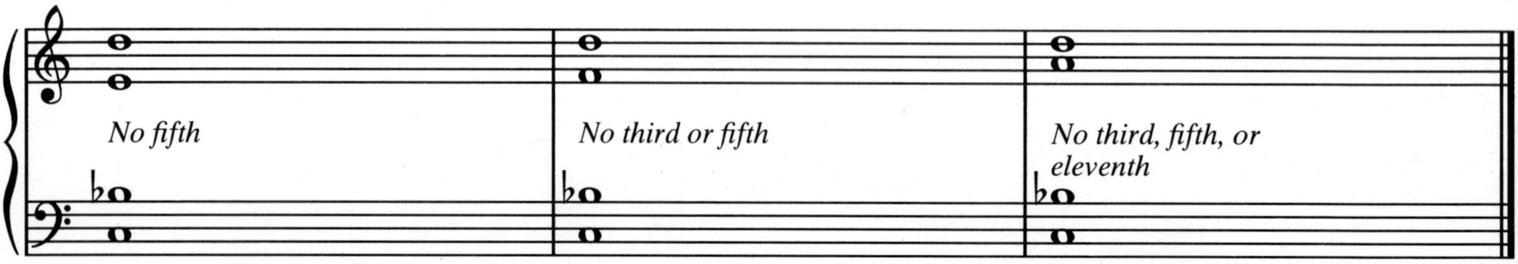

Glossary

a cappella unaccompanied
a tempo return to original tempo
accelerando (accel.) gradually faster
ad libitum (ad lib.) at your pleasure
Adagio slow
agitato restless
al Fine to the end
Alla marcia in the style of a march
alla trombe in the style of trumpets
allargando getting broader
Allegro in a lively manner
Allegro moderato used to indicate moderately brisk movement
Andante a moderate tempo; leaning toward slower
Andantino moderately slow
appoggiatura non-chord tone occurring on a strong beat
arco bow (violins, etc.)
authentic cadence dominant to tonic

brioso vigorously

cantabile to make the music "sing"
cesura (//) a complete break in sound
chorale style four-part texture usually voiced "two and two"
come sopra the same as above
con with
Con moto with motion
continuo bass line with figures to indicate harmonies to be played on keyboard instrument
crescendo (cresc.) gradually louder

Da Capo (D.C.) from the beginning
Dal Segno (D.S.) from the sign
deciso decidedly
diminuendo (dim.) gradually softer
dolce sweetly; gently
dolente sorrowful

espressivo (espr.) expressively

geschwind quickly
getragen sustained
grazioso gracefully

hemiola rhythmic relation of three notes in the time of two

keyboard style in harmonization, "three and one" voicing; melody as highest sounding voice

Kräftig strong

Langsam slow
Larghetto slow; not quite as slow as Largo
legato in a smooth, connected manner
leggiero (legg.) light; delicate
loco play as written

ma non troppo but not too much
maestoso stately
Maßig (Mässig) moderate
mezza voce half voice
Moderato at a moderate speed
morendo gradually dying away
Munter lively

Nicht zu schnell not too fast

piú more
pizzicato plucking of a string
poco little
portato indicates a non-legato tone; not as short as staccato

quatuor quartet

rallentando (rall.) gradually slower
Rasch fast
ritardando (rit.) gradually slower
roulade as a florid vocal phrase
rubato to extend the length of one note at the expense of another

scat syllables used to verbalize blues and jazz rhythms
sempre always
senza without
sforzando (sfz) giving a strong accent
simile (sim.) in a similar manner
smorzando (smorz.) dying away
Sostenuto sustained
staccato detached; usually an upward motion
subito suddenly

un poco a little

Vivace quite fast

Zeitmass tempo

Index of Titles

Index of Composers